■ ■ ■ ALL AROUND THE TOWN

■ ■ ALL AROUND
■ ■ THE TOWN

Amazing Manhattan Facts and Curiosities

Patrick Bunyan

Fordham University Press

New York

1999

Library of Congress Cataloging-in-Publication Data

    Bunyan, Patrick.
        All around the town : amazing Manhattan facts and curiosities /
    Patrick Bunyan. – 1st ed.
            p.   cm.
        Includes bibliographical references and index.
        ISBN 0–8232–1940–2 (hc.). – ISBN 0–8232–1941–0 (pbk.)
        1. New York (N.Y.)—Miscellanea. 2. New York (N.Y.)—Guidebooks.
    I. Title.
    F128.36.B86 1999
    917.47'10443—dc21   99–19769
                                                                         CIP

Printed in the United States of America
03 02 01 00 99   5 4 3 2 1
First Edition

To Scott Burns

■ CONTENTS

■ ACKNOWLEDGMENTS

I would like to thank the following people for all their support and help on this book over the years: Nava Atlas, Leonard Kniffel, Dale Neighbors, Marsha Adams, Margaret Glover, Richard Foster, Peter Jaffe, my editor Jacky Philpotts, and my friends at FPG International.

■ INTRODUCTION

Manhattan is an amazing, energetic place, forever changing. Much has happened here in the four hundred years since the first Europeans arrived. Events that reflect not only the story of New York City but the story of the United States as well. Events as varied as the first exhibition of an elephant in the New World to the last known sighting of Judge Crater.

Much of this history is not so easy to see. In Manhattan, the reminders of the past are often torn down and replaced with something new. New Yorkers, who are always striving "to get ahead," rarely have time to look back. This book is a look back, a record of an assortment of Manhattan sites where history happened, a compendium of facts, history, birthplaces, and "firsts."

More than a thousand entries, arranged by their street address, were culled from many sources—histories, biographies, newspapers, guidebooks, and maps. They range from amusing anecdotes to familiar historical events and from the Dutch New Amsterdam period to the present day.

The entries are arranged by today's street addresses. Manhattan is divided into four sections:

■ Downtown: all addresses south of and including Chambers Street and the Brooklyn Bridge.
■ The Village (which includes the Lower East Side and Soho): all addresses north of Chambers Street to and including 14th Street.
■ Midtown: all addresses north of 14th Street to and including 59th Street.
■ Above 59th Street: the rest of Manhattan.

Within each of these sections, the alphabetical streets are listed first, followed by the numbered avenues and then the numbered streets in sequence. Last, each street or avenue is then arranged by individual address or house number.

For example, 137 McDougal Street would be in the Village section, listed alphabetically under the street name, McDougal, then in order at 137. The entry for 124 West 55th Street would be in the Midtown section, listed in numerical order under 55th Street, both East and West, then in order at 124.

The major parks are arranged by name in the alphabetical street section. Streets are arranged by their most common usage. A street with several different names will be listed under each name. An address on East 59th Street will be listed with the numbered streets, while a Central Park South address will appear with the alphabetical streets.

Proper names appear in italics, and an asterisk marks what is currently at a site. An asterisk at an address denotes the structure is the same as referred to in the entry.

■ ■ ALL AROUND THE TOWN

City Hall in 1826. *(Library of Congress)*

■ ■

DOWNTOWN

■ ■

BARCLAY STREET

22 Barclay Street
St. Peter's Roman Catholic Church*—The serene Ionic temple church on this site is the second St. Peter's. The first was consecrated on November 4, 1786, and was the first permanent Roman Catholic parish in New York State. The once-surrounding burial ground was the first Roman Catholic cemetery in the state. The current church was built in 1836 to replace the original, which was severely damaged in the Great Fire of 1835.

BATTERY PARK

Castle Garden*—The U.S. government built this one-time fort in 1807 on what was originally an artificial island about three hundred feet from shore. Constructed along with four other new fortifications in anticipation of the War of 1812, the West Battery, as it was called, never fired a shot in defense. Renamed Castle Clinton, it was vacated by the U.S. Army in 1823, and the fort was turned over to the city, which used it as an official greeting site. The Marquis de Lafayette in 1824, President John Tyler in 1843, and Hungarian patriot Louis Kossuth in 1851 were all welcomed here. One rather unceremonious welcoming was for President

Castle Garden was still an island attached by a causeway at the tip of Battery Park in this view of 1830. The popular waterfront park was later expanded with landfill, which connected the old fort to Manhattan in the 1850s. *(Library of Congress)*

Andrew Jackson on June 12, 1833. The timber bridge from the fort to the battery collapsed from the weight of the president's procession, dumping a number of men and horses into the harbor. The president was slightly ahead of the crash and unhurt.

Jenny Lind, the "Swedish Nightingale," had her tumultuous American debut concert here in the now-roofed-over converted theater on September 11, 1850. More than six thousand music lovers paid at least three dollars a seat, a major coup for master showman P. T. Barnum, who convinced her to perform.

From 1855 until Ellis Island opened in 1890, seven and a half million immigrants passed through this building while it was the country's premier immigrant-landing depot.

The fort's last incarnation was as the city's aquarium, from 1896 until 1941. It was the largest aquarium in the world when it opened, and its tanks were stocked with exotic fish from around the world collected by local sea captains. It was popular with several generations of New Yorkers.

Robert Moses, who forced the aquarium to move to Coney Island, tried to have the old fort removed for his proposed Brooklyn-Battery bridge. A public outcry stopped the bridge and the demolition of the fort. It was declared a National Historic Monument in 1946.

BATTERY PLACE AT THE HARBOR

Pier A*—Recently restored, this pier has served as the gateway for many celebrities upon their arrival in New York City: Charles A. Lindbergh's triumphal return after the first transatlantic flight on June 13, 1927; "Wrong Way" Corrigan Douglas for his off-course Atlantic flight on August 5, 1938; and King George VI on June 10, 1939, are among many.

But one visitor stands above all the rest: it was here that the legendary elephant Jumbo arrived on the *Assyrian Monarch* and first stepped on American soil with all the fanfare P. T. Barnum could muster, on Easter Sunday, April 10, 1882. Barnum had recently purchased the elephant from the London Zoo for $10,000, much to the disappointment of English children, who started a letter campaign asking Queen Victoria to intervene and save the pachyderm. Nevertheless, Jumbo came to the United States to be the star attraction in Barnum's circus. Ever after his death three years later in a train accident, Jumbo's fame lived on. No other animal's name has been so widely adopted into the English language.

There was a notable departure from Pier A on the evening of June 30, 1893. President Grover Cleveland was secretly ferried to the yacht *Oneida* anchored in the East River. The purpose of the trip, a presidential operation, was kept from the public and the press. Five doctors and one dentist removed a large cancerous growth from Cleveland's upper jaw during the shipboard operation. The administration denied the rumors and insisted the president had had routine dental surgery. The truth remained hidden for more than twenty-five years, long after Cleveland's death.

P. T. Barnum's most famous circus attraction, "Jumbo," paraded to the opening of "The Greatest Show on Earth" at Madison Square Garden. Jumbo arrived in America with Matthew Scott, his beloved keeper of twenty years. The pair became inseparable when Scott nursed the sick baby elephant back to health. *(Frank Leslie's, April 22, 1882)*

BEEKMAN STREET

Beekman Street and Nassau Street, Southwest Corner

Beekman (Chapel) Street Theater—The earliest New York performance of *Hamlet* took place here on November 26, 1761. Twenty-one-year-old Lewis Hallam Jr. played the title role. Hallam was the first star known to Colonial audiences and the first leading actor whose debut and early experiences were American. The theater was closed down by a riot over the Stamp Act controversy on May 5, 1766.

101 Beekman Street

The fourteen-year-old aspiring artist Ben Shahn was apprenticed to Hessenberg's Lithography Shop at this address from 1913 to 1917. The Lithuanian-born teenager was attending high school at night.

BOWLING GREEN

1 Bowling Green between State and Whitehall Streets

A small clearing in the primal forest, this area of lower Manhattan was the likely site of Peter Minuit's celebrated exchange with the indigenous "Indians" in the late spring of 1626. The end of an age-old Native American trail that began north in Westchester, this is the beginning of today's Broadway, or "Breede Wegh" as the Dutch called it. Minuit, the French-born director-general of the Dutch colony of New Netherland, met with the natives and "bought" the island for sixty guilders, or twenty-four dollars, worth of beads and tools.

Fort Amsterdam—Early Dutch settlers built this fort, designed in 1626 by Kryn Frederycks. It was a four-bastioned compound that contained the governor's house, the officers' quarters, the barracks, the prison, and a church. The fort was the site of the first recorded murder in New Amsterdam, when Gerrit Jansen, a gunner, was stabbed to death in front of the gate in May of 1638. The murderer, Jan Gysbertsen, quickly fled the settlement, never to be seen again. The fort went through several name changes and additions with each succeeding tenant—the Dutch, the English, and the Americans—until it was torn down in 1790.

Government House—An impressive two-story porticoed mansion was built here as a home for the president of the new country, but by the time it was completed the newly formed federal government had left for Philadelphia. The house then served as New York's Governor's Mansion until the state capital left for Albany in 1797. It was during this period that Governors George Clinton and John Jay lived here. The mansion was demolished in 1815 and replaced by a row of smaller townhouses. As business drove out residences in lower Manhattan in the mid-nineteenth century, these townhouses eventually became headquarters for the leading shipping companies, and the block became known as "Steamship Row."

Alexander Hamilton United States Customhouse*—In 1907 the country's largest and most profitable customhouse occupied this site. The elaborate building was designed by Cass Gilbert and decorated with sculpture by Daniel Chester French. After the Customs Service moved to the World Trade Center in 1973, the building stood empty for more than twenty years. As a fitting memorial, this spot—long ago a meeting ground between the native population, the ancestors of the Delaware Nation, and the first European settlers—is now the New York branch of the National Museum of the American Indian. The Delaware people called the tip of lower Manhattan *hay-la-py-ee chen-quay-hee-laas,* "the place where the sun is born."

BOWLING GREEN PARK

A Dutch cattle market from 1638 to 1647, this spot was later the city's first park. In 1732, while under British rule, it was fenced in and rented to Frederick Philipse, John Chamber, and John Roosevelt, local merchants, for use as a bowling area. The ten-year lease was for one peppercorn per year "for the recreation and delight of the inhabitants." It was here that American patriots pulled down a gilded-lead equestrian statue of George III on July 9, 1776. They melted down the statue and used the lead for musket balls to shoot at the British.

BROAD STREET

8 Broad Street
New York Stock Exchange*—This current home of the exchange dates from 1903. All great booms and busts in the market will be measured against what happened here during the Stock Market Crash of 1929. The great boom of the 1920s ended here on "Black Thursday," October 24, 1929, when thirteen million shares were traded. Within a week, the losses totaled $26 billion. One of the reasons for the crash was that speculators had bought stock on margin, paying only a portion of the price, then borrowing the rest and using the stock as security for further loans.

This continued to fuel the boom as long as the market rose. But when prices fell, the borrowers needed more money to back up the drop in the value of their collateral. This forced panic selling. Later, one of the reforms in the market was to have the Federal Reserve Board fix margin rates.

15 Broad Street

This was the address of the law offices of Bangs, Stetson, Tracy and MacVeagh. President Grover Cleveland accepted a job here after losing the election of 1888 to Benjamin Harrison. Cleveland lived in New York until he returned to Washington after winning the presidential election of 1892.

26 Broad Street

The first Latin school in New York was established at this address in the summer of 1659. Alexander Carolus Curtius, a professor from Lithuania, was hired as headmaster. He didn't last very long. He was unhappy about his salary, and parents complained he was a poor disciplinarian. Dutch governor Peter Stuyvesant closed the school two years later, and Curtius sailed back to Europe. The school reopened a year later with a new teacher.

38 Broad Street

When the Fire of 1845 reached the warehouse of Crooker and Warren on the night of July 19, a tremendous explosion shook the city. The saltpeter stored here blew up with such force that the entire building was blown away, except for some bricks. The blast was felt in Brooklyn and Jersey City and heard as far away as Sandy Hook.

44 Broad Street

Woodhull, Clafin & Company—On February 4, 1870, investors, traders, and the curious crowded the sidewalk at this address, straining to see something never before seen on Wall Street, the country's first brokerage firm operated by women. Victoria C. Woodhull and her sister Tennessee Clafin opened their company with the aid of their patron Commo. Cornelius Vanderbilt, a client from Victoria's earlier career as a clairvoyant. This office also served as campaign headquarters for Woodhull's candidacy for the U.S. presidency, forty-eight years before women could vote.

60* Broad Street

This office building was once the headquarters of Drexel Burnham Lambert, one of the country's largest brokerage firms. On December 21, 1988, the company pleaded guilty in federal court to insider trading and stock manipulation and agreed to pay penalties of $650 million. The chairman of Drexel, Michael "Junk Bond King" Milken, and his friend and fellow trader Ivan Boskey both received jail terms for their involvement in the scandal. The firm, which closed in February of 1990, came to symbolize the worst excesses of Wall Street during the freewheeling and freedealing of the Reagan era.

Broad Street and Beaver Street

In the heady days leading to the Revolutionary War, this intersection marked a milestone on the road to war for American independence. On June 6, 1775, British soldiers garrisoned in the city were about to embark on the frigate *Asia* to join their fellow troops in a more receptive and safer Boston. They were stopped at this spot by Marinus Willett, an officer in the New York militia, who seized a cart full of their weapons. Willett, acting under local authority that had permitted the troops to depart but with only their own personal arms, insisted they leave the cart of weapons. The showdown ended with the British leaving peaceably without the additional weapons. These confiscated arms were later used by the first American troops raised in New York under the orders of Congress to fight the British. Willett served with distinction in the war and later served as mayor of the city.

Broad Street and South William

On the night of February 28, 1741, a chain of events began here that became known as the "Great Negro Plot," one of the saddest chapters in race relations in the city's history. On that winter night, someone broke into the home of Robert Hogg, who lived at this corner. Some of Hogg's stolen linens later fell into the hands of John Hughson, the shady owner of a tavern that catered to slaves. Within the next few weeks, Fort George burned to the ground, and there were several more mysterious fires. Determined to make a connection between the robbery and the fires, authorities arrested and questioned Hughson's young servant girl, Mary Burton. Offered money and threatened with damnation, Mary spun a tale of a plot to burn the city and kill all the white people, except her boss Hughson, who would then be crowned "King of New York." The rumored slave revolt inflamed the White colonists, whose resulting rampage ended with the execution of thirty-one African Americans, many of whom were burned at the stake. Another 154 were cast into prison, and 71 were transported to the West Indies. John Hughson and his wife were executed.

101 Broad Street

The German-born C. T. Pachelbel, son of the renowned Johann, performed the first documented concert held in the city at this site, the house of Robert Todd, a vintner, on January 21, 1736. The program was of instrumental music for harpsichord, flute, and violin.

*The Anglers' Club of New York**—A lunchtime blast on January 24, 1975, rocked this club, an annex of next door's Fraunces Tavern, killing four people. The F.A.L.N., a Puerto Rican nationalist group, claimed responsibility for the bombing.

Broad Street West of Water Street

The Exchange Building—Besides being the first capital of the United States, New York City was also the first capital of New York State. The state legislature's opening session took place in this building in January of 1784. The senators and assemblymen continued to meet here until 1796, when the new capital was moved to Albany. On November 3, 1789, the U.S. District Court convened here. Established under the Judiciary Act of 1789, it was the first federal court organized under the new Constitution. President Washington appointed James Duane, former mayor of the city, to be the First District U.S. Judge. The highest court in the land, the U.S. Supreme Court, held its opening session here on February 17, 1790, presided over by Chief Justice John Jay. The building was demolished in 1799.

BROADWAY

1 Broadway

Kennedy Mansion—Built by Capt. Archibald Kennedy of the Royal Navy in 1760, this elegant home, on the site of an earlier tavern, served as the Revolutionary War headquarters of Gen. George Washington until the British occupied the city in September of 1776 and used the house as their headquarters. It was converted into a hotel and lasted another hundred years before being replaced by the current Washington Building, the tallest office building in the world when built in 1884. This building was dramatically remodeled in 1921.

4 Broadway

Aaron Burr, one-time vice president of the United States, lived at this address in 1790–94.

5 Broadway

This address was the home of Robert Livingston, chancellor of New York State and a member of the Continental Congress. He is famous for administering the oath of office to George Washington. When he lived here in the early days of the Republic, his garden extended down to the banks of the Hudson River.

9–11 Broadway

Bowling Green Offices Building*—This Egyptian-style building once housed the offices of the White Star Line. For several days in April of 1912 anxious relatives and friends of the passengers of the company's ship *Titanic* crowded the sidewalk out front and overflowed into Bowling Green Park. They had gathered here, hoping to learn word of the survivors of the doomed ship. Many famous New Yorkers lost their lives on this voyage, including wealthy businessmen John Jacob Astor IV and Benjamin Guggenheim. Also drowned were Isidor Straus, philanthropist and co-owner of R. H. Macy's Department store, and his wife, Ida, whose bravery and devotion to one another has become part of *Titanic* folklore.

The crowd outside 9 Broadway, the offices of the White Star Line, waits for a list of *Titanic* survivors after the ship sank on April 15, 1912. More than 1,493 passengers and crewmembers perished on the ship's maiden voyage to New York. *(FPG)*

Broadway and Beaver Street

The first time an elephant was exhibited in North America was near this intersection on April 29, 1796. The three-year-old female had arrived two weeks earlier from Bengal, India. The ship's captain Jacob Crowninshield paid $450 for her. The elephant was a sensation. Crowninshield quickly resold his prize for $10,000 to a Philadelphian, who exhibited the animal all over the East Coast.

26* Broadway

Allegedly, this corner was the site of the city's first recorded play, perhaps so considered by biased theater historians because of its Broadway address. On December 6, 1732, *The Recruiting Officer* was performed in what was likely the barn of Mr. Rip Van Dam.

The play, a farce written by George Farquhar, had a company of English actors. Both Alexander Hamilton and John Jay, at different times, had homes at this location.

Standard Oil Building—In 1886 the Standard Oil Trust, the world's largest and richest manufacturing organization, moved to 26 Broadway from Cleveland. That modest ten-story building was remodeled and expanded several times into the present building. John D. Rockefeller had his office here until the turn of the twentieth century. After he retired and turned to charitable work, the oilman-turned-philanthropist received at this address up to fifteen thousand letters a week asking for some of his money. One of Rockefeller's most trusted partners, Charles Pratt, died here in his office on May 4, 1891. Pratt used his fortune to build the Pratt Institute and Pratt Institute Free Library, one of the first public libraries in the city. The Standard Oil Company moved to Midtown in 1956.

27–37 Broadway

This site is the first recorded location of a burial ground in Manhattan. In 1649 it was referred to as the "Old Church Yard" in early Dutch records. By 1676 all the lots were full. Within a few years, all the bodies were removed to a site farther north on Broadway, and this land was sold at auction.

39–41 Broadway

This is the legendary site of the first European dwellings on Manhattan Island. Capt. Adriaen Block and his crew were forced to spend the winter of 1613–14 here after their ship, the *Tiger,* anchored in the bay, had caught fire and burned that November. The Dutch sailors built four small crude huts assembled in Native American fashion by bending over and joining the tops of two parallel rows of saplings. The following spring, Block salvaged wood from the *Tiger* and built a new ship, which he named the *Restless.* Only forty-four and a half feet long, the *Restless* took the crew back to Holland.

Alexander McComb Mansion—President George Washington leased this mansion in February of 1790. He lived here only several months before moving to the nation's new capital in Philadelphia. On August 30, 1790, Washington took his final leave of New York City on a Hudson River wharf behind this house. The first president and first lady received a thirteen-gun farewell salute.

Bunker's Mansion House—John Quincy Adams was a guest here at the old McComb Mansion, which had been converted into a hotel in 1821. The ex-president was in town for a dinner honoring the New-York Historical Society on November 19, 1844.

Broadway between Morris Street and Exchange Place, West Side

At this site was the home and orchard of Hendrick Van Dyck. A Native American woman was trying to steal some peaches when Van Dyck spied her and killed her. Several days later, on September 15, 1655, Native Americans attacked the settlement in revenge. Over a period of two days, fifty settlers were killed, and many women and children were taken as prisoners. This was the last major attack by native dwellers on the settlers.

50 Broadway

Tower Building—A major advancement in the development of skyscrapers was skeleton-frame construction. The narrow 21½-feet-wide, thirteen-story building that once stood at this location was the first to use this innovation, albeit only partially. The first seven floors were built with the new method, an iron armature supporting the weight of each floor. The top floors were constructed with the usual load-bearing walls, so those walls had to be increasingly thicker to support the weight of higher ones. This key development allowed architects to build higher into the sky and not waste valuable lower floor space to thick exterior walls. One problem yet unsolved was how to reassure the public that these tall buildings wouldn't fall down. Bradford Lee Gilbert, the architect, solved this dilemma by putting his own office on the top floor to prove it was safe. This innovative monument was torn down in 1914 with little fanfare to make way for an even taller building.

57 Broadway

On September 7, 1879, two days after returning home from a trip abroad, Stanford White started his first day as a new partner with Charles McKim and William Mead. The three partners would create some of the most beautiful buildings in America. They mastered a classical style particularly suited to America's new wealthy class. They were to stay at this address until 1894.

71 Broadway

Empire Building—Russell Sage, the wealthy financier and namesake of the philanthropic foundation, had a brokerage office on the second floor of an office building that once stood on this corner. On December 4, 1891, a madman named Henry W. Norcross entered the office and demanded $1.2 million from Sage. When Sage refused, Norcross set off a dynamite bomb, killing himself and a clerk. The blast injured seven others, including Sage. In addition to damaging the building, the explosion blew valuable securities out onto the street. The current Empire Building at this site was built in 1898.

Broadway at the Head of Wall Street

Trinity Church*—Richard Upjohn designed the present Gothic Revival church, the third on this spot, and it was consecrated on May 21, 1846, Ascension Day. The ornate 281-foot stone spire made the church the highest structure in Manhattan for thirty years until eclipsed by the towers of the Brooklyn Bridge. During the nineteenth century the church became a popular gathering place on New Year's Eve. The hushed crowd would listen for the lofty steeple's midnight chimes to welcome in the New Year with hymns. The party moved uptown to Times Square in 1904. The first church, chartered by British King William III in 1697, was destroyed in the Great Fire of 1776.

Queen Elizabeth II visited here during the Bicentennial Celebrations, on July 9, 1976. The date of this visit was two hundred years to the day that American patriots had pulled down a statue of her great-great-great-great-grandfather King George III in Bowling Green Park. While here, the queen also collected 279 years' worth of "rent due the Monarchy"—279 peppercorns—since the royal charter on the church had never expired.

Like most of lower Manhattan, Trinity Church was destroyed in the fire of 1776. The British, who had just occupied the city during the Revolutionary War, were accused of not effectively fighting the three-day fire that destroyed 493 homes and a third of the city. *(Author's collection)*

The churchyard is the final resting place for several famous Trinity parishioners, including Robert Fulton, Alexander Hamilton, and Francis Lewis, the only signer of the Declaration of Independence buried in Manhattan. The yard also contains the nation's first tomb to unknown soldiers, the Martyr's Monument, honoring unidentified colonials who died in British prisons in the city during the American Revolution.

111 Broadway

Trinity Building—This five-story building, with the same name as the current building and replacement, was built in 1852. The structure was an early example of the modern office building, with specially designed space for multiple tenants. One of those tenants was architect Richard Upjohn, who designed the building and Trinity Church next door.

115 Broadway

City Arm's Tavern—An important event on the American road to independence from England took place here on October 31, 1765: a meeting of two hundred merchants and the "Sons of Liberty" to protest the Stamp Act, when the participants decided on a nonimportation agreement. Originally the mansion of Etienne De Lancey built around 1700, the tavern went through several name and owner changes. It was the site of President George Washington's inaugural ball on May 5, 1789. Vice President John Adams, John Hancock, James Madison, Alexander Hamilton, and John Jay were guests. Because Martha Washington, who did not arrive until the twenty-seventh, missed the party, George danced with Mrs. Peter Livingston and Mrs. Alexander Hamilton.

City Hotel—This early example of a true hotel, rather than an inn, was erected in 1794. The five-story brick structure with seventy-eight rooms was covered with the first slate roof in the city. The ground floor had fashionable shops along the Broadway side. Seven hundred guests attended a grand military ball here on Washington's birthday, February 22, 1819, in honor of Gen. Andrew Jackson, a hero of the War of 1812.

Broadway between Pine and Cedar Streets

The National Hotel—Johann Maelzel and his invention "The Turk," a fanciful chess machine, made their American debut at this hotel that once stood on the corner of Cedar Street on April 13, 1826. "The Turk" was a turbaned figure made of wood and filled with whirling gears, wheels, cogs, and metal parts that sat in front of a

Built in 1870, the Equitable Life Assurance Society headquarters at 120 Broadway was one of the first office buildings to incorporate elevators. Fire fighters continue to hose the building's shell in sub-zero weather during a fire on January 9, 1912. *(Author's collection)*

large box with a chess board on top. Maelzel and his mechanical marvel had only recently amazed European audiences. "The Turk" had even played a chess game with Napoleon and won. Americans, too, were amazed, at least for a few years until the hoax was exposed. It was then learned that a small but skilled chess player was inside, operating "The Turk." This hidden assistant managed to fool everyone by darting between inner compartments just before Maelzel opened a series of doors exposing "The Turk's" supposed mechanical workings.

*Equitable Building**—An earlier beaux arts headquarters of the insurance company on this block was destroyed in a spectacular fire on January 9, 1912. The replacement and current structure with more than 1.2 million square feet of floor space was the world's largest office building when completed in 1915. The overwhelming bulk of this edifice rising forty-two stories straight up from the narrow streets confirmed the need for the long-proposed zoning laws. The city passed its first zoning law on July 25, 1916. The law restricted the total height of buildings relative to their site and encouraged the use of setbacks on higher floors to allow more sunlight to reach the street.

133 Broadway
John Jay lived here when he coauthored *The Federalist* in 1787.

140 Broadway
Marine Midland Bank—A bomb exploded here on August 20, 1969, in protest of the Vietnam War. Twenty people were injured.

149 Broadway
From 1794 to 1803 this was the site of the home and office of John Jacob Astor.

165 Broadway
Singer Building—From 1908 to 1967 this location was home to the beautiful forty-seven–story Singer Building. The rococo-style skyscraper, with innovative setbacks, was the world's tallest building for eighteen months until the Metropolitan Life Tower at Madison Square was completed. The destruction of this landmark, the tallest building ever demolished, was a great loss to the city's architectural heritage.

176 Broadway
Howard's Hotel—President John Tyler stayed here on the night of June 25, 1844. The president had secretly arrived early in the day by train from Washington, D.C.,

Two of the city's most beautiful early skyscrapers, the now demolished Singer and the Woolworth Buildings, lined up along Broadway. Seen between the two flagpoles is "Golden Boy," who stood atop the Telephone Company Building until the 1980s when he moved with AT&T to the new Madison Avenue Chippendale-topped highrise. (FPG)

for his wedding to New Yorker Julia Gardiner. The clandestine marriage at the Church of the Ascension the following day was kept from the public to ensure the newlyweds' privacy.

195* Broadway
American Telephone and Telegraph Company Building—The first transcontinental telephone call from the fifteenth-floor office of the president of AT&T to San Francisco over a 3,400-mile-long wire was held on January 25, 1915. Alexander Graham Bell, from this address, spoke to his long-time assistant Thomas Watson on the West Coast. They reenacted the world's first spoken words on the telephone they had made in 1876. But this time, when Bell said, "Mr. Watson, come here, I want you," Watson replied, "It would take me a week now." Shortly after their historic demonstration, President Woodrow Wilson called from Washington, D.C., with his congratulations.

Broadway and Fulton Street, Southwest Corner

Brady's National Gallery of Daguerrotypes—Mathew Brady opened his first daguerreotype studio on Broadway at Fulton Street in 1844. The new medium was a tremendous success in America. Within ten years, there were more daguerreotype studios in Manhattan alone than in all of England, where legal restraints interfered with their commercialization. Brady, who learned his craft from innovator Samuel F. B. Morse, was quick to see the commercial and documentary potential of photography. All the leading politicians of the day—Henry Clay, Daniel Webster, Martin Van Buren, and Millard Fillmore—had their photographs taken here.

BRADY'S NATIONAL GALLERY OF DAGUERREOTYPES

This collection embraces some of the most distinguished men of this country. The President and Cabinet, also the late President Polk and his Cabinet, Members of the United States Senate and House of Representatives, Judges of the Supreme Court at Washington, and many other eminent persons are included in this Gallery. The Proprietor being much of his time in Washington, has the advantage of adding to these portraits any others that may interest the public. This establishment is one of the most extensive in the world, its facilities for the production of portraits by the Daguerrean art being unrivalled. It now occupies two large buildings, 205 and 207 Broadway. The operating department is arranged in the most scientific manner, and directed by persons of acknowledged skill in the profession. In the department arranged for copying paintings, daguerreotypes, engravings, statuary, &c., the light and instruments have been expressly designed for this purpose. It is the aim of the proprietor to render in every part of his business that attention which the public are entitled to from the patronage he has received. At the annual exhibitions of the American Institute for five years, the pictures from this establishment have received the first prize, consisting of a silver medal. The last year the first gold medal ever awarded to Daguerreotypes was bestowed on the pictures from this Gallery. The portraits taken for the "Gallery of Illustrious Americans," a work so favorably received throughout the United States, are engraved from these Daguerreotypes. Strangers and citizens will be interested and pleased by devoting an hour to the inspection of Brady's National Gallery, Nos. 205 and 207 Broadway, corner of Fulton-street, New York.

By the 1850s there were hundreds of daguerreotype galleries in the city, particularly along Broadway from Fulton to Canal Streets. This advertisement was designed to attract sitters to Mathew Brady's studio at 205-7 Broadway. *(Author's collection)*

Broadway and Fulton Street

Loew's Bridge—A lacy Gothic pedestrian bridge was built over this busy and dangerous intersection in 1867. Philip Genin, a hatter on the southwest corner, had encouraged the span's construction. A year later his archrival, Knox the Hatter from the northeast corner, had the bridge removed by a court order. The mad hatter Knox claimed it blocked light and air to his store and attracted loiterers.

Broadway between Fulton and Vesey Streets

St. Paul's Chapel*—Completed in 1766, this is the oldest public building still in use in Manhattan. On April 30, 1789, almost the entire newly formed U.S. government—the vice president, the speaker of the House, and both houses of Congress—accompanied their hour-old, newly inaugurated president, George Washington, on a walk to this chapel for a special thanksgiving service. The president worshiped here for most of the time he lived in New York. His pew, in the north aisle, is adorned with the first depiction in oil of the Great Seal of the United States. President George Bush used this same pew on April 30, 1989, while attending a special two hundredth–anniversary service commemorating that first inauguration. Former President James Monroe's funeral was held here on July 7, 1831.

Broadway and Ann Street, Southeast Corner

Spring Garden—This corner was the location of the first pleasure garden in New York. Pleasure gardens, an idea imported from England, were outdoor restaurants in a landscaped setting. The Spring Garden, begun in the early 1700s, lasted until 1768.

American Museum—This site later became the home of P. T. Barnum's museum, a collection of natural history exhibits, "scientific" displays, and freaks. It was here that the self-proclaimed "Prince of Humbugs" introduced the Siamese twins Chang and Eng to the United States, along with Gen. Tom Thumb, the famous midget. The building caught fire on July 13, 1865, killing most of the assembled menagerie. One Bengal tiger did manage to escape but was killed by a fire fighter on Broadway. Barnum moved his new show uptown to 539 Broadway, only to have that museum burn three years later.

New York Herald Building—Another version of nineteenth-century mass entertainment occupied this site in 1866: the *New York Herald* newspaper. It was from this building that editor James Gordon Bennett Jr. sent his correspondent Henry Stanley to find the missing missionary David Livingstone on March 21, 1871. Seven months later Stanley found the good doctor at Lake Tanganyika in Africa and

greeted him with the words, "Dr. Livingstone, I presume?" In 1896 this building was torn down, and the *Herald* moved uptown to 35th Street at Herald Square. The last vestige of the *Herald* is the newspaper's elaborate clock in the triangular plot in front of R. H. Macy's.

Broadway between Vesey and Murray Streets
The city's first sidewalk lined these three blocks of Broadway in 1790. The narrow walkways were paved with stones and bricks.

Broadway between Vesey and Barclay Streets
Astor Hotel—The Park Hotel—later renamed the Astor House Hotel—was built in 1834 on the site of a home once lived in by Rufus King, a member of the Continental Congress. John Jacob Astor, the hotel's builder, purchased the King home, lived in it awhile, and had it demolished along with the rest of the block to pre-

The offices of the New York Herald are on the left in this view of Broadway looking south from Vesey Street in 1867. St. Paul's Chapel is on the right. The packed pedestrian bridge crossing busy Broadway is Loew's Bridge, an early effort at traffic control. *(Harper's Weekly, June 8, 1867)*

The Astor House Hotel on Broadway and Vesey Street shortly before it was torn down in 1914; note the "Must Vacate" sign. The bar, famous for its "free lunch," continued to be a popular meeting place long after newer uptown hotels became more fashionable. *(FPG)*

pare for his innovative hotel. Opened two years later on June 1, 1836, it became the nation's favorite hotel. Davy Crockett was one of the first guests. Andrew Jackson, Henry Clay, James Polk, Abraham Lincoln, Jefferson Davis, Sam Houston all stayed here. William James, the psychologist, was born in the hotel on January 11, 1842. English author Charles Dickens stayed at this hotel on his first trip to New York in 1842, and it was here seventy years later that his eldest surviving son Alfred D'Orsay Tennyson Dickens died suddenly on January 2, 1912. Alfred was in New York to plan his father's centenary celebration.

Broadway between Barclay Street and Park Place

This was once the site of Mayor Philip Hone's home. Mayor from 1826 to 1827, Hone was also a bank director, trustee of Columbia College, vice president of the New-York Historical Society, and founder of the Union Club. This brilliant Renaissance man is known today chiefly through his diary. His chronicle, kept from 1823 to 1851, has been a blessing to generations of historians eager to learn of New York City life in the mid-nineteenth century. In 1836 Hone recorded in his diary a now-familiar New York phenomenon: how rising real-estate values had prompted him to sell his home to the American Hotel next door and move uptown. The hotel was host to President Andrew Jackson, Daniel Webster, and other notables.

*Woolworth Building**—This Gothic-style masterpiece is nicknamed "the Cathedral of Commerce." Opening celebrations on April 24, 1913, included a twenty-seventh–floor dinner for three U.S. senators and seventy-eight congressmen. That night, President Woodrow Wilson, sitting in Washington, D.C., pushed a button that lit eighty thousand light bulbs in the world's tallest skyscraper. The Woolworth held that title until the early 1930s.

253–254 Broadway

Peale's Museum and Gallery of the Fine Arts—The first rhinoceros ever exhibited in America was seen here September 13–25, 1826.

Broadway and Warren Street, Southwest Corner

On September 21, 1837, Charles Lewis Tiffany and John B. Young opened a "fancy goods" and stationery shop at 259 Broadway. Sales for the first day totalled $4.98, with a profit the first week of $334. The store remained at this location until 1841.

Devlin & Company Clothing—The basement of a later corner building was the hidden entrance to a subterranean chamber furnished with a grand piano, fountain, and goldfish tank. This sumptuous room served as the waiting room and ticket office for New York's earliest subway. The project, completed after fifty-eight nights of tunneling, was built secretly to avoid the city corruption and graft kickbacks of the Tammany political bosses. The tunnel, 12 feet below Broadway, was designed for compressed-air propulsion and was only 9 feet in diameter and 312 feet long. This prototype, invented by the publisher of *Scientific American* Alfred Ely Beach, was unveiled to the public on February 26, 1870. It was an immediate sensation. The *New York Herald* reported the tunnel was an "Aladdin's cave" full of hidden magic. Over the next year, four hundred thousand people rode the fancy car at twenty-five

Elegant ladies and gentlemen await their turn on New York City's first subway platform in February of 1870. The subway beneath Broadway and Warren Street was an experimental pneumatic subway tunnel powered with a huge helix fan. *(Author's collection)*

cents a ride, the proceeds going to charity. But this type of subway system was never built. It was too expensive to produce the tremendous volume of air needed to propel the train. Beach rented out his tunnel for a shooting gallery and wine cellar, but soon after he had it sealed. The station and the tunnel were forgotten—until February 8, 1912, when subway workers, working on the current BMT, were astonished to rediscover it.

263 Broadway

The drugstore of Dr. James R. Chilton was once at this address. He was a chemist and early photography buff. It was here that the first successful daguerreotype ever taken in the Western Hemisphere was displayed on September 16, 1839. The picture was taken on a sensitized copper plate by D. W. Seager, an Englishman living in New York. The subject matter was St. Paul's Chapel, just down Broadway. The camera exposure for this picture was more than eight minutes long. This streetscape has been lost, as have other early photographs of the city. Samuel F. B. Morse was known to have made several cityscapes, but these too are either lost or were destroyed. The earliest known and identified photographs of New York City were made by Victor Prevost in the 1850s.

BROOKLYN BRIDGE

A wonder of the nineteenth century, the East River Bridge, as it was first called, was a result of the engineering genius of its chief designer, John A. Roebling. He was one of the first to use steel cable on such a colossal scale in a suspension bridge. Roebling, who died while working on the project, was replaced by his son Washington. While working in the caissons on the riverbed, Washington was disabled by the pressure, what is now understood as the "bends." It took fourteen years to complete the world's longest suspension bridge, a proud symbol of the Industrial Age. Its Gothic towers strung with harplike cables towered over the city. During opening-day ceremonies, on May 24, 1883, New York–born President Chester A. Arthur led a walk across the span from the nation's largest city, New York, to the nation's third-largest city, Brooklyn. A week later, on Memorial Day weekend, a tragic stampede that killed twelve people, including two children, marred the celebrations. A man named Steve Brodie claimed to have jumped on July 23, 1886. Although no one saw him take the plunge, he was seen being pulled from the East River, and that was enough for him to become an actor, bar owner, and folk hero.

On May 30, 1883, after hearing the screams of a woman, who had fallen on a staircase, the crowd panicked, believing the new Brooklyn Bridge was collapsing. The resulting stampede killed a dozen people, including two children, and injured several more. *(Frank Leslie's, June 9, 1883)*

CHAMBERS STREET

During a devastating yellow fever epidemic—in August of 1822—a fence was erected along Chambers Street. This barricade was intended to prevent citizens from returning to their homes and businesses in lower Manhattan. Earlier, the authorities had forced the evacuation of much of the population in the hopes of stemming the epidemic. A contemporary account recorded the scene: "Saturday the 24th August, our city presented the appearance of a town besieged. From daybreak till night one line of carts, containing boxes, merchandise, and the effects, were seen moving towards Greenwich Village [from] the upper parts of the city." These summer outbreaks of yellow fever accelerated the development of the city northward up the island of Manhattan.

Chambers Street and Centre Street, Southwest Corner

The Rotunda—This classical, domed, templelike structure, erected in 1818 by the painter John Vanderlyn with the help of his patron Aaron Burr, was intended as an art center for the new nation. The paintings of Thomas Cole, John Trumbull, Samuel F. B. Morse, and Asher Durand were exhibited along with Vanderlyn's own panorama of the Gardens of Versailles. The space beneath the dome served as a viewing room for the elaborate painted panorama. Guests, who stood in the center on an elevated platform, were surrounded by the painted garden. The venture was a financial failure. The city took over the building, and it housed government offices until it was demolished in 1870.

31–33 Chambers Street

Manhattan Company Reservoir—An ancient Egyptian–style reservoir topped with a reclining statue of Aquarius, the water-bearer, stood at this spot. Aaron Burr founded this enterprise, called the Manhattan Company, in 1799. It supplied the growing city with fresh water from pine-wood pipes coated with tar for tightness and longevity. An unusual charter from the state legislature allowed the company to engage in banking activities. (The company was an early parent of the Chase Manhattan Bank.) One vocal critic of this reservoir company's involvement in the banking business was Alexander Hamilton. This disagreement between Burr and Hamilton was the first of many that eventually led to their fatal duel in 1804.

39–41 Chambers Street

Palmo's Opera House—Opened by Signor Ferdinando Palmo in 1844, this small theater was built to bring Italian opera to New York on a permanent basis. Palmo lost his opera house and all his money within two years. It later reopened as Burton's Chambers Street Theater. It was the first theater in the city to sell numbered seats, and late theater-goers were assured of an empty seat. This theater was one of many that staged risqué "artist model shows" in the middle of the nineteenth century. A contemporary account of the show described "living men and women in almost the same state in which Gabriel saw them in the Garden of Eden on the first morning of creation." The shows were eventually outlawed.

52 Chambers Street

New York Institution—Originally the city's second almshouse in the park, this building was set aside for a variety of other benevolent purposes in 1816, when the poor were moved to Bellevue. It was an early home to the New-York Historical Society, the New York Society Library, and the American Academy of Fine Arts. Another early tenant was the Bank for Savings, the first savings bank in the United States. It opened for business on July 3, 1819, in the Institution's basement.

Old New York Courthouse*—The "Tweed" Courthouse has come to symbolize the most corrupt era in the city's government. A bill in 1858 set aside $250,000 for construction of this Victorian pile. But when it was completed in 1872, the total cost to the taxpayers came to more than $12 million. The difference ended up lining the pockets of Boss William Tweed and his cronies. The eventual cost for New York's new courthouse was twice the price the United States had paid for Alaska just five years earlier. This courthouse served as a fitting stage for Judge Samuel Seabury's investigation into city corruption. On May 25, 1932, Mayor Jimmy Walker took the stand and confirmed what even his admirers suspected—that the popular "Night Mayor" wasn't very honest, even by New York standards. The mayor was summoned to Albany by fellow Democrat Governor Franklin D. Roosevelt to face charges. Walker resigned on September 1, 1932, and promptly left for a European vacation.

During a state committee investigation into New York City government, Judge Samuel Seabury questions Mayor Jimmy Walker in Old New York County Courthouse in May of 1932. The corruption scandals forced the mayor to resign. *(FPG)*

CHERRY STREET

1 Cherry Street

From April 23, 1789, until February 23, 1790, President George Washington lived at this address in a red brick mansion owned by Walter Franklin. De Witt Clinton occupied the same house in 1817 before he moved to Albany to be governor of New York.

5 Cherry Street

This address was once the home of John Hancock. It was later the birthplace, on April 3, 1823, of New York City's most notorious politician, William Marcy Tweed. Tweed's father ran his chair-making business from his home at this address. This entire stretch of Cherry Street no longer exists; it was replaced by the Manhattan approach to the Brooklyn Bridge.

27 Cherry Street

New York City's answer to Betsy Ross, Samuel Chester Reid, lived in a house that once stood at this address. Reid, who was a naval officer in the War of 1812, is credited with designing the U.S. flag in its present modern form, the thirteen stripes with a varying number of stars. The first flag of his design, sewn by his wife, Mary, in their dining room, was raised over the U.S. Capitol on April 12, 1818.

CHURCH STREET

Church Street and Vesey Street

In 1859 this intersection was part of the wharf district where George H. Hartford and his partner, George F. Gillman, began their small tea company. This fledgling enterprise, which sold tea directly from ships arriving from Asia to their New York City customers, would grow to be one of the largest companies on earth, the Great Atlantic and Pacific Tea Company, commonly known as A & P.

85 Church Street

This address was once the home of John Wesley Jarvis, an important early American portrait painter. His friend, the writer Thomas Paine, lived with him here for six months in 1806.

Church Street between Park Place and Murray Street and to West Broadway

King's College—Here was the first permanent home of King's College, which was renamed Columbia College after the Revolutionary War. Alexander Hamilton, John Jay, Robert Livingston, Gouverneur Morris, and De Witt Clinton, all leaders of the newly independent nation, studied at this campus. Columbia was here from 1760 until 1857, when the school moved to Madison Avenue and East 49th Street.

City Hall*

This delicate French Renaissance–style structure has served as City Hall since its dedication just before the outbreak of the War of 1812. For almost 190 years it has been a focal point for the city's triumphs and tragedies. It has been a site for the mourning of fallen leaders and heroes who lay in state: Henry Clay on July 3, 1852; John Quincy Adams on March 8, 1858; and Ulysses S. Grant on August 5, 1885. Abraham Lincoln's body was placed on the circular staircase. More than 120,000 mourners paid their respects to the Great Emancipator in the twenty-four hours his body was on

City Hall was draped in mourning for President Abraham Lincoln on April 25, 1865. Lincoln's body lay in state here on the long funeral journey from Washington, D.C., to Springfield, Illinois. *(Collection of the New-York Historical Society)*

view. The front steps have been a stage for mayoral inaugurations, protests, and speeches. These steps often serve as the finish line for Broadway ticker-tape parades honoring foreign dignitaries, winning athletes, politicians, and explorers.

City Hall Subway Station*—After an hour and a half of speeches above ground, newly inaugurated Mayor George B. McClellan, the son of the Civil War general, and other dignitaries made their way down to this station underneath the drive in front of City Hall to officially open the subway on October 27, 1904. This beautifully tiled station, unfortunately now closed to the public, was the start of that first ride at 2:35 p.m. With the words "I now, as Mayor, in the name of the people declare the subway open," McClellan pulled the Tiffany-made solid-silver control handle, and the train lurched uptown. The enthusiastic mayor refused to relinquish the controls, as planned, and continued in his role as conductor. He overshot several stations and jerked a few of his notable passengers off their seats. Despite the mayor's unsure hand, that first subway arrived at the last stop at 145th Street, twenty-six minutes later. At 7:00, the Interborough Rapid Transit, or IRT as it became known, was opened to the public. By the end of the day, more than 110,000 passengers had entered the system.

CLIFF STREET

97 Cliff Street
An eighteen-year-old Samuel Clemens worked at this address in 1853 as a journeyman printer. He was living in a boardinghouse on Duane Street.

CORTLANDT STREET

Cortlandt Street and West Street
This spot—now covered by the World Trade Center—was the landing dock of the world's first steam ferryboat. On July 2, 1812, the *Jersey* carried the first passengers from here to New Jersey just south of Hoboken. Designed and operated by Robert Fulton, the innovative all-wooden ship was 118 tons, 30 feet wide, and 80 feet long. The open double-ended design made it unnecessary to come around 180 degrees before or after each landing, enabling wagons to disembark from the same direction in which they had boarded. This saved time and effort on every crossing and docking. Before steam, ferries were powered by draft horses harnessed to treadmills connected to the paddle wheels.

DEY STREET

Dey Street and Greenwich Street

During an excavation at this intersection in 1916, the earliest known artifacts of European explorers in New York were discovered: the charred timbers of the Dutch ship the *Tiger*. The ship's captain, Adriaen Block, and his men were forced to camp on Manhattan Island for the winter of 1613–14. The *Tiger* burned, and the crew built a new, smaller ship. This part of lower Manhattan, rich in early New York City archaeological history, is buried beneath the present World Trade Center.

DOVER STREET

Dover Street and Pearl Street

Cornelis Dircksen established the first ferry to Long Island around 1640 at this site on what was then the East River shoreline. The passengers signaled Dircksen and his rowboat with a blow on a conch shell horn hung on trees on each side of the shore. These passengers, the earliest recorded New York City commuters, were Dutch planters who farmed small plots in Brooklyn. The land, just recently purchased from Native Americans, was still the property of the Dutch West Indian Company and leased to the planters until their debt was paid. This arrangement gave the borough its name: the word *Brjikenleen* is derived from two Dutch words, *Brjiken* for "use," and *leen* for "loan."

FRANKFORT STREET

39 Frankfort Street

George B. Smith, a member of Engine Company No. 12, placed the first modern fire hydrant in New York City at this address in 1817. Mr. Smith installed the hydrant, an octagon-shaped wooden enclosure held together with iron straps, in front of his own house at his own expense. Unfortunately, low pressure in the water main reduced the effectiveness of the new device, and it wasn't until the 1840s that hydrants became widespread.

FRANKLIN SQUARE

Now replaced by the anchorage to the Brooklyn Bridge, this square was at the end of Cherry Street. It was the location for a public demonstration of the city's first gas street lamp on June 11, 1824. Two years later these new gas-burning lamps were lighting up Broadway from the Battery to Grand Street.

FULTON STREET

Fulton Street at the East River

The Fulton Ferry Company, headed by engineer and businessman Robert Fulton, began the first steamboat ferry service to Brooklyn on Saturday, May 10, 1814. The ship, *Nassau,* made the trip in about eight minutes at a speed of five miles per hour. Fulton's ferry hastened the development of Brooklyn as a residential community, the nation's first suburb. The ferry landings were later honored and renamed Fulton Street, one in New York and the other across the river in Brooklyn. Now further inland, the ferry landing site is currently the South Street Seaport. The *Nassau,* after many years in service, was converted into a floating chapel tied to a New York wharf.

71 Fulton Street

Situated in a courtyard at the back of this lot was the city's first recorded permanent fire station. Built in the early 1820s, this "Fireman's Hall" served as both a headquarters and social club for the volunteer fire fighters. Prior to construction of this structure, crude neighborhood sheds filled with ladders, hand engines, and buckets were the only means of defense against fire in the predominantly wooden city.

148 Fulton Street

On October 25, 1857, Joseph Wedemeyer, a friend of both Karl Marx and Friedrich Engels, founded the Communist Club of New York. His club, which met at this address, was the first Marxist organization in the Western Hemisphere.

168–172 Fulton Street

Opened in 1795, this was the warehouse, workshop, and showroom of America's leading furniture craftsman, Duncan Phyfe. He lived across the street at number 169.

252 Fulton Street

Jimmy the Priest's Saloon—This building, with a saloon on the ground floor and a flophouse above, was often home to sailors in town between voyages. One of those long-ago sailors was Eugene O'Neill. It was here, upstairs in his room, that the future playwright attempted suicide in December of 1911. The saloon, complete with an old mahogany bar and sawdust on the floor, served as a model for his plays *The Iceman Cometh* and *Anna Christie.* The World Trade Center replaced this literary landmark.

GREENWICH STREET

Greenwich Street from Battery Place to Cortlandt Street

This length of Greenwich Street was the test section of the world's first elevated railway. The inventor, Charles T. Harvey, rode the cable-driven car on its initial run on July 3, 1867. The line was built on a row of iron supports and consisted of a single track. Steam engines housed in underground vaults supplied the power to pull the continuously moving three-quarter-inch steel cable. The car edged forward when the driver engaged a clamp that extended below the wooden car and gripped the cable. Repeated cable breakdowns doomed the system until locomotive power replaced the cable system in 1871. Harvey's mass-transit innovation evolved into the Ninth Avenue Elevated Line.

82–84 Greenwich Street

These two lots extending through to Washington Street were once the site of one of the earliest circuses in America. Scottish showman John Bill Ricketts put together some equestrian acts, an acrobat, and a rope walker, called his show a circus, and brought his troop up from Philadelphia in 1793, first to a site on Broadway and Exchange Alley, then to this site in 1797. It was here that President John Adams watched the show on October 24 of that year.

HANOVER STREET

Hanover Street and Beaver Street

Comstock and Adams Dry Goods Store—The fire, caused by a gas-pipe explosion, that started in this store on December 15, 1835, was the origin of the Great Fire of

1835. This conflagration burned for two days and engulfed the heart of the business section, everything south of Wall Street and east of Broad Street. More than six hundred buildings were totally consumed. In addition to the enormous loss to the financial community, nearly all the city's fire-insurance companies were destroyed or bankrupted—which left their clients with no possibility for compensation. Yet for all the destruction, there was miraculously no loss of life.

JOHN STREET

15–21 John Street

John Street Theater—One of the earliest theaters built in New York, the John Street Theater stood here from its opening on December 7, 1767, until 1798. The building was described as "principally of wood; an unsightly object, painted red."

Looking almost bucolic, this engraving is based on a painting by Joseph Beekman Smith of 1768. The large building in the middle of the block is the Wesley Chapel, the first Methodist Episcopal Church in America. *(Author's collection)*

Royall Tyler's *The Contrast,* the first comedy in America produced by a native author, was performed at this theater on April 16, 1787. It introduced the character of Jonathan, the stereotypical rustic Yankee. President and Mrs. Washington, who had their own box, were welcomed each performance with the "President's March," later known as "Hail Columbia." Washington's attendance here helped mollify local religious opposition to the theater.

44 John Street
John Street United Methodist Church—*This is the site of the oldest Methodist Society in America. Philip Embury preached at the dedication service here at a small "Wesley Chapel" on October 30, 1768. The current church, the third on this site, was erected in 1840.

John Street between Nassau and William Streets
The Battle of Golden Hill was fought on this spot on January 19, 1770, shedding the first blood of the American Revolution, several weeks before the Boston Massacre. The Sons of Liberty and their sympathizers rioted on this site of a British Army barracks, outraged by the British removal of their liberty pole and over the issue of quartering British soldiers in their homes. One patriot was killed, and several were wounded.

81 John Street

This address was once the office of J. L. Haiger. In 1877 he became the first paid telephone subscriber in the city. A five-mile-long wire was laid across the half-finished Brooklyn Bridge, connecting this office to his steel-wire plant in Brooklyn.

LIBERTY STREET

28–36 Liberty Street

Livingston Sugar House—A warehouse once on this spot served as a British military prison for American Revolutionary War soldiers from 1776 until 1783. The British commonly used sugar houses as jails. Built of stone walls, with small windows and low ceilings, they were adept at holding prisoners as well as sugar. This is now the site of Chase Manhattan Bank Plaza.

55 Liberty Street

Liberty Tower*—The current co-operative apartment house was once the twenty-ninth–floor headquarters of the Sinclair Consolidated Oil Company run by Harry Sinclair. In the early 1920s U.S. Secretary of the Interior Albert B. Fall secretly transferred government oil lands here to Sinclair's company. The deals, exposed by the end of the decade, became known as the "Teapot Dome" Scandal and resulted in prison terms for both Sinclair and Fall. Franklin D. Roosevelt had a first-floor office here in the mid-1920s. He was then vice president and New York representative of the Fidelity and Deposit Insurance Company of Maryland.

59 Liberty Street

In the early 1870s Charles Guiteau had a struggling law practice in a building that once stood at this address. Guiteau become infamous about ten years later for assassinating President James A. Garfield on July 2, 1881, in a Washington, D.C., train station.

MAIDEN LANE

19 Maiden Lane

James Madison was living in Elsworth's Boarding House, which once stood at this address, in 1787. It was here that the future president of the United States co-wrote *The Federalist,* essays explaining the new Constitution and advocating its adoption.

57 Maiden Lane

After moving to the city in 1790, as the country's first secretary of state Thomas Jefferson wrote, "My first object was to look out a house on the Broadway as being the centre of my business. Finding none there vacant for the present, I have taken a small one in Maiden Lane, which may give me time to look about." He lived here three months, in a house that stood at this address until 1929.

Maiden Lane near William Street

It was near this spot, in an orchard once owned by Mr. Cook but long ago replaced by modern office buildings, that a group of twenty-five African American and three Native American slaves met after midnight on April 7, 1712, to plan an insurrection against their white masters. They waited until the moon was setting at two o'clock, and then their leader, a slave named Coffee, set fire to the outhouse of his owner, Peter Van Tilburgh. The plotters watched and waited as a crowd gathered, drawn by the blaze. The slaves attacked, killing nine people and wounding six others. The local militia caught and killed some of the insurrectionaries within hours. The rest were rounded up and brutally executed—most burned alive—as an gruesome example to the colony's slaves.

NASSAU STREET

Nassau Street between Cedar and Liberty Streets, East Side

Middle Dutch Church—Dating from 1727, this gabled church was used as a prison and riding school for the British during the Revolution. On April 29, 1839, the city celebrated the fiftieth anniversary of the inaugural of George Washington here. The guest of honor was sixty-nine-year-old ex-president John Quincy Adams, who spoke for two hours. Mr. Adams shared the stage with a chair used by Washington at his inauguration. In 1845 the building was leased to the federal government as a post office. It was here, in a second-floor office, that the first U.S. stamps were issued on July 1, 1847. The stamps, a five-cent issue with Benjamin Franklin's image and a ten-cent issue with George Washington's image, were a new innovation: prepaid postage. Prior to this, all letters were delivered with postage due.

82 Nassau Street

New York Telephone Exchange—The Bell Company opened the first telephone exchange here in March of 1878. Later, in October, the city's first telephone directory, with 252 names, was issued on a small card. In the early days, there

were no telephone numbers. Calls were made by asking the operator for the name of the person being called.

115 Nassau Street

Currier & Ives Shop—The offices and salesroom of America's foremost lithographic team were at this address in the 1880s. Nathaniel Currier started his print shop in 1834. For the next seventy years he and James Merritt Ives, his partner after 1857, produced thousands of cherished prints. These prints, whose subject matter range from domestic scenes to disasters, are an important visual record of nineteenth-century America.

126 Nassau Street

A boardinghouse at this address was once home to Mary Cecilia Rogers, a beautiful young woman who sold cigars and tobacco on Broadway near Duane Street. She was a familiar and beloved figure in the neighborhood. Her disappearance on July 28, 1841, and the finding of her strangled body floating in the Hudson River shocked the city. Her murder was never solved. Edgar Allan Poe, an admirer who frequented her shop, later based his "Mystery of Marie Roget" on this case.

Two Currier & Ives employees pose in front of the shop at 115 Nassau Street in August of 1885. The firm is displaying portraits of Ulysses S. Grant and is draped in mourning for the New York City funeral of the former president. *(Museum City of New York)*

135 Nassau Street

Clinton Hall—Built by the Mercantile Library Association as their circulating library, this building was the office of Lorenzo and Orson Fowler in 1835. The two brothers were the country's leading proponents and practitioners of phrenology, the art of analyzing character from the conformation of the skull. The "head reading" fad swept the nation in the mid-nineteenth century. As with many pseudo-sciences, phrenology had many unshakable devotees, including Walt Whitman and Edgar Allan Poe. This address served as the Fowlers' base of operations, with examination rooms, a museum, a lecture hall, and publishing center for their numerous books and journals.

140* Nassau Street

Morse Building—This twelve-story structure, now converted to an apartment house, was once home to one of the world's earliest film studios, the American Vitagraph Company. Founded by two English vaudeville performers, J. Stuart Blackton and Albert E. Smith, the company made silent motion pictures here from 1897 until 1903. The roof served as a studio to take full advantage of the sunlight needed for early cameras. Vitagraph's first feature, aptly named *The Burglar on the Roof,* was a sixty-second melodrama starring Blackton as the burglar.

Nassau Street and Spruce Street, Northeast Corner

Tribune Building—It was from here in a rented office in the building of a competing newspaper that the young millionaire William Randolph Hearst set up shop after buying the *New York Journal* on October 7, 1895. He spent much of his own fortune to boost the readership of this paper. Hearst then launched a circulation war with the powerful Joseph Pulitzer's *World.* This rivalry spawned the era of yellow journalism in America. Both papers' sensational coverage of the conditions in Spain's colony, Cuba, helped push the United States into the Spanish-American War.

Nassau Street and Frankfort Street, Southeast Corner

This was the first permanent home of Tammany Hall, which opened in 1812. Founded as a fraternal society in 1789, it became the Democratic Party organization in the city. It grew in political power with the arrival of Irish immigrants. The party supplied the jobs, and the Irish supplied the votes. By the 1880s it had become completely corrupt.

NEW STREET

7 New Street

Exchange Buffet—Opened on September 4, 1885, this was the world's first self-service restaurant.

34 New Street

On July 19, 1845, at 3:00 a.m., a fire began at this address, then the sperm whale–oil shop of J. L. Van Doren. Before it was extinguished twelve hours later, three hundred buildings were destroyed and thirty people died. There was also more than

$6 million in property loss, due largely to the destruction of the imported goods stored in the warehouses. The extent of the damage was almost as severe as that from the earlier Great Fire of 1835. These two blazes virtually destroyed the last remnants of seventeenth-century Dutch Colonial architecture in the city.

58 New Street

New York Gold Exchange—The building that once stood at this address was the center of a financial whirlwind surrounded by anxious brokers on September 24, 1869, later to be known as Black Friday. It was here in the Gold Room, where gold was sold as a commodity, that traders began to feel the effects of Jay Gould and Jim Fisk's attempt to corner the market. Gould and his partner had hoped to buy all $15 million worth of gold then in circulation and thus drive up its price. President Ulysses S. Grant prevented this by allowing the U.S. Treasury's gold to be sold in the market. However, Gould's Washington spies, including Grant's brother-in-law, leaked him the news of Grant's decision, and Gould was still able to make an $11 million profit. Many brokerage firms and individual speculators were financially ruined.

PARK ROW

21–25 Park Row

Park Theater—The theater that once stood on this site opened on January 29, 1798, with a performance of *As You Like It*. It was also the site of America's first grand opera ever presented in full in its original language, Rossini's *The Barber of Seville,* on November 29, 1825. On the night of February 14, 1842, 2,500 guests attended the "Boz Ball" in honor of English author Charles Dickens's first visit to America. The stage and orchestra pit were covered over to accommodate the crowd. Between the cotillions and waltzes, a curtain would rise revealing a small stage with tableaux vivants from the storyteller's writings. Violinist virtuoso Ole Bull made his American debut on this same stage on November 25, 1843.

31 Park Row

New York World Newspaper Offices—A *World* reporter, Nellie Bly, returned to this address after her journey around the world on January 26, 1890. Bly, the nom de plume of Elizabeth Cochrane, was hoping to beat the record set by Jules Verne's

Before federal government regulations, the nineteenth-century stock exchanges were susceptible to rogue traders. This was the case on Black Friday, September 24, 1869, in the Gold Room on New Street. Jay Gould and Jim Fisk financially ruined hundreds of investors by trying to corner the market on gold. *(Author's collection)*

fictional character Phileas Fogg in *Around the World in 80 Days*. She did it in 72 days, 6 hours, 11 minutes, and 14 seconds—including a short detour to meet the author in Amiens, France. The front-page headline on the day of her return trumpeted, "Father Time Outdone." Later that year Joseph Pulitzer would move his paper into the new World Building down the block at the corner of Park Row and Frankfort.

37 Park Row

The first public demonstration of the phonograph took place here at the offices of the *Scientific American* on December 7, 1877. Thomas Edison brought one of his two working models (the only other was already at the patent office) to the magazine's editor, Alfred Ely Beach. The inventor set the machine down and turned the crank, and the machine promptly bid the editor a good morning. The modest talking machine was created with just a needle and a tinfoil cylinder attached to a hand crank.

Park Row and Frankfort Street, West Side

On Friday, April 17, 1914, Mayor John Purroy Mitchel left City Hall to attend a luncheon and was approaching a waiting car when a man walked up and shot him point-blank. The mayor was only grazed and escaped serious injury, but an aid was hit in the mouth. The attacker, Michael Mahoney, was declared insane and sent to an asylum. Ironically, five years earlier, Mitchel, who was then the president of the board of aldermen, was made acting mayor during the previous mayor William J. Gaynor's recuperation from an attempted assassination. Mayor Gaynor resumed his duties but died three years later as a result of his wound. Gaynor's death during the next mayoral election campaign help paved the way for Mitchel's election win.

PEARL STREET

6 Pearl Street

At 11:30 p.m. on August 1, 1819, author Herman Melville was born at this address. His mother, Maria, was the only daughter of the Revolutionary War hero Gen. Peter Gansevoort, and his father, Allan, was in the import business on the nearby docks. The future author of *Moby Dick* lived here until 1824.

Pearl Street and Whitehall Street

This was the site of the first market in the city for the townspeople to buy country produce. Governor Peter Stuyvesant and the city council established the weekly Saturday market on September 12, 1656.

39 Pearl Street

Under the director-general of New Netherland, Wouter Van Twiller, the first building solely dedicated to religious purposes was built here in 1633. This wooden structure was abandoned in 1642 when a church was built inside Fort Amsterdam.

54* Pearl Street

Fraunces Tavern—As was the case with many taverns of the Colonial Period, Fraunces Tavern was an important gathering place, particularly for early business meetings. The New York State Chamber of Commerce was founded here on April 5, 1768. But this tavern is best known for its connections to Gen. George Washington. It served for ten days as his last residence while general of the American Revolutionary forces. He delivered his famous farewell speech to his officers here on December 4, 1783. The newly formed government's Departments of War, Treasury, and Foreign Affairs, which were later combined as the State Department, were quartered here while the city served as the nation's capital. The current building, completed in 1907, is not the actual tavern but an educated guess as to what the building looked like. This reconstruction served as the locale for a special breakfast on April 30, 1989, celebrating the two hundredth anniversary of George Washington's inauguration. The invited guests were all descendants of former U.S. presidents, from Lacey Washington, the first president's sixth great-niece, to Karen Denis, President Reagan's third cousin.

61 Pearl Street

The deed for this property was the first to be recorded in the Register's Office of New York County. Dated October 12, 1654, it documents that Cornelius Van Tienhoven sold this address and 26 Stone Street to Jacob Hendricks, one of the first surgeons in New Amsterdam. The doctor didn't own this real estate long; he resold it the same day to Jacob Steendam.

66 Pearl Street

This address sits on a portion of the city's earliest landfill project. In 1684 this property across from the Stadt Huys was created with earth and debris from nearby hills. Called "water lots," this landfill was the first of many devised by generations of Manhattan developers and city bureaucrats who sought to add more land to sell and tax. A small, gabled, Dutch-style house that was the first built on this lot was owned by Peter and Mary Jay, who were most likely living here when their son, John, was born on December 12, 1745. John Jay went on to become the first chief justice of the U.S. Supreme Court.

71–73 Pearl Street

Stadt Huys—Rising above the neighboring Dutch gabled homes, this five-story stone building was a prominent landmark along the shoreline when it was built by

Governor Willem Kieft. On New Year's Day of 1642, it was leased for a Stadt Herbergh (Public Inn) to Philip Gerritsen for three hundred guilders a year. For the next several years, outlying Dutch settlers sought refuge here from Native American raids during Governor Kieft's War. In 1653 the building became the Stadt Huys (City Hall), New York City's first. A cupola was added, and its entrance, which had faced Fort Amsterdam, was changed to face the East River. It served as the seat of government until 1699. In 1979 excavations revealed the foundation, only 42 feet by 52 feet, of the old Stadt Huys. Archaeologists found many colonial artifacts, including fragments of Dutch and English pottery and even some Native American wampum.

81 Pearl Street

This was the site of the first printing press in the New York colony. William Bradford was appointed public printer on April 10, 1693. He was involved in several firsts in the history of printing in America: the first legislative proceedings published, the first New York paper money, and the first newspaper to appear in New York, the *New York Gazette,* on October 16, 1725. Bradford is buried in Trinity Churchyard.

119–21 Pearl Street

On May 16, 1691, Capt. William Kidd, the shipowner and sea captain, married Mrs. Sarah Oort, who was probably the richest widow in New York at the time. The happy couple moved into her mansion, which once stood approximately in the rear of this lot. The captain lived here for eight years, then sailed for the Indian Ocean. It was at this point that Captain Kidd began his infamous career as a pirate. After he was hanged in London on May 12, 1701, rumors spread that he had buried his plunder along the coast near the city.

218 Pearl Street

This site once held the home of Hercules Mulligan, a member of the Sons of Liberty and an Irish-born secret agent for the Americans during the Revolutionary War. On November 25, 1783, when the British left the city, George Washington and four of his officers visited this house to pay their respects to Mulligan for helping the Patriot cause.

255–257 Pearl Street

The two dilapidated buildings that once stood at this site, in what was then a run-down section of the waterfront, were home to Thomas Edison's first commercial electric generators. At exactly 3 p.m. on September 4, 1882, the Pearl Street Station started supplying fifty-nine downtown customers with electricity. Edison had chosen this location, paying little for the two buildings at a time when his capital was low, because he wanted to be near the financial section and potential investors.

326 Pearl Street

Walton House—Built in 1752, a four-story house on this site was considered "the most beautiful home in America." The extravagant parties held here during Colonial rule were referred to in the British Parliament as proof that the Americans could afford to pay higher taxes. By the end of the Revolutionary War, Pearl Street was turning more commercial. The building became the first home of the newly established Bank of New York, which opened on June 9, 1784. Alexander Hamilton, who bought a single share of stock, was elected one of the bank directors. It later became a boardinghouse, before it was torn down in 1881.

362 Pearl Street

Within a year of moving permanently to New York City and marring Sarah Todd, John Jacob Astor moved to this address owned by his new mother-in-law in 1786. This was the first home and office of America's earliest self-made multimillionaire. At this address he sold musical instruments and sheet music, one of the first music dealers in the city, before moving on to the more lucrative fur trade and real-estate businesses, in which he amassed his fortune.

PECK'S SLIP

Peck's Slip and South Street

During a small blizzard on January 5, 1818, the packet ship *James Monroe* of the Black Ball shipping line set sail for Liverpool. The departure of this 424-ton vessel with two decks and three masts marked a high point in the economic development of New York City. What made this sailing a historic improvement was that the ship sailed on the very day her owners had said she would sail. The *James Monroe* inaugurated the first regular dependable shipping service to Europe. Prior to this, ships left only when they were full and the weather was good. Now, full or not, sun or snow, the Black Ball ships would guarantee merchants the delivery of their goods. The journey was also the first transatlantic scheduled departure for the eight pioneer passengers on the ship.

PINE STREET

45 Pine Street

In 1798 Charles Brockden Brown, the first American novelist to gain an international reputation, lived in a house that once stood on this spot.

POLICE PLAZA

Rhinelander's Sugar House—Part of this plaza was once the intersection of Duane and Rose Streets, and it was here that a notorious Revolutionary War British prison once stood. Originally built as a warehouse in 1763, the building housed American prisoners, many of whom died of starvation and disease. A window from the building serves as a present-day memorial.

Newsboy's Lodging House—Another building now gone that stood in this vicinity at Duane and New Chambers Streets was one of the most successful city charities of the nineteenth century, the Newsboy's Lodging House. Founded in 1853 for homeless boys, the home supplied reasonable meals and shelter for the thousands of homeless orphans in the city. Horatio Alger, the author of industrious-boy-makes-good, rags-to-riches stories, was a guiding spirit and role model to the newsboys.

READE STREET

57 Reade Street

Abercrombie and Fitch Company—This world-famous sporting-goods company made the news in 1908 by selling Theodore Roosevelt equipment for his upcoming African safari. The ex-president returned on June 18, 1910, to a welcoming parade on Fifth Avenue.

RECTOR STREET

2* Rector Street

United Express Building—Four hundred and twenty-five plate-glass windows were broken as a result of the Black Tom Island explosion on Sunday morning, July 30, 1916. The United Express Building, particularly the side facing the harbor, was the most severely damaged. Two tremendous explosions, heard as far away as Maryland, shook the entire tri-state area. Black Tom Island, a man-made peninsula along the New Jersey shore in New York Harbor, was a storage facility for more than 2,138,000 pounds of munitions bound for wartime England and France. At first only suspected, and not proved until 1939, the explosion was an act of German espionage—before America's entry into World War I. Remarkably, only seven people were killed, but $50 million in damage were caused to the Allies.

SOUTH STREET

174 South Street
This was the birthplace of Alfred E. Smith, governor of New York and U.S. presidential nominee of 1928, on December 30, 1873. This site is now the Alfred E. Smith Houses, a housing development.

Photographed for posterity, this room was the birthplace of Alfred E. Smith on December 30, 1873. The stalwart Democratic Party politician was the son of Irish immigrant parents. (FPG)

SOUTH WILLIAM STREET

26 South William Street
The first synagogue in North America was built on this site. Congregation Shearith Israel, a Spanish and Portuguese synagogue, was dedicated on the seventh day of Passover, April 8, 1730. The one-story brick building remained in use for nearly a century.

STATE STREET

7* State Street
Watson House—This mansion is the lone survivor on a block once lined with the homes of wealthy New Yorkers. Attributed to John McComb Jr., the architect of City Hall, it was home to Elizabeth Ann Seton from 1801 to 1803. Mother Seton was canonized, the first American-born saint, in 1975.

STONE STREET

10 Stone Street
In the Dutch Colonial Period, this block was called Brouwers Straet because of the breweries between Whitehall Street and a canal along the present Broad Street. The West India Company brewery was operating at this address in 1646. By 1656 Oloff Stevense Van Cortlandt, patriarch of the prominent New York family, also opened his brewery on this block. One year later this street was the first in the city to be paved—hence the name Stone Street.

59 Stone Street
Asser Levy, one of the original Jewish settlers in New Amsterdam in 1654, had a home at this address in 1663 and had also lived at number 33 down the block. Levy fought and won an early discrimination battle with city authorities. Governor Peter Stuyvesant ordered all Jews exempt from military guard duty but imposed a special monthly tax in lieu of such service. Levy appealed to authorities in Holland, who then ordered Stuyvesant to allow Levy to stand guard. He became the first Jewish soldier in America.

Number 7 State Street was the Shrine of Saint Elizabeth Seton and the last grand mansion on the block. This photograph shows the building as the Mission of our Lady of the Rosary before it had skyscrapers for neighbors. *(Author's collection)*

VESEY STREET

24 Vesey Street

George Washington's dentist, John Greenwood, had his office at this address in the 1790s. Dr. Greenwood, a former cabinet maker and maker of nautical instruments, built a set of the president's false teeth. Not wooden, the dentures, made from human teeth attached to an ivory base, were held in place by Washington's lone remaining tooth. The renowned dentures are now in the collection of the New York Academy of Medicine.

WALL STREET

Wall Street, now synonymous with high finance, was named after a wooden stockade fence with a twelve-foot ditch on the northern side, built here at the boundary of the settlement in 1653. Governor Peter Stuyvesant ordered the barricade built by all male residents "without exception" as a defense against the British colonists of New England and not, as is widely believed, as protection against the indigenous people. The wall ran from the Hudson River to the East River and had one entrance, at Wall and Pearl Streets. Called the Watergate, it was shut every night at nine o'clock under the Dutch rules. It stood until 1699, when it was taken down by the British.

7 Wall Street

At this address on October 15, 1915, Charles E. Merrill took on the first of many partners, Edmund C. Lynch, and changed his company's name to Merrill Lynch. In business for only a year himself, Merrill would go on to head the country's largest retail stockbrokerage firm.

23 Wall Street

Downing's Oyster House—In the years before the Civil War, this corner restaurant was famous for its tasty menu. The owner, Thomas Downing, an African American man, was a popular host to his Wall Street power-broker customers. The restaurant's basement also played host to runaway slaves as a station on the Underground Railroad.

   Morgan Guaranty Trust Company*—An earlier Drexel, Morgan and Company bank building on this same site was the scene of one of the first commercial uses of electricity. On September 4, 1882, Thomas Edison personally connected the electric lamps in the office of his friend and enthusiastic supporter John Pierpont Morgan. The power was supplied from the inventor's Pearl Street generators. The current building, built in 1913, was the scene of a noon-time bomb blast that killed thirty-three and injured four hundred on the crowded sidewalk outside on September 16, 1920. Despite an $80,000 reward, the bomber or bombers were never caught, and their motive was equally mysterious. The most common explanation was that the blast was the work of foreign anarchists. A lasting reminder of the explosion is the damaged marble still visible on the façade.

Police and investigators surround the offices of the Morgan Guaranty Trust Company on the afternoon of September 16, 1920. A worker with a crane, left, towers over the sidewalk at the site of a bomb explosion on the Wall Street side of the building. *(FPG)*

Wall Street and Nassau Street, Northwest Corner

Simmon's Tavern—At a special meeting of the City Council, James Duane was sworn into office as the mayor of New York City at this tavern on February 7, 1784. Duane, the country's first American-born mayor, had been appointed by Governor De Witt Clinton. The new mayor replaced the State Provisional Council, which had managed the city.

28 Wall Street

Federal Hall—This is one of the most important sites in the history of the United States. In 1703 this was the location of New York City's second City Hall. The trial of John Peter Zenger, editor of the *New York Weekly Journal,* for libel against the English colonial governor William Cosby began here on August 4, 1735. Zenger's acquittal, with the help of his "Philadelphia lawyer" Andrew Hamilton, established the principle of freedom of the press. Another significant step toward American independence from England also took place here: the Stamp Act Congress met in the same building to draft a Declaration of Rights and Grievances on October 7, 1765. Twenty-eight delegates from the American colonies met to outline the fourteen articles, chief among them the protest against "taxation without representation" and the demand for the right to a trial by jury. After the Revolution, the building was remodeled by expatriate French architect Pierre L'Enfant as Federal Hall, and the government of the newly organized United States began to function in a second-floor chamber. Outside this room on a balcony, on April 30, 1789, George Washington was inaugurated as the nation's first president and John Adams as the first vice president. The new Congress adopted the Bill of Rights here on September 25, 1789.

Federal Hall National Memorial*—The current Greek Revival building was built in 1842 to house the first U.S. customhouse and served for a time as a subtreasury. John Quincy Adams Ward's statue of Washington, dedicated on November 26, 1883, by President Chester A. Arthur, stands on the approximate spot where Washington took the oath in 1789.

40* Wall Street

A contender for the title of "world's tallest building," this 1929 tower lost out to the Chrysler Building when a 175-foot art-deco spire was added to the Chrysler after 40 Wall Street was too far along to be changed. The tower proved too high, though, for a twin-engine Army Air Force C-45 Beechcraft airplane. The doomed plane, flying at 650 feet, crashed into the fifty-eighth floor of what was then called

FEDERAL HALL
The Seat of CONGRESS

The only eyewitness rendering of the nation's first inauguration, Amos Dolittle's engraving depicted the April 30, 1789, event. George Washington, with his hand on a Bible, is being given the oath of office by Judge Robert Livingston. *(Library of Congress)*

The wrecked tail section of the Army Air Force plane hangs over the twelfth-floor setback roof after it fell forty-six stories at 40 Wall Street after it crashed there May 20, 1946. All the occupants of the plane were killed. *(FPG)*

the Manhattan Bank Building. Apparently lost, it hit the building on a foggy evening, May 20, 1946. The crash killed all five occupants of the plane, but none of the five hundred night workers in the building.

52 Wall Street

This was the first and long-time home of City Bank, now Citibank. The nation's first bank robbery took place here on Sunday, March 20, 1831. The theft was undiscovered until Monday morning when the bank opened. More than $200,000 in bank bills and two hundred Spanish doubloons were missing. Edward Smith was caught within a week and sentenced to five years in Sing Sing for the crime.

55* Wall Street

Merchant's Exchange—The first exchange on this site was only eight years old when it was destroyed in the Great Fire of 1835. The present structure, a masterpiece of Greek Revival architecture, was converted to the U.S. Custom House in 1862. Chester A. Arthur, before he became president, worked here as collector of the Port of New York from 1871 to 1878. In 1904 architect Charles McKim added five floors in his sensitive remodeling for conversion to the headquarters of National City Bank, later renamed Citibank. After ninety years the bank moved out, making way for the building's current incarnation as a dining space in the grand hall and lavish hotel of the 1904 addition.

56 Wall Street

The pirate Captain Kidd owned but did not occupy this property in 1691. He sold the lot a year later for thirty-five dollars and made a five-dollar profit.

58 Wall Street

This address was the home and law office of Alexander Hamilton from 1783 to 1790.

Wall Street between William and Pearl Streets

The legendary birthplace of the New York Stock Exchange is in the vicinity of number 72 Wall Street. When the new Congress had issued $80 million worth of bonds to pay for the Revolutionary War, traders began meeting here in the open air to trade the securities. On May 17, 1792, under a buttonwood tree, twenty-four of these merchants and auctioneers, future stockbrokers, established the new Exchange. They initiated rules of conduct and pledged themselves to give preference to the other members. That famous buttonwood tree, another name for a sycamore, survived until June 21, 1865, when it was felled by a storm.

74 Wall Street

Edward Livingston lived at this address in the early part of the nineteenth century. Livingston was mayor of the city and a member of the House of Representatives. He served with Andrew Jackson at the Battle of New Orleans and later became a U.S. senator from Louisiana.

The architect Isaiah Rogers designed the Merchant's Exchange at 55 Wall Street in 1842. This monumental building still stands as the base for the handsome and sympathetic Charles McKim addition of 1904. *(Author's collection)*

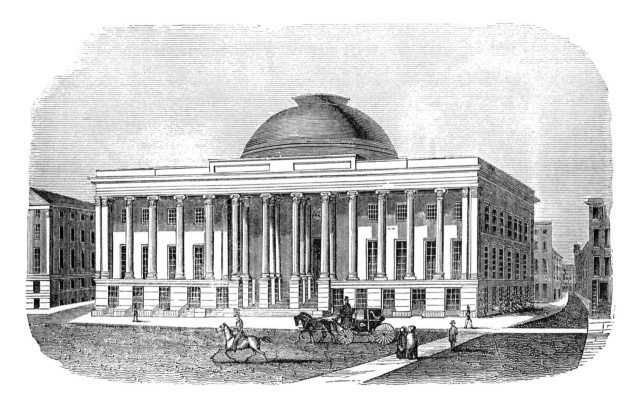

Wall Street and Water Street, Southeast Corner

Merchants' Coffee House—This was the second site of this tavern that earlier had stood on the opposite corner. Paul Revere, on one of his many rides, delivered a dispatch from the Boston Committee of Correspondence to the New York compatriots on May 17, 1774, encouraging them to protest a British order to close Boston Harbor. On February 24, 1784, a meeting was held here to establish the Bank of New York, the oldest commercial bank in the country.

Wall Street and Water Street, Northwest Corner

Tontine Coffee House—Opened in 1793 on the site of the first Merchant's Coffee House, this establishment was built with money raised by early brokers looking for a home for the new stock market. The first floor was used as a place for trading, and the rest of the building housed a ballroom, a dining room, and a bar.

Wall Street and South Street

For much of the eighteenth century this was the foot of Wall Street. Landfills have since extended the shoreline. By 1709 this was the site of a thriving slave market. The city was the second-largest slave-owning city in the British colonies, second only to Charleston, South Carolina. The auctioned slaves were not only African Americans but whites, dependent women, orphaned children, and debtors.

On the night of April 22, 1774, the New York equivalent of the Boston Tea Party took place here on Murray's Wharf.

Future first president George Washington arrived in New York at this spot on April 23, 1789, for his inaugural. He stepped off an elaborately decorated barge manned by thirteen oarsmen representing the first colonies. The journey had begun nine days earlier at his Mount Vernon home. Washington's landing was reenacted on April 29, 1889—somewhat farther east—by then-President Benjamin Harrison. The arrival was again recreated here in 1989 by an actor who portrayed the first president on his journey all the way from Virginia. A retinue of reporters recorded every step of the reenacted journey.

WARREN STREET

57 Warren Street

Master glassmaker and artist Louis Comfort Tiffany was born at this address on February 18, 1848. He was the son of Charles Lewis Tiffany, the founder of the famous jewelry store.

WASHINGTON STREET

Washington Street between Dey and Cortlandt Streets

Eli Hart and Company Warehouse—Citizens protesting flour and grain prices broke into two warehouses here on February 13, 1837. They dumped flour and wheat into the streets. Mayor Cornelius W. Lawrence tried to quell the riot but was pelted with stones and forced to flee for his life. This site is now part of the World Trade Center Complex.

WATER STREET

58 Water Street

James Hamlet, a freed African American man, was a porter working here at the store of Tilton and Mahone. He was the first person seized under the provisions of the Fugitive Slave Law. Within two weeks of Congress's passing the law, the U.S. Commissioner had issued a warrant for Hamlet, and he was arrested here on September 30, 1850. Hamlet was forced to return to his former owner, Mary Brown of Baltimore. Hamlet was later ransomed back for $800 raised by the Union Safety Committee.

74 Water Street

Bowen's Waxworks—President George Washington and his family visited this popular attraction to view a wax likeness of the new president on September 14, 1789.

273* Water Street

Captain Joseph Rose House—From the 1840s to the 1860s this small house was Kit Burns' Sportsman's Hall, a saloon. It was a popular hangout for the notorious gangs of the period, such as the Daybreak Boys, the Border Gang, the Patsy Conroys, and the Shirt Tails. The patrons were kept entertained in a first-floor amphitheater by bloody dog and rat fights. Built before 1780 for sea captain Joseph Rose, the structure is the third oldest in Manhattan. For more than two hundred years, this building has been the captain's home, an apothecary shop, a rooming house, a brothel, and later still a "home for fallen women." Life goes on at 273 Water Street, which was beautifully restored in 1997. It is now a four-unit luxury apartment house.

286 Water Street

On April 22, 1824, this address was the site of the first house in the city to be lighted with gas. Directly behind this lot stood number 7 Cherry Street, the home of Samuel Leggett, the first president of the New York Gas Company. Mr. Leggett had his own home illuminated with gas six months later.

304 Water Street

John Allen's Dance Hall—This was an infamous dance hall and brothel of the 1850s and 1860s. The dancers/prostitutes who worked here were known for wearing red-topped black boots with sleigh bells around their ankles—and often little else. Nicknamed the "Wickedest Man in New York" by a journalist, the proprietor, Mr. Allen, proudly had the title printed on his business cards. About 1868 Allen, perhaps converted by one of his three brothers, who were all respectable clergymen, decided that he had found God and started giving sermons in his dance hall. His "conversion" did not last long, especially when business dropped off. But when he tried to reopen under the old policies, his regular customers abandoned him.

This engraving is of John Allen's Dance hall in 1868, probably depicted more rambunctiously than the small room could handle. The infamous dance hall was frequented by criminals, prostitutes, and sailors. *(Frank Leslie's, August 8, 1868)*

WEST STREET

19 West Street
Downtown Athletic Club—In 1935 the first Heisman Trophy was given to Jay Berwanger, a halfback for the University of Chicago. The award is given annually here to the individual voted best college football player of the year.

West Street and Cedar Street, Southeast Corner
This was the birthplace of colorful financier James "Diamond Jim" Brady. He was born on August 12, 1856, above his father's saloon.

WHITEHALL STREET

Whitehall Street and Bridge Street
The first meat market in New Amsterdam was established at this intersection in April of 1659.

39* Whitehall Street
United States Army Building—This former army induction center was a popular target of the antiwar movement of the 1960s. Activists Dr. Benjamin Spock and Allen Ginsberg were both arrested here. At one such rally on October 15, 1965, twenty-two-year-old David Miller, a volunteer relief worker, stood atop a sound truck and used a cigarette lighter to burn his draft card. Several days later he was arrested in New Hampshire. He became the first person to be arrested under a federal law that prohibited the destruction of a draft card. Two months later at another demonstration, sixty-one people were arrested for picketing and singing Christmas carols. The building was extensively remodeled in the mid-1980s.

Whitehall Street and State Street
Stuyvesant's Great House—Peter Stuyvesant, the peg-legged Dutch governor of New Netherland, built a two-story stone house on this spot in 1655. After the British took control of New York, the house was used for the British governors. The street and the building were renamed "Whitehall" in honor of the English seat of government in London. It was home to Sir Edmund Andros while he was in office between 1674 and 1681. The house was destroyed by fire on October 25, 1715. Robert Fulton died in a house on this same site on February 23, 1815. He had contracted a cold while inspecting his steamboats along the Hudson River.

Whitehall Street near Water Street

This was the site of the city's first pier, a small wooden jetty, which was built in 1648–49 by Dutch governor Peter Stuyvesant. Before landfills changed the shoreline, this spot was called Schreyer's Hook or Weepers' Point, so named because loved ones said their goodbyes here to travelers leaving on ships to their mothercountries. By the time of the Revolutionary War the shoreline had moved another block south to just short of South Street. It was from this spot that George Washington boarded the Whitehall ferry to begin his journey home to Mount Vernon after bidding farewell to his officers at Fraunces Tavern on December 4, 1783. Six years later he returned to the city, farther upstream at Wall Street, for his inauguration.

Whitehall Street and Water Street

Tavern of the Fighting Cocks—Between one and two in the morning of September 21, 1772, this small tavern and brothel, near the original shoreline, was the likely origin of the Fire of 1776. Winds spread the blaze up Beaver and Broad Streets, the fire destroying everything west of Broadway to the Hudson River. With little rain for weeks, the wells were too dry to supply water to fight the blaze. The conflagration spread unchecked until it reached Barclay Street and the open campus surrounding King's College, later Columbia University. This disaster happened only one week after the British began their occupation of the city during the Revolutionary War. The animosity between citizens and the British authorities hampered efforts to combat the fire.

Whitehall Street and South Street, Northeast Corner

Eagle Hotel—Statesman Daniel Webster married his second wife, Caroline LeRoy, in the parlor of this hotel on December 12, 1829. The hotel, built in 1822 and later renamed the Eastern, stood on this spot for more than ninety-eight years, a longevity record in the history of New York real estate.

WILLIAM STREET

21–23 William Street

Delmonico's Restaurant—This first home of the famous restaurant, considered by some as the first American restaurant, opened in 1827. The two Swiss brothers, John and Peter Delmonico, introduced haute cuisine to America. Their chef,

Charles Ranhofer, created baked Alaska and lobster Newburg. The building was destroyed, along with half the downtown area, in the Great Fire of 1835. Two years later the brothers built a new building, still standing today as an apartment house, nearby at 56 Beaver Street.

131 William Street

This was the birthplace of Washington Irving on April 3, 1783. His childhood home was down the block at 128 William, where he began to write in the year 1802.

WORLD TRADE CENTER

1 World Trade Center

Windows on the World*—Nelson Mandela, the former political prisoner of apartheid South Africa, met with business leaders at a breakfast here in the 110th-floor restaurant on June 22, 1990. He urged continued business sanctions against the South African government. Three days earlier, Mandela had been given a hero's welcome to New York with a parade up Broadway to City Hall.

33 World Trade Center

Vista Hotel—At 12:18 p.m. on Friday, February 26, 1993, a tremendous blast not only rocked the World Trade Center complex with the force of an earthquake but shook the psyche of the entire nation. The United States was no longer spared the nightmare of terrorism on its home ground. The massive explosion created a crater sixty yards wide and several levels deep in the underground parking garage directly below this hotel. Six people died and more than one thousand were injured in the blast. Most of the injured were overcome with smoke inhalation, as smoke permeated the complex and rose up more than one hundred stories in the city's two tallest buildings. All electric power was knocked out, and without the aid of elevators or instructions over the public-address system, thousands of frightened office workers were forced to flee through the crowded, dark, and smoky stairwells down to the safety of the street. Within a week the first suspect, Mohammed A. Salameh, was arrested in New Jersey while trying to get his $200 deposit back on the rented van traced to the explosion. The FBI swiftly rounded up a small group of Islamic fundamentalists, followers of cleric Sheikh Omar Abdel-Rahman, and arrested them in connection with the explosion. Five of the conspirators were convicted, and each was sentenced to 240 years in prison.

Washington Square Park, late 1920s. *(FPG)*

THE VILLAGE

13 Astor Place

Astor Place Opera House—On May 10, 1849, an angry crowd of more than ten thousand fans of the American actor Edwin Forrest surrounded this building during a performance of *Macbeth* starring the English tragedian Charles Macready. The ensuing riot that night was the culmination of a bitter feud between the two rival actors and their fervent admirers. Macready had come to symbolize and magnify a deep-rooted anti-English resentment held by many of the city's poor. Thirty-one people died and 150 were injured in what became known as the "Astor Place Riots." The damaged hall was reconstructed and renamed Clinton Hall. It was the second home of the Mercantile Library. It was also home to the Book Sales Room and Art Galleries, where on May 28, 1870, the first U.S. philatelic auction was held and more than fourteen thousand stamps were offered for sale.

This view of Astor Place Theater was published in 1850, one year after the riot. The building was the second home of the Mercantile Library, a membership library. Still in operation today, the Mercantile was the largest circulation library in the United States in the decades after the Civil War. *(Library of Congress)*

AVENUE B

151* Avenue B

Jazz innovator and alto saxophonist Charlie "Bird" Parker lived in the basement apartment of this brownstone, now on the National Register of Historic Places. This address was home to Parker and his family from 1950 until late 1954.

BANK STREET

5 Bank Street

This address was once the residence of the writer Willa Cather. It was her home from 1913 until 1927, when it was torn down during the construction of the Seventh Avenue subway line. A plaque on a later apartment house marks the site.

63* Bank Street

Sid Vicious, former punk-rock guitarist of the Sex Pistols, died of a heroin overdose at this address on February 2, 1979. Released from jail on bail only thirteen hours earlier, he was here, at the apartment of an actress friend, to attend a party to celebrate his recent freedom. Vicious, whose real name was John Simon Ritchie, was awaiting trial for murdering his girlfriend and acting manager Nancy Spungen four months earlier at the Chelsea Hotel.

Bank Street near Hudson Street

On Halloween night, 1974, Ralph Lee, a mask designer and theater director, with a group of friends wearing masks and carrying large puppets all made by Lee, began a lively and meandering procession to Washington Square Park. This rag-tag band has evolved over the years into the celebrated and uninhibited Greenwich Village Halloween Parade. More than a million costumed and uncostumed revelers now attend the event annually, and it is one of the city's largest parades.

155 Bank Street

Westbeth*—This building was once home of the famous Bell Telephone/Western Electric Laboratories in 1897. Several important inventions were developed here, including the vacuum tube, the electrical digital and analog computer, and sound movies. Dr. Herbert E. Ives gave one of the first demonstrations of television here, on April 7, 1927. A tap dancer on the roof, to take advantage of full sunlight, performed before an early camera, while the image was broadcast to a tiny screen in Dr. Ives's office below. In 1969 the complex was converted into the nation's biggest federally subsidized artist colony. Diane Arbus, photographer of the bizarre, committed suicide in her apartment here on July 28, 1971.

BARROW STREET

43* Barrow Street
Friends and fellow editors at *The Nation,* Mark Van Doren and Joseph Wood Krutch lived together in this brick house in the 1920s.

BAYARD STREET

33 Bayard Street
The nineteenth-century American composer of German birth Anthony Philip Heinrich, called the "Beethoven of America," died at this address—the home of his friend, Dr. Wolf—on May 3, 1861. His funeral was held here two days later.

BEACH STREET

3 Beach Street
James Fenimore Cooper wrote *The Pilot* here in 1823. The novel, whose main character is based on John Paul Jones, is credited with creating the genre of the sea novel.

36 Beach Street
This stretch of Beach Street, Ericsson Place, was named after the naval engineer John Ericsson, who lived here between 1864 and 1889. The engineer of the *Monitor,* the first ironclad battleship, he died here on March 8, 1889.

Beach Street at the Hudson River
West Point Foundry Works—In the early part of the nineteenth century, Beach Street ran through to the Hudson River. On this site the first steam locomotive in America, the Stourbridge Lion, arrived from England in May of 1829. The train was then sent on to Pennsylvania, where it had a successful test run on August 8, 1829. It traveled ten miles per hour.

BEDFORD STREET

75 1/2* Bedford Street

Renowned as an architectural oddity, "the narrowest house in New York City," this address was home for a short time to Edna St. Vincent Millay and her new husband, Eugen Jan Boissevain, in 1923. Often overlooked, the house next door at 77 Bedford carries the distinction of being the oldest house in Greenwich Village.

86* Bedford Street

Chumley's Restaurant—This former speakeasy with another discreet entrance on Barrow Street was a literary hangout in the 1920s for writers John Dos Passos, Upton Sinclair, Theodore Dreiser, and Edna St. Vincent Millay.

BETHUNE STREET

23 Bethune Street

The photographer Walker Evans and the photographer/painter Ben Shahn were roommates here in the early 1930s for two years.

BLEECKER STREET

4 Washington Square Village South

This stretch of Bleecker Street, now called Washington Square Village South, was once named Leroy Place. And it was from here, at a house numbered 13, on the morning of October 3, 1839, that John Lloyd Stephens left on a journey that would transform modern archaeology. Stephens, the owner of the house, a lawyer and amateur archaeologist, left along with his friend and artist Fredric Catherwood on a voyage of discovery to Central America. In the next few years these early explorers "discovered" the Mayan Empire and challenged the prevailing view of the pre-Columbian history of the Americas.

33 Bleecker Street

From the age of five to nine, Herman Melville lived at this address with his family. The family moved one more time to 675 Broadway, the site of the Central Hotel, before his father's business failed and they left New York to live in Albany.

Bleecker Street and Broadway

This intersection marked the beginning of the end for the last horse-drawn trolley in the city. On the morning of July 26, 1917, several railroad officials and dignitaries boarded the last trolley, number 97, for a final trip to the horse barn and into history. The Interborough Rapid Transit (IRT) Company was retiring the old-fashioned trolley because of a lack of revenue and passengers.

Bleecker Street and Mercer Street, Southeast Corner

African Grove Theater—The first African American theater in the United States opened in 1821. The theater's location, still debated, was most likely at this corner in what was then an established African American neighborhood. The theater advertised, "Neither time nor expense has been spared in rendering this entertainment agreeable to the ladies and gentlemen of color." The company performed *Othello* and other Shakespearean dramas. Ira Aldridge, one of the first African American actors to achieve an international reputation, appeared at this theater. The theater lasted only two seasons. The reasons for the closing have been lost to history, but a popular version places the blame on a segregated seating policy requiring whites to sit in the rear of the theater.

On July 26, 1917, the city discontinued horse-drawn trolleys as public transportation. A major improvement over horse-drawn carriages, the world's first horsecars began in New York City in 1832. By the late 1870s they were being replaced by faster and more efficient cable and electric cars. *(FPG)*

145* Bleecker Street

James Fenimore Cooper lived at this address for three years after returning from Europe in 1833.

152* Bleecker Street

Cafe au Go Go—Dirty-talking stand-up comic Lenny Bruce's most publicized arrest was made at this basement coffeehouse on April 3, 1964, even before he appeared on stage. Two plainclothes police officers had attended the show two days earlier on April Fool's Day and determined the show was obscene by New York City standards. In November, a criminal court convicted Bruce of giving an obscene performance. Bruce died in 1966 of a drug overdose; two years later the New York Appellate Court reversed his conviction. The club was a milestone in the career of another Bruce, Bruce Springsteen. He made his New York City debut here in 1966 with his high school band, the Castilles.

157* Bleecker Street

The Slide—This dance hall, named after the slang term for male prostitutes in drag, was one of the first widely known gay clubs in the city. The Slide, along with exotic Chinatown and the city's bordellos, became a late-night stop for urban sophisticates out "slumming" in the 1890s. In addition to amusing the tourist trade, these early gay clubs served as a safe haven and meeting place for gay men drawn to America's cities as the country changed from a rural society to an urban one. The club's notoriety was its undoing; the police closed it after a few years of operation.

160* Bleecker Street

The Greenwich—In 1897 this was the first New York City address of author Theodore Dreiser. At that time this building was a "hotel for gentlemen," and a bed for the night cost twenty-five cents. Originally called the Mills House, the hotel was built a year earlier by philanthropist Darius O. Mills as a cheap but moral lodging for unmarried workingmen. There were 1,500 units surrounding an enclosed courtyard. In 1976 the building was converted into a private residence call the Atrium.

172* Bleecker Street

Author, playwright, and critic James Agee lived on the top floor of this building from 1941 to 1951. It was here that he wrote the screenplay for *The African Queen.*

The curious, gathering outside the home of Dr. Harvey Burdell at 31 Bond Street on January 31, 1857. His murder the night before was only the beginning of a long and tawdry melodrama. *(Frank Leslie's Illustrated Newspaper)*

190 Bleecker Street

Beat poet Gregory Corso was born at this address, above a funeral parlor, on March 26, 1930.

BOND STREET

5 Bond Street

This address was the home of Albert Gallatin, financier, U.S. secretary of the treasury, and statesman, from 1820 to 1833. He was also a founding trustee of New York University. It was also later home to Maj. Gen. Winfield Scott.

31 Bond Street

The sensational stabbing murder of Dr. Harvey Burdell, a well-known dentist, took place here in his home on the night of January 30, 1857. Emma Cunningham, his one-time tempestuous lover and boarder, quickly declared that she was the doctor's secret wife and was entitled to his estate. Her surprising claim aroused suspicion, and she was arrested. The prosecution lacking a murder weapon or an eyewitness, she was acquitted for insufficient evidence. A later court declared she had married an impostor, not Burdell, and the marriage was declared illegal. Cunningham's final attempt to inherit the murdered victim's money was to pretend she was pregnant with his child. The police exposed this deception, too, catching her trying to buy a newborn baby.

44 Bond Street
This address was the residence of Susan B. Anthony in 1868–69.

BOWERY

Bowery and Bayard Street, Northwest Corner
New England Hotel—Stephen Foster, the composer of many of America's favorite songs, was found in this run-down hotel when he suffered a fatal accident on January 10, 1864. He was on the floor of his room, naked and bleeding, having gashed his neck on a porcelain washbasin. He was taken to Bellevue Hospital, where he died three days later. The near-destitute songwriter had long been battling alcoholism. "Beautiful Dreamer," one of his popular songs, was published posthumously.

37–39 Bowery
Zoological Institute—More a menagerie than a zoo, the institute was the first permanent display of imported "exotic" animals for the paying public in the 1830s. America's first lion tamer, Isaac A. Van Amburgh, got his start here as a cage cleaner.

   Bowery Amphitheater—The Virginia Minstrels appeared at this theater on January 31, 1843, and forever changed the image of African Americans in popular American culture. Four unemployed white actors, Billy Whitlock, Dan Emmett, Frank Pelham, and Frank Brower, originated a variety troupe done entirely in blackface. Whites in blackface had already become a theatrical standard by the early nineteenth century, but the minstrel shows created a sensation by ridiculing African Americans as happy simpleton entertainers. These cruel characterizations, written with a romantic misconception of plantation life, appealed to the unsophisticated white audiences in the years around the Civil War. It reinforced their idea that African Americans, whether enslaved or free, were inferior and, more insidiously, etched this racist image on the American consciousness to this day.

40–42 Bowery

A saloon that once stood at this address was the headquarters of the Bowery Boys, a tough gang who allied themselves with the Native American Party. They were united in their hatred of the poor immigrant Irish population. The Bowery Boys' rivals were the Dead Rabbits, a gang of Irish Democrats. This long-standing political animosity came to a head in a riot on July 4, 1857. The violence lasted for two days and spread over several blocks, including Bayard, Mulberry, and Baxter Streets. There were many deaths and injuries on both sides.

46–48 Bowery

Bull's Head Tavern—General Washington and Governor George Clinton stopped here on their triumphal public entry into the city on November 25, 1783, after the final British troops withdrew after the Revolution.

Bowery Theater—This theater that opened on this site in 1826 can claim two "firsts" in theater history. It was the first to be lighted with gas and the first in the United States to have a ballet performance. The ballet was *The Deserter* and opened on February 7, 1827. Seven years later, on July 9, 1834, the theater was the target of an anti-abolitionist mob, which sacked the auditorium in search of the English actor George Percy Farren. The actor's allegedly anti-American comments were interpreted as being against slavery, an unpopular stand with many New Yorkers at the time. A later rebuilt theater was the scene of a serious accident on the night of June 18, 1868. The fire department had just put out a blaze across the street when the boiler of their steam engine exploded, hurling scalding water into a crowd outside the theater during an intermission.

49 Bowery

Cafe Logeling—In 1877 the Manhattan Chess Club was founded in a room behind this restaurant. The club is the oldest in the country. Members have included Wilhelm Steinitz, José Raúl Capablanca, and Brooklyn's own Bobby Fischer. The current clubhouse is on 46th Street.

114 Bowery

Steve Brodie, one of the most colorful characters of the Bowery, owned a saloon here in the late 1880s. Steve's claim to fame was his presumed jump off the Brooklyn Bridge in July of 1886, three years after the bridge opened. He became an actor, a singer, a bartender, and a tireless self-promoter. He also became part of the language. *Webster's* defines a "brodie" as "a suicidal leap, hence a fall or flop."

Steve Brodie tends the bar in his saloon at 114 Bowery. Every available wall and ceiling space is devoted to framed portraits of famous fighters in this photograph from about 1890. *(Museum City of New York)*

201 Bowery

Tony Pastor's Opera House—Tony Pastor, a comic singer and former P. T. Barnum employee, opened his concert saloon in 1865. Called "the Father of American Vaudeville," he helped transform the bawdy music-hall tradition of the mid-nineteenth century into an acceptable form of entertainment for the middle class and women. He banned smoking and alcohol and instructed his performers to keep their acts "clean" of offensive language and behavior. He even offered door prizes of dress patterns and kitchenware to entice women into the theater. Lillian Russell made her debut here on November 22, 1880, and a year later he moved his playhouse uptown to Tammany Hall on East 14th Street in the Union Square theater district.

222* Bowery

When built in 1884, this structure was the first branch of the Young Men's Christian Association in New York City. Over the years, it was home to writer William Burroughs and painters Fernand Leger and Mark Rothko. The Queen Anne–style building designed by Bradford Lee Gilbert was designated a landmark in 1998.

Bowery from Prince Street to Union Square

On November 14, 1832, the world's first streetcar carried Mayor Walter Bowne and other dignitaries up this section of the Bowery. John Stephenson was the twenty-three-year-old inventor and patent holder of this "horse-drawn carriage running on rails." That first car, built at Stephenson's Elizabeth Street workshop, was christened the *John Mason* after the president of the New York and Harlem Railroad. The car was equipped with padded seats and glass windows and was pulled by a team of two horses. The fare was less than a nickel.

315 Bowery

CBGB-OMFUG—The initials stand for Country Blue-Grass Blues and Other Music for Uplifting Gormandizers, and the club was the American birthplace of punk and New Wave music. Opened in December of 1973, this venerated dive is a continuing forum for new music. Famous alumni like Blondie, the Talking Heads, the Ramones, and the Patti Smith Group have performed here, along with an estimated ten thousand not-so-famous bands over the years.

BROADWAY

Broadway and Chambers Street, Northwest Corner

Irving House—Louis Kossuth, the leader of the short-lived rebellion against the Hapsburgs, made this hotel his headquarters in December of 1851. The Hungarian patriot was in this country to help further the cause of independence for his native land.

Broadway and Reade Street, Southeast Corner

Washington Hotel—Completed in 1812, this hotel was a gathering place for many important figures of the early nineteenth century. It served as the Federalist Party headquarters in the city. The hotel's most regal guest was Prince Louis Napoleon, the nephew of Napoleon Bonaparte, who stayed here while he was in exile in America for several months in the spring of 1837. The future Napoleon III, emperor of

In the 1820s New York's first literary club, the Bread & Cheese, met at the Washington Hotel on Broadway and Reade Street. Founded by James Fenimore Cooper, the club included William Cullen Bryant, Fitz-Greene Halleck, and S. F. Morse as members. *(Author's collection)*

France, spent his time being entertained by New York society. The building was destroyed by a fire in 1844 and replaced by the A. T. Stewart department store, which eventually covered the entire block front.

A. T. Stewart Dry Goods Store—This building housed the first true department store, and at the time it opened in 1846 it was the largest in the world. A glorious commercial monument to the emerging American consumer, it was nicknamed the "Marble Palace." The store was decorated with mahogany counters, frescoes, and chandeliers and was served by an all-male army of three hundred salesmen and clerks. The building is still here. It was home to the newspaper *The New York Sun* from 1919 until 1952 and now is office space for the city.

Broadway and Thomas Street, West Side

New York Hospital—It was here at the hospital's first home that the Doctor's Riot began on April 13, 1788, after some boys observed medical students in Dr. Richard Bayley's anatomy class working on cadavers. Word of this discovery and rumors of body snatching inflamed a crowd, which set out for the hospital. Mayor James

Duane managed to calm and disperse the crowd. The next day, the jail where the doctors and students had taken refuge was stormed. This time the militia fired into the rioters; five were killed. The following year a law was passed allowing only the corpses of executed murderers, arsonists, and burglars to be used for medical dissection.

340–44 Broadway

Broadway Tabernacle—A two-day Women's Rights Movement Convention attended by Lucretia Mott, Susan B. Anthony, Elizabeth Cady Stanton, and Lucy Stone was held here, beginning on September 7, 1853. The participants had gathered to discuss prosperity and political power for women, especially the right to vote. Preacher William Lloyd Garrison and former slave Sojourner Truth spoke on the evils of slavery. In this same hall in 1856 ex-president Millard Fillmore was nominated as presidential candidate for the American, or Know-Nothing, Party.

Broadway and Leonard Street, Southeast Corner

New York Society Library—This was the second home of the library, and in the 1840s it was also the home of the National Academy of Design. It was here in Sep-

Built on a slight mound west of Broadway and today's Thomas Street, New York Hospital was the center of a green campus. A description in 1817 remarked, "No spot on the whole island could be better chosen on which to build a hospital." *(Author's collection)*

tember of 1847 that the Academy held the first public exhibition of the statue *The Greek Slave* by Hiram Powers. The first public display of a nude female statue in America, it caused a sensation. Normally a life-size statue of a female nude would have horrified puritan American tastes, but the sculptor shrewdly justified the subject's nudity by explaining it was beyond her control, taken, as she was, a slave by the Turks. Moreover, he wrote in the exhibition program, his subject represented the triumph of Christian virtue over her humiliating fate. Powers became the most popular sculptor in America, and reproductions of *The Greek Slave* became a fixture in every well-appointed parlor.

402 Broadway

Allen Dodworth Dancing Academy—Nineteenth-century commentator Thomas I. Nichols reported, "If there is anything New Yorkers are more given to than making money, it is dancing...." And where were they learning to dance? Why, here at Allen Dodworth's first academy, which opened in 1842. Dodworth was a violinist with the New York Philharmonic and an influential social arbitrator. He operated an exclusive school for the sons and daughters of the upper crust, where letters of introduction were required to attend. At the end of his long career he wrote a dance/etiquette manual called *Dancing and Its Relation to Education and Social Life* in 1885.

412 Broadway

Apollo Hall—On December 7, 1842, at 8:00 in the evening, the New York Philharmonic (then called the Philharmonic Society of New York) gave its first concert, to about six hundred music lovers. Three conductors took turns leading the sixty-three-piece orchestra, including the orchestra's founder, Ureli Corelli Hill, a German-trained musician from Connecticut, who led Beethoven's *Fifth Symphony.* The society has the distinction of being the oldest permanent orchestra in the English-speaking world.

This same hall was the historic site of the National Radical Reformers Convention on May 10, 1872. They formed the Equal Rights Party, the first political party in American history to nominate a woman, Victoria C. Woodhull, for president of the United States. In another equally radical move, they nominated an African American man, Frederick Douglass, for vice president. The party, led by the onetime spiritualist and Wall Street broker Woodhull, advocated free love, birth control, vegetarianism, easier divorce laws, and the end of the death penalty.

434 Broadway

Barnum's Hotel—Margaret Fox and her sister Kate, who launched the modern spiritualism movement in America, amazed New York with their mysterious "rapping" seances at this hotel in the summer of 1850. Mystically minded Victorians flocked to attend these performances for a dollar per person. *Tribune* editor Horace Greeley, one of many influential people thoroughly convinced of their powers, regaled his readers with their exploits. Almost forty years later, on October 21, 1888, Margaret confessed her longtime deception at an Academy of Music meeting of spiritualists. Rather than messages from the "other side," Margaret admitted that she produced the rappings by cracking her joints.

472 Broadway

Mechanics Hall—This was home to the famous E. P. Christy's Minstrels, whose blackface musical show set an American-stage longevity record of a decade of continuous run. Also on this stage the song "I Wish I Was in Dixie's Land," now know simply as "Dixie," by Dan Emmett, was introduced on April 4, 1859, by a later group called Bryant's Minstrels. Emmett, an originating member of the first true blackface minstrel troupe, the Virginia Minstrels, was a Northerner who never intended his song to become the battle cry of the Confederacy.

488–92 Broadway

Haughwout Building*—Mr. Elisha Otis installed the first practical passenger elevator in this cast-iron gem on April of 1857. It made the five-story trip in less than a minute. Not only was it considered fast, it was also secure, coming fully equipped with an automatic safety device. Haughwout, a prototype for the larger modern department stores, sold china, porcelains, and silverware on the first three floors and used the upper floors for manufacturing. The building had fallen on hard times by the 1960s and was slated for destruction, as was a huge stretch across Manhattan, for Robert Moses's plan for the Lower Manhattan Expressway. Thankfully, the expressway proposal was killed, but it wasn't until 1995 that this architectural masterpiece was restored.

509 Broadway

The first giraffes in America were exhibited in a vacant lot at this address in July of 1838. The two giraffes were the only survivors of a total of eleven that made the trip from southern Africa.

513–27 Broadway

St. Nicholas Hotel (* the middle portion 521–23 still remains)—Opened on January 6, 1853, this white marble hotel cost more than a million dollars to build. It included the novelty of a central heating plant that piped warm air, through registers, into every guest room. Mayor George Opdyke used a suite at this hotel as headquarters for the city government during the Draft Riots of July of 1863. The mayor met here with Governor Horatio Seymour and the city police, the Union Army, and the National Guard commanders to plan a strategy to stop the insurrection.

Another Civil War episode in the city's history also took place at this hotel. On November 25, 1864, the St. Nicholas was seriously damaged in a Confederate sabotage plot to burn down the city. More than eleven different hotels and Barnum's American Museum were set ablaze in a desperate attempt by Southern spies, who hoped to stave off defeat in the waning months of the war. The fire in this hotel was set in room 175 with "Greek fire," the same flammable mixture used to start the fires in the other hotels. No lives were lost, and the fires were quickly put out. Only one of the conspirators was ever caught. He was Capt. Robert Kennedy, a veteran of the Battle of Shiloh. Kennedy was found guilty of spying and arson. He was hanged at Fort Lafayette on March 25, 1865, fifteen days before the surrender at Appomattox.

Opened to accommodate wealthy visitors to the Exhibition of 1853, St. Nicholas Hotel at 521 Broadway had many modern conveniences, including a bridal chamber decorated entirely in white satin. The middle section of the once grand hotel is still standing. *(Author's collection)*

548 Broadway

Church of Divine Unity—William Thackeray made his first American appearance at this Unitarian church, now gone, on November 19, 1852. He delivered a lecture titled "On the Humorous Writers of Queen Anne's Reign."

Broadway and Prince Street, Northeast Corner

Niblo's Garden—Dating from the 1820s, this celebrated pleasure garden and theater was at this location until the 1890s. In 1837 Daniel Webster, the great orator and jurist, spoke on political issues, as did the leading actors of their day, such as Edwin Forrest and Joseph Jefferson.

Metropolitan Hotel—The Metropolitan Hotel opened in 1852 and shared this site with Niblo's. The hotel's most famous guest was Japan's Crown Prince Tateish Onojero, quickly dubbed "Tommy" by the American press, on June 16, 1860. The first Japanese royal to visit the United States, the teenaged "Tommy" was the object of intense public curiosity and affection. Another famous Tom is also associated with this hotel, its bartender Professor Jerry Thomas. In 1862 Professor Thomas was the author of The *Bon-Vivants Companion or How to Mix Drinks,* the first authoritative bar manual. He was also the inventor of the "Tom and Jerry" and "Blue Blazer" cocktails. Another invention had its birthplace here. What is considered the first American musical production, *The Black Crook,* opened on September 12, 1866. By all accounts, it was a disjointed variety show, which included ballet dancers, music, and melodrama. But it was a big hit and ran for a record 475 continuous performances.

Broadway near Prince Street

A great log cabin was built near this intersection to advertise the presidential campaign of Gen. William Henry Harrison on June 16, 1840. He won the election in November, but he died after being president for only thirty-one days. He had caught a cold while delivering his two-hour inaugural address in a freezing rain.

584* Broadway

The international writers' group, PEN, sponsored a public reading of the book *The Satanic Verses* by Salman Rushdie on February 22, 1989. Mr. Rushdie, along with his publishers, had been threatened with execution by the Iranian leader Ayatollah Khomeini, who considered the book blasphemous to the Muslim faith. American writers Susan Sontag, Gay Talese, E. L. Doctorow, and others spoke out against censorship.

The Gothic Revival-style St. Thomas' Church was located on the northwest corner of Broadway and West Houston, the site of the current Cable Building. This neighborhood was a thriving red-light district, where brothels openly advertised, during the second half of the nineteenth century. *(Author's collection)*

585 Broadway

This was the final address of John Jacob Astor. When he died at the age of eighty-four, on March 29, 1848, in a brick house that stood on this spot, he was the wealthiest man in America. He had made much of his fortune in real estate. Shortly before his death, he was quoted as saying, "Could I begin my life again, knowing what I know now, and I had the money to invest, I would buy every foot of land on the island of Manhattan."

Broadway and West Houston Street, Northwest Corner

St. Thomas' Episcopal Church—The funeral for John Jacob Astor was held here on March 31, 1848. Honorary pallbearers were friends Washington Irving and Philip Hone. After the service, Astor was buried in the family vault at the back of the church. By 1866 the once-fashionable neighborhood had changed dramatically, and the church shared the street with bawdy dance halls and saloons. Consequently, the congregation moved the church to its present location on Fifth Avenue at West 53rd Street. John Jacob Astor and the remains of his family left even sooner, in 1851, for a better neighborhood, the Upper West Side's Trinity Church Cemetery on Broadway and West 155th Street.

624 Broadway

Laura Keene's Varieties Theater—Ms. Keene, the actress and impresario, opened this theater on November 18, 1856. She later became well known for performing in the play *Our American Cousin* at Ford's Theater in Washington, D.C., the night Abraham Lincoln was assassinated. This theater went though various name changes before being demolished in 1881.

643 Broadway

The third daguerreotype gallery of Mathew Brady was in a building that once stood at this address. It was here that Brady took his most famous photograph, a portrait of Abraham Lincoln. While campaigning for the Republican nomination for president, Lincoln had his photo taken at this studio on February 27, 1860, the day of his famous speech at Cooper Union. Lincoln credited the widely distributed Brady photo with helping him win the election.

647* Broadway

Pfaff's—The basement of this same building was the site of the rathskeller restaurant Charlie Pfaff's, a hotbed of the early Greenwich Village bohemians in the years before the Civil War. Nonconformists, writers and hacks, thespians and intellectuals gathered here for lively debates with regulars such as socialist and free-love champion Henry Clapp; satirist George Farrar Browne (pseudonym Artemus Ward); early drug experimenter Fitz-Hugh Ludlow; and the scandalous actress Ada Clare, the "Queen of Bohemia." Clapp's weekly *The Saturday Press,* founded in 1858, was a forum for another Pfaff's favorite, Walt Whitman, the great American poet.

663 Broadway

National Academy of Design—Opened in 1850, this was the first building of the academy that was founded in 1826 by the artist and inventor Samuel F. B. Morse

Mathew Brady's influential photograph of Abraham Lincoln helped convince voters that he was not a country-bumpkin lawyer but a respectable leader. Still in the suit he wore for his Cooper Union speech, Lincoln had his portrait taken in a building that once stood at 643 Broadway on February 27, 1860. *(Library of Congress)*

and thirty other artists. Louis Comfort Tiffany and Augustus Saint-Gaudens were students here in the years before the Civil War.

667–77 Broadway

Metropolitan Hall—This auditorium was the site of the World's Temperance Convention on September 1, 1853. Delegates, including Susan B. Anthony, Horace Greeley, Lucretia Mott, and P. T. Barnum, passed resolutions pledging to work for total abstinence, to label drunkenness a crime, and to "end the reign of Satan among Christians." The meeting helped bring together several expanding nineteenth-century social movements: temperance, women's rights, vegetarianism, and nativism.

Winter Garden Theater—This theater replaced the burned Metropolitan in 1859. All three Booth Brothers—Junius, Edwin, and John Wilkes—performed only once together during their careers, appearing on this stage in *Julius Caesar* on November 25, 1864. It was a benefit performance to raise money for a statue of Shakespeare in Central Park to commemorate the Bard's three hundredth birthday. Less than five months later the youngest brother, John Wilkes Booth, assassinated Abraham Lincoln in Washington, D.C. It was at this same theater that Edwin

A. S. Hosier painted this watercolor of the Samuel Ward mansion at Broadway and Bond Street about 1835. The rear addition with the columns housed the art gallery and one of the finest libraries in New York.
(Museum City of New York)

made his return to the stage in January of 1866. After the assassination, he had vowed never to act again, but financial necessity forced him to return. The forgiving audience welcomed him back with wild applause.

Grand Central Hotel—In turn, this hotel replaced the Winter Garden. Jim Fisk, the stock-market speculator and partner of Jay Gould, was shot on a staircase here on January 6, 1872. He died the next day. Edward S. Stokes, the killer, and Fisk were in love with the same woman, Josie Mansfield, an actress the press nicknamed "Twenty-third Street Cleopatra." The hotel lasted another hundred years and collapsed on August 3, 1973, killing four people who were living in the then-welfare hotel.

Broadway and Bond Street, Northeast Corner

Samuel Ward's mansion and the adjacent art gallery, said to have been the first private gallery in America, once stood on this corner. Known as "The Corner," the handsome square building was topped with a delicate cupola. Mr. Ward was a patron of the arts, a civic leader, and a trustee of Columbia College in the first half of the nineteenth century. He was also the father of Julia Ward Howe, the composer of "The Battle Hymn of the Republic." The current building was home to the Brooks Brothers store from 1874 until 1884.

682 Broadway

This was the last home of diarist Philip Hone, who was mayor of New York City in 1825. He built a house here on land he purchased from his neighbor Samuel Ward in 1837. He died in 1851.

721 Broadway

New York Hotel—Opened in 1844, this innovative hotel was the first to introduce room service and an "à la carte" menu. August Brentano began his book-selling business with a small newsstand in the lobby in 1853. Because of the hotel's popularity with Southerners at the time of the Civil War, it was widely believed to be a hotbed of Confederate spies and blockade runners. The fact that it was spared during the Confederate plot to burn down several hotels in November of 1864 only seemed to confirm these Northern suspicions.

757 Broadway

This address was in 1870 the first shop of F. A. O. Schwarz, the founder of what is now reputed to be the world's largest toy store. Schwarz opened this small toy shop after having moved to New York from Baltimore.

Broadway from East 8th Street to East 23rd Street

This stretch of Broadway, only recently labeled "Ladies Mile," was the city's major shopping artery in the second half of the nineteenth century. Middle-class prosperity, the availability of massproduced consumer goods, changing roles for women, and increasingly sophisticated advertising helped create a shopper's paradise. The clever displays of goods and plate-glass windows gave birth to "window shopping." These remaining grand shopping emporiums were designated part of a historic district in 1989, and today the area is again a flourishing shopping district.

764 Broadway

Descombe Rooms—The first chess tournament of importance won by an American-born player, twenty-year-old Paul Charles Morphy, was held at this address from October 6 to November 10, 1857. The American Chess Congress, sponsored in part by the New York Chess Club, sent invitations to the world's best-known players, including James Thompson and C. H. Stanley. The brilliant Morphy beat the sixteen other participants and won first prize, $300. He became a somewhat reluctant popular native hero, having a cigar and a hat named after him. Sales of chess sets skyrocketed, and he was asked to write a column for *Chess Monthly* and the New York *Ledger*. Within a few years, the fad passed, and Morphy gladly faded into oblivion.

Broadway and East 9th Street, Northwest Corner

This corner was the approximate site of the home of Capt. Robert Richard Randall, a wealthy shipmaster and merchant. In 1801 he bequeathed his house and the surrounding twenty-one acres, from roughly Waverly Place to 10th Street and from Fifth Avenue to Fourth Avenue, for the founding of Sailors' Snug Harbor, for "the purpose of maintaining and supporting aged, decrepit, and worn-out sailors." The Harbor home moved to Staten Island in 1833, and then on to North Carolina in 1976, but continues to lease its twenty-one acres of prime real estate in the Village to this day.

Broadway between East 9th Street and East 10th Street, East Side

A. T. Stewart's Department Store—Opened as A. T. Stewart's second department store in 1862, the huge cast-iron building covered two and a half acres and, like the flagship store on lower Broadway, was a tremendous success. By this time Stewart's business, both retail and wholesale, was so vast that it generated 10 percent of the imports into the port of New York. Purchased by John Wanamaker in 1896, it became Wanamaker's Department Store and was expanded into an annex built in

1907, still standing one block south. The store survived until 1954, long after most of the retail trade had moved north to Herald Square and Fifth Avenue. On July 15, 1956, 208 fire fighters were injured during the twenty-five hour blaze that engulfed the empty, legendary store.

Broadway and East 10th Street, Northeast Corner

Fleischmann's Vienna Model Bakery—Now a leafy churchyard, this was once a bake shop popular with women shoppers in the heyday of "Ladies Mile." The term "breadline" originated on this corner as the needy lined up after hours to receive free baked goods from the charitable owners.

The large building on the right is A. T. Stewart's Department Store on Broadway and West 9th Street about 1910. Grace Church is at the end of Broadway, and a slice of Fleischmann's Vienna Model Bakery can be seen between the two buildings. *(Author's collection)*

800 Broadway

*Grace Church**—This Gothic Revival masterpiece was the scene of the marriage of Gen. Tom Thumb, the country's most popular sideshow performer, and Lavinia Warren on February 10, 1863. More than 1,200 guests, described by the *New York Times* as "the elite, the creme de la creme, the upper ten, the bon ton, the select few, the very first families of the city—nay of the country," witnessed the vows of the happy couple, whose combined height was only five feet, six inches. The newlyweds traveled to Washington, D.C., where they were received by America's tallest president, Abraham Lincoln, who remarked on their respective heights, "God likes to do funny things, here you have the long and the short of it."

Broadway and East 11th Street, Southwest Corner

*Saint Denis Hotel**—Mary Todd Lincoln, the wife of assassinated President Abraham Lincoln, was a guest at this hotel on September 17, 1867. Mrs. Lincoln had stayed here before with the president, but this time she was traveling incognito and registered under the pseudonym "Mrs. Clark." The former first lady and her African American servant, a former slave named Lizzie Keckley, were forced to stay in the hotel's only integrated quarters, an attic room. They were in New York on a desperate scheme to raise money by selling Mrs. Lincoln's old clothes and jewelry. The whole affair ended badly a few days later when they were taken in by hucksters interested only in capitalizing on the Lincoln name. She also created a political uproar after her unflattering correspondence to the slain president's allies appeared in the newspapers. She had tried to enlist them in her sale of the old clothes. This incident was one of the first public signs of Mrs. Lincoln's mental instability, which eventually led to her son Robert's request for a hearing to determine her sanity. In 1875 she was formally committed to an Illinois institution for the insane. She was released after four months, but the public was never convinced of her stability.

On May 11, 1877, the Saint Denis's second-floor "gentlemen's parlor" was the scene of Alexander Graham Bell's first public demonstration of the telephone. This call was the first to use wire invented for the telephone and not telegraph wire, which Bell had used earlier. Two hundred invited guests watched Bell as he called an assistant in Brooklyn.

839 Broadway

*Roosevelt Building**—The rooftop of this building served as the first movie studio of the American Mutoscope and Biograph Company in the 1890s. William Kennedy Laurie Dickson, a pioneer filmmaker who first worked with Thomas Edison, designed a rotating stage on tracks to keep the sun at the best lighting angle for filming. Dickson, the company's chief cameraman, became a part owner of the studio by 1896. The company moved to an indoor studio at 11 East 14th Street in 1906.

851 Broadway

Cornelius van Schaanck Roosevelt, a wealthy real-estate broker, played host here to society and literary figures of the mid-nineteenth century. Some of his guests included James Fenimore Cooper, Washington Irving, and Louis Napoleon. One of Mr. Roosevelt's grandsons, Theodore Roosevelt, became the twenty-sixth president of the United States. It was from a second-story window of this house that six-year-old "Teedie" watched the funeral procession of another president, Abraham Lincoln, pass by on April 25, 1865.

On April 25, 1865, the funeral procession for President Lincoln passed the house of Cornelius van Schaanck Roosevelt on Broadway south of Union Square Park. The two small children in the second-story window are probably Theodore Roosevelt and his brother Elliot. *(Theodore Roosevelt Collection, Harvard College Library)*

CANAL STREET

54–58 Canal Street

S. Jarmulovsky's Bank Building*—This private bank, founded in 1873, grew with the hard-earned savings of new immigrants living on the Lower East Side. But as political instability in Europe grew before World War I, depositors withdrew savings to send to their families overseas. Rumors and runs on this bank forced it to close on August 4, 1914, financially ruining the lives of thousands of trusting immigrants.

CATHERINE STREET

47 Catherine Street

In 1826 Samuel Lord, a new immigrant from England, and George W. Taylor, his wife's cousin, opened their dry-goods store at this address. The Lord and Taylor store prospered and outgrew this and several other uptown addresses before settling at its present location at Fifth Avenue and West 38th Street in 1914.

90 Catherine Street

This address was the birthplace of Jimmy Durante on February 10, 1893. The famous comedian was the fourth and youngest child born to Rosa and Bartolomeo Durante.

CENTRE STREET

12 Centre Street

Although he spent much of his time in the borough of Brooklyn, Walt Whitman did live at several boardinghouses in Manhattan. The poet lived at one at this address—run by a Mrs. Chipman—in 1842. His stay here was documented for posterity in an amusing story he wrote for the *New York Aurora*. It relates his getting home late one night, being locked out, and being forced to spend the night in a city shelter.

40 Centre Street

Foley Square—*U.S. Courthouse**—The 1949 Communist Party conspiracy trial, the 1951 Ethel and Julius Rosenberg espionage trial, and the 1984 General Westmoreland vs. CBS libel case are among the celebrated trials that have been con-

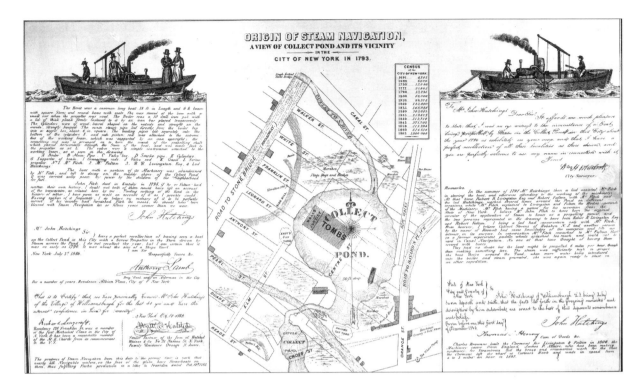

A map of Collect Pond superimposed over the current street grid. This pond was the location of John Fitch's experiments with steam-powered screw-propeller vessels in 1793. Less than twenty years later, slaughterhouses and tanneries on the southern shore polluted the water, and the pond was filled. *(Author's collection)*

ducted here. Defendants faced with dodging an army of reporters on these front steps have included former Philippines first lady Imelda Marcos and former Miss America Bess Myerson.

Centre Street and Leonard Street

Collect Pond—In the long geological development of the island of Manhattan, the site of this present-day intersection was the island's largest source of natural fresh water. The pond was about the size of three city blocks and surrounded by pristine wilderness. Archaeological studies have confirmed the existence of an early Native American settlement along the western shore. By the Colonial Period it supplied the locals with an abundant supply of fish, oysters, and fresh water. It drained into the Hudson River by way of a ditch that became Canal Street. In 1796 the inventor John Fitch used the pond to experiment with his steamboat, almost ten years before Robert Fulton was to launch the *North River*, or the *Clermont* as the ship has been recorded in history. Fitch's ships were successful, but he was unable to obtain financial backing. In despair he killed himself two years later. By 1811 the

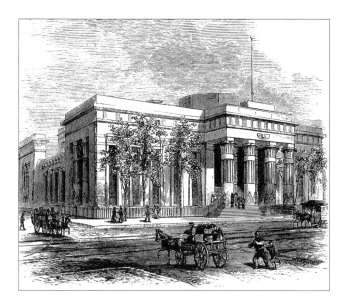

The Tombs on Centre and Franklin Streets is pictured in an early engraving. Charles Dickens, on a visit in 1842, wrote, "Such indecent and disgusting dungeons as these cells would bring disgrace upon the most despotic empire in the world." (Author's collection)

pond, which had become polluted as the city grew around it, was filled in.

Centre Street and Franklin Street, Northwest Corner

Halls of Justice—This prison, named The Tombs because of its exotic Egyptian Revival–style architecture, was built in 1839. One of its most famous inmates, John C. Colt, the brother of Samuel Colt, inventor of the revolver, was convicted of the murder of his printer, Samuel Adams. He was to be hanged here on November 18, 1842. On that day two strange events took place: Colt was allowed to marry his common-law wife, Caroline Henshaw, and a mysterious fire broke out. Once the fire was put out, it was discovered that several prisoners had escaped, and a body was found in Colt's cell with a knife in its heart. Officials had the body buried within three hours and announced Colt's suicide. Within days his bride disappeared, never to be seen again. It was widely speculated that Colt had faked his own "suicide" and escaped with the aid of his wealthy brother. A second prison was erected on this site in 1902 and lasted until 1939. The current incarnation of The Tombs, built in 1939, is across the street.

Centre Street and Grand Street

Bayard's Mount—Once a natural hill, this spot was fortified by American rebels before the British occupation during the Revolutionary War. On July 23, 1788, the city's first great parade ended here, at the home of merchant William Bayard, with a huge picnic. The parade, which had started at the commons, present-day City Hall Park, at 8:00 that morning was held to demonstrate local support for the ratification of the new Federal Constitution. Maj. Pierre L'Enfant, the future designer of Washington, D.C., designed the parade, along with the picnic pavilions. The procession was composed of all the city's major trade groups: merchants, carpenters, printers, and doctors. Elaborate floats, including a model of the Federal ship *Hamilton* under full sail carried by sailors, were interspersed between the marchers. The parade was a great success. Three days later, in Poughkeepsie, the New York State Convention ratified the Constitution of the United States.

240 Centre Street

*Old Police Headquarters**—After World War I, at the height of the "Red Terror," the public was near hysteria over Communist, socialist, and revolutionary influences in America. On November 7–8, 1919, there were nationwide raids to round up people who were considered Bolsheviks and subversives. These raids were called "Palmer raids" after the then-attorney general of the United States A. Mitchell Palmer. In New York City more than two thousand people were brought here to be questioned. All noncitizens were deported. The building is still a bastion of capitalist power, only now it is a luxury co-operative apartment house.

CHARLTON STREET

Charlton Street near Hudson Street

Richmond Hill—A beautiful Georgian mansion sat atop what was once a high hill that covered several blocks of this neighborhood. The mansion, built in 1767, overlooked the Hudson River, a brook, and a pond. It served briefly as George Washington's headquarters during the American Revolution and was also home to the country's first vice president, John Adams. It was also the home of another vice president, Aaron Burr, who lived here from 1797 until his duel with Alexander Hamilton forced him to leave New York in 1804. John Jacob Astor purchased the estate and developed the property. He moved the mansion down the hill, cut through present-day Charlton Street, leveled the hill, and laid out building lots. Many of the houses, built in the mid-1820s as a result of Astor's development, are still standing today on the nearby blocks. The Richmond Hill mansion didn't fare so well. Moved yet again, it was converted into a theater in 1831 and later a circus. During this period, in 1833, Isaac A. Van Amburgh presented the first wild animal act in America on its stage. American-born animal trainer Van Amburgh is reputed to be the first man to put his head in the mouth of a lion. Finally a tavern, the Richmond Hill was demolished in 1849.

CHATHAM SQUARE

5 Chatham Square

This address was the barber shop of Samuel F. O'Reilly in 1899. It was here that modern mechanical tattooing was invented. O'Reilly, who adapted the ink tube and tip of Thomas Edison's new electric engraving pen, changed his shop into the country's first tattoo parlor.

Brooks Brothers Clothing was at this location, the northwest corner of Cherry and Catharine Streets, for fifty-six years until 1874. The firm outfitted Civil War Generals Ulysses S. Grant, William T. Sherman, and Philip Sheridan. President Abraham Lincoln was wearing a Brooks Brothers suit when assassinated.
(*Author's collection*)

CHERRY STREET

Cherry Street and Catharine Street, Northeast Corner

Brooks Brothers Clothing Store—Henry Sands Brooks founded his menswear firm here on April 7, 1818. His two elder brothers, Henry and Daniel, joined him: therefore, Brooks Brothers. Because the firm supplied uniforms for the Union Army during the Civil War, looters sacked the store during the Draft Riots of 1863. The store stayed in the neighborhood long after it was no longer fashionable, not moving uptown until 1874.

Cherry Street between Clinton and Montgomery to Monroe Streets

Belvedere House—The tavern that once stood on this site and surrounding land is considered the first "country club" in America, opened in 1793. Membership was limited to just thirty-three gentlemen. In 1804 Jerome Bonaparte, Napoleon's brother and the future king of Westphalia, rented the property for the summer and fall seasons while seeking refuge in New York from the British. The building was razed in 1830.

CHRISTOPHER STREET

51* Christopher Street

The Stonewall Inn—A routine police raid on this gay bar gave birth to the gay-rights movement. On June 28, 1969, at 1:20 a.m., Deputy Inspector Seymour Pine and seven other policemen from the Public Moral Section closed the bar on pretense that liquor was being sold without a license and announced that all the employees would be arrested. In addition to the employees, customers without proper identification and likely cross-dressers were detained for questioning. As these suspects were being loaded into a paddy wagon, their friends and fellow patrons surprised the police and began throwing pennies, cans, bottles, and bricks at the officers, who retreated into the bar. The fight escalated when the mob broke the front window and set the bar on fire. What started as just another example of police harassment against gay people sparked a revolution. This act of defiance and the four days of rioting that followed marked a turning point in the quest for equal rights for gays and lesbians. The Stonewall Rebellion victory is commemorated each year in the Gay Pride March in June in New York and throughout the country.

CHURCH STREET

236 Church Street between Worth Street and Leonard Street, West Side

The first newspaper in the United States owned and published by African Americans, *Freedom's Journal,* was launched at this site in 1827, the same year slavery was abolished in New York State. The Reverend Samuel Cornish and John Russwurm, the first African American to receive a college education in the United States, edited the paper. The paper's goal was printed in the first issue: "We wish to plead our own cause. Too long have others spoken for us...."

Church Street and Leonard Street, Southwest Corner

Mother African Methodist Episcopal Zion Church—In 1796 this was the site of the first church built by and for African Americans in New York City. Before this time, African Americans were unable to be full members of the city's churches. They were banished to balconies or back pews and not allowed to bury their dead in sanctified churchyards. One of the founders of this new church was Peter Williams, who as a slave had been purchased by the trustees of the John Street Methodist Episcopal Church, where he was made a sexton. Williams—who later purchased his freedom—became a wealthy tobacconist and donated the land and much of the money to build the church. Later, Sojourner Truth renounced her slave name here. The church was sacked during an anti-abolitionist riot on July 9, 1834, and was damaged by a fire that started across Leonard Street at the National Theater in 1839. The congregation is now located at West 137th Street near Lenox Avenue.

Church Street and Leonard Street, Northwest Corner

Italian Opera House—On November 18, 1833, Rossini's *La Gazza Ladra* was performed here in the first theater in the United States designed exclusively for opera. Lorenzo da Ponte, a librettist for Mozart and professor of Italian at Columbia College, financed and built the theater. This cultural beachhead closed within two years, most likely due to its poor location and limited Italian opera repertoire. The building became the National Theater, burned to the ground on September 23, 1839, was rebuilt, and burned again.

The promise of that glorious first night at the Italian Opera House was unfulfilled. The ambitious cultural enterprise at Church and Leonard Streets failed after two seasons. Renamed the National Theater, it burned along with three neighboring churches—Northwest Reform Dutch, Eglise du St. Esprit, and Mother African Methodist Episcopal Zion Churches—in a spectacular fire on September 23, 1839. *(Author's collection)*

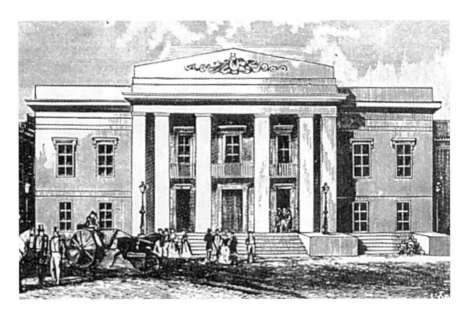

CLINTON STREET

79 Clinton Street

A little frame house that once stood on this spot was the home and headquarters of "Mother" Fredericka Mandelbaum, reputedly the most successful fence for stolen property in the annals of New York City crime. Beginning in 1862 and for the next twenty years, she was believed to have handled almost $10 million in stolen goods. "Mother," who weighed more than 250 pounds, also gave lessons in pickpocketing and burglary to eager students. When the police finally closed down her profitable operation, she fled to Canada.

220 Clinton Street

The classical composer Edward Alexander MacDowell was born at this address on December 18, 1861.

COOPER SQUARE

41 Cooper Square

Cooper Union for the Advancement of Science and Art*—Built by inventor and industrialist Peter Cooper in 1859, this school was the first free nonsectarian coeducational college in the nation. Cooper, a great social reformer who never received a formal education, wanted to help educate gifted students from the working class. Cooper Union is still free to all students who qualify.

Abraham Lincoln delivered his first New York speech in the Great Hall of this building on February 27, 1860. Introduced by William Cullen Bryant and sponsored by the Young Men's Republican Union, this appearance before an audience of 1,500 New Yorkers launched Lincoln's presidential candidacy. The speech included the famous passage "Let us have faith that right makes might, and in that faith let us to the end dare to do our duty as we understand it." Others have also used this forum for great causes: Victoria C. Woodhull on women's rights, Jacob Riis on the needs of the poor, and Booker T. Washington on African American rights.

DELANCEY STREET

Delancey Street and Chrystie Street, Northwest Corner

The country home of James de Lancey once stood near this corner on a street now named for him. He was both the chief justice of New York Colony and lieutenant

Completed in 1859, Cooper Union was one of the earliest buildings in the world to use wrought-iron beams. This innovative structure was equipped with a floor-to-roof circular shaft anticipating improvements in the newly invented elevator. *(FPG)*

governor. He died suddenly here on July 30, 1760. Delancey Street marks the northern boundary of the family's estate, which extended from the Bowery to the East River and from Stanton to Division Streets. Over 120 blocks, it was the largest estate then owned by a single family on Manhattan.

DESBROSSES STREET

Desbrosses Street at the Hudson River

On the morning of April 24, 1865, the body of slain President Abraham Lincoln arrived at this spot at what was then a ferry landing. This was the beginning of the two-day New York City portion of the long emotional journey from Washington, D.C., to Springfield, Illinois, for burial. Six gray horses covered in black pulled the coffin in a hearse with glass sides topped with huge plumes of black and white feathers. The procession, which moved down Hudson Street to Canal Street then on to Broadway, was escorted by the city's own 7th Regiment to City Hall, where the body lay in state. The almost complete silence of the spectacle was broken only by the muffled drums in various bands and the slow tolling of church bells.

EAST BROADWAY

165* East Broadway

Garden Cafeteria—An earlier restaurant on this site was a popular gathering place for Yiddish intellectuals, many of whom worked at the nearby *Jewish Daily Forward*. It was also a place for spirited discussions between the Russian anarchists Alexander Berkman, Emma Goldman, and Leon Trotsky in the years before World War I. The writer Isaac Bashevis Singer was a frequent diner.

173–75* East Broadway

The Jewish Daily Forward—Part of what was once called the Yiddish "Publisher's Row," the *Forward* was founded by Abraham Cahan in 1897. The beloved advice column "Bintel Brief," or "bundle of letters," helped educate, amuse, and assimilate the new Jewish immigrants on the rocky road to their American dream. The building is now a church for the neighborhood's latest immigrants, the Chinese.

197 East Broadway

The Education Alliance*—Wealthy German Jews established this Jewish community center, originally known as the Hebrew Institute, in 1889. It has helped Americanize three generations of later Eastern European Jewish immigrants. The Alliance offered day and evening classes in English and citizenship. A free library was available before there were public libraries in New York City. This is where David Sarnoff learned English, Arthur Murray learned to dance, and Sir Jacob Epstein took art classes.

EAST HOUSTON STREET

26 East Houston Street

Harry Hill's Concert Saloon—Hill's was a bawdy dance hall that also staged special diversions for its low-life customers and "slumming" tourists, such as weekly poetry readings by the owner or Punch-and-Judy shows. Another specialty of the house was impromptu boxing matches, at a time when they were illegal in New York State. At a "testimonial benefit" for John L. Sullivan on March 31, 1881, the future champ offered $50 to anyone who could stay with him in the ring for four 3-minute rounds. Steve Taylor, a boxer from New Jersey, tried and admitted defeat after two rounds. Sullivan gave Taylor $25 for his trouble.

ELDRIDGE STREET

60 Eldridge Street

Lyricist Ira Gershwin was born at this address, above Simpson's Pawnshop, on December 6, 1896. His brother George, the composer, was born in Brooklyn two years later.

ELIZABETH STREET

206 Elizabeth Street

On June 5, 1900, a tenement at this address was one of the first stops on an unannounced tour of sweatshops by New York Governor Theodore Roosevelt. The progressive governor was accompanied by his personal friend Jacob Riis, who was a social reformer, photographer, journalist, and author of *How the Other Half Lives*. They also visited about twenty other tenements on this street and Mulberry Street to investigate apartments that served as a factory for the immigrants of the neighborhood. They found many violations, including overcrowding, unlicensed manufacturing, and filthy conditions. Roosevelt's interest in housing and sweatshop reform helped focus public attention on the appalling living conditions of the poor.

ESSEX STREET

64–66 Essex Street

Sinsheimer Saloon—The long-ago restaurant at this address was the birthplace of the Jewish B'nai B'rith on October 13, 1843. This secular fraternal society was one of the nation's first service organizations. B'nai B'rith, which translates to "Sons of the Covenant," was founded mostly by German Jews in reaction to the potent anti-immigrant movement of the time.

FORSYTH STREET

102 Forsyth Street
This address was the birthplace of comedian Fanny Brice on October 29, 1891.

GANSEVOORT STREET

Gansevoort Street and Little West 12th Street
The area from here to the Hudson River was once the location of a Sapokanickan Indian trading site. This native tribe traded with the Dutch settlers in the 1600s. The word *sapokanickan* means "farm in the woods."

GAY STREET

12* Gay Street
Betty Compton lived in this two-story house in the 1920s. In addition to being an actress, she was the girlfriend of Mayor "Jimmy" Walker. Their scandalous extramarital affair was a further embarrassment for the already embattled mayor, who was fighting corruption charges. After the mayor resigned from office and obtained a divorce, he married Compton while in France in 1933.

14* Gay Street
Writer Ruth McKenney and her sister Eileen lived in the basement apartment of this house in the 1920s. Her "My Sister Eileen" stories of their adventures in the big city were first published in *The New Yorker* and were later made into a book, play, musical, and movie.

GRAND STREET

504 Grand Street
R. Hoe and Company—The most violent anti-Semitic riot in U.S. history took place at this loca-

Former mayor Jimmy Walker and his wife, Betty Compton, arrive in New York City aboard the *Manhattan* on October 31, 1935, after a three-year exile in Europe. The couple, who had married while in France, returned once they learned Walker would not be prosecuted for income-tax evasion. *(New York Daily News)*

tion. On July 30, 1902, the employees of R. Hoe and Company, a prestigious old printing press company at this address, during their lunch break began jeering at the fifty thousand Jewish mourners following the hearse carrying the body of their leader Rabbi Jacob Joseph. The taunting escalated to throwing printing paraphernalia, bits of iron, and wood from the upper floors of the factory. The Jews ran for cover and began throwing back the projectiles. When the police reserves arrived, they sided with the predominantly Irish workers and set upon the Jews. By the time the assault ended, more than three hundred Jews required medical attention. The police arrested eleven Jews and one Hoe employee. Mayor Seth Low appointed an investigative commission, which placed much of the blame on Irish and police anti-Semitism.

GREAT JONES STREET

57* Great Jones Street

This building was home and studio for twenty-seven-year-old artist Jean-Michel Basquiat, found dead here on August 12, 1988, of a heroin overdose. He had rented this space from his friend and mentor, and owner of the building, Andy Warhol, who had died a year earlier.

GREENWICH AVENUE

Greenwich Avenue between Christopher Street and West 10th Street

Women's House of Detention—In October of 1970 a prison once on this block held Angela Davis, the 1960s Communist radical. Davis, who had made the FBI's "Ten Most Wanted List," was eventually extradited to California for her involvement with the attempt to free the Soledad Brothers, a group of Marxist prison inmates. Her stay here was accompanied by daily sidewalk protests demanding freedom for political prisoners. Always unwelcome and out of scale with the neighborhood, the jail was torn down in 1974, and this area is now the site of a lush community garden.

86 Greenwich Avenue

A triangular tenement that once stood here was the address of James and Susan Light. Their spacious seventeen-room apartment served as home and gathering

The gloomy art-deco prison once located on Greenwich Avenue at West 10th Street, right, housed women awaiting trail in the adjoining Jefferson Market Courthouse. The courthouse's Victorian fire watchtower with clock is in the center. *(FPG)*

place for many Greenwich Village intellectuals around the time of World War I. Some residents included photographer Berenice Abbott, writers Djuna Barnes and Matthew Josephson, and critics Malcolm Cowley and Kenneth Burke. Suffragist Dorothy Day lived downstairs. The Greenwich Theater now stands on this site.

GROVE STREET

59 Grove Street
Thomas Paine died in the farmhouse of his friend Marguerite de Bonneville, located here, on June 8, 1809. The current structure houses a restaurant, Marie's Crisis Cafe, named after Paine's *Crisis Papers*.

HAGUE STREET

3–5 Hague Street
Neither this address nor this street exists today. The entire street was eradicated to build the Alfred Smith Housing projects now occupying several former blocks just north of the Brooklyn Bridge to Catherine Street. On the morning of February 4, 1850, this was the site of the city's greatest loss of life up to that time. Sixty-seven people died and fifty were injured in a steam-boiler explosion that completely destroyed the two tenement buildings that stood here.

HESTER STREET

128 Hester Street
This address, as well as the whole block between Forsyth and Christie Streets, is now a park. But on December 18, 1819, it was the birthplace of Isaac Thomas Hecker, the founder of the Roman Catholic order the Paulists.

HORATIO STREET

Horatio Street and the Block Bounded by Greenwich, Jane, and Washington Streets
William Bayard's Home—The dying Alexander Hamilton was brought to a house at this site on July 11, 1804. He had been shot during his duel with Vice President Aaron Burr in Weehawken, New Jersey. Dr. David Hosack, the physician who attended the duel, did what he could for the mortally wounded patriot. Semi-conscious, Hamilton was placed in a boat and rowed across the Hudson River. On the Manhattan shore, he was met by his friend William Bayard, who had him

taken to his home. Hamilton died the next day, surrounded by his family. On July 14, 1804, he was buried in Trinity Churchyard. Burr fled to Philadelphia but was never prosecuted for the death of his political enemy. The marker on the house at 82 Jane Street identifying it as the Bayard home is incorrect. The actual house was torn down.

HUDSON STREET

487* Hudson Street
In the 1840s this was the childhood home of the writer Bret Harte.

490 Hudson Street
The Marquis de Lafayette visited an earlier school at this location on his triumphal visit to the United States on September 10, 1824. He had asked to see "the best example of the public school system."

567 Hudson Street
White Horse Tavern—Poet Dylan Thomas spent the afternoon of November 4, 1953, here, drinking at his favorite bar. Popular with the neighborhood crowd and longshoremen, it reminded the poet of an English pub. He staggered home to the Chelsea Hotel and announced, "I've had eighteen straight whiskeys. I think that's the record." He promptly collapsed and was taken to St. Vincent's Hospital, where he died five days later.

JAMES STREET

32 James Street
St. James Church—The heart of the Irish immigrant community in the nineteenth century, this church was where the Ancient Order of the Hibernians, a fraternal organization, was founded in May of 1836. The order was created to protect members of the Roman Catholic clergy and Church at a time of extreme anti-Catholic bigotry in the United States. The Nativism movement, formed in reaction to increased immigration, favored the interests of native Americans over those of recent immigrants. Proponents supported laws that would have required twenty-one years to become a citizen and denied public offices to Roman Catholics.

JEFFERSON STREET

Jefferson Street and Henry Street

The area surrounding this intersection was once the site of the Native American village of Recktauck in the early seventeenth century. After midnight on February 25, 1643, Dutch soldiers under the command of Maryn Adrianesen massacred forty tribesmen in their sleep. Another eighty natives were also killed in the village of Pavonia, on the site of Jersey City, the same night. Governor Kieft ordered these raids in retaliation for earlier Native American attacks on Dutch settlements. Called the Governor Kieft's War, these attacks were the most violent in the long-running tension caused by the European invasion of North America. The Dutch settlers and the Native Americans kept fighting for two more years until August 30, 1645, when peace was agreed upon at a meeting in Fort Amsterdam. The fighting began again in September of 1655.

Jefferson Street and South Street

Pier 46—Unlike today, on July 29, 1897, the East River was busy with boat traffic and lined with piers. It was here that the bedeviled battleship USS *Maine* rammed Pier 46 to avoid an excursion boat named the *Isabel*. Captain Sigsbee was fully exonerated by a naval board of inquiry that termed the crash unavoidable. A year and a half later, on February 15, 1898, the *Maine* mysteriously exploded in Havana Harbor, with a loss of 260 sailors. The incident helped spark the Spanish-American War.

LA GUARDIA PLACE

542* La Guardia Place

Artist Keith Haring had a home in this building. Initially a subway graffiti artist, Haring was welcomed into the New York art-gallery scene of the 1980s. His lively cartoons, instantly recognizable, were a tremendous commercial success. He died here on February 16, 1990, of complications from AIDS.

LAFAYETTE STREET

142 Lafayette Street

On February 2, 1860, a tragic tenement-house fire at this address prompted the widespread installation of fire escapes. The blaze started in a ground-floor bakery and spread throughout the six-story building. Twenty people either died in the flames or perished by trying to leap to safety. Less than four months later, the city passed a much-needed law requiring all residences housing more than eight families to have either interior fireproof stairwells or outside fireproof balconies and stairs.

425* Lafayette Street

Astor Library—Opened on January 9, 1854, with $400,000 bequeathed by John Jacob Astor, this handsome Romanesque structure became the city's first free library. Washington Irving, the first librarian, cared for its one thousand volumes, the country's largest collection at the time. The famous library attracted other eminent writers, such as William Thackeray, Henry Wadsworth Longfellow, and Ralph Waldo Emerson. The expanded building later became home to the Hebrew Immigrant Aid Society (H.I.A.S.), responsible for sheltering and relocating thousands of Jewish refugees. The city's recently enacted Landmark Preservation Law and theater producer Joseph Papp saved the library from demolition in 1965, and the building's interiors were renovated and became the Public Theater. The company's premier production, *Hair*, the archetypal sixties musical, opened on October 17, 1967. This theater also served as the site for Joseph Papp's funeral on November 11, 1991.

The Astor Library, now the Public Theater at 425 Lafayette Street, was the principal charity of the Astor family. Both John Jacob Astor and his eldest son, William B. Astor, gave financial support to this library, which helped educate the city's poor and immigrant populations. *(Harper's Weekly, October 2, 1875)*

428–34 Lafayette Street

Colonnade Row*—These four surviving townhouses were originally part of a group of nine houses that extended farther south along the street. Once named La Grange Terrace, after Marquis de Lafayette's country home in France, the 1833 design is attributed to Seth Geer and not, as was often thought, to Alexander Jackson Davis. These gracious homes were the first row-house development in the city unified behind one façade, a common first-floor façade topped with two-story-high slender Corinthian columns. Considered too far north of downtown for some, the complex nevertheless proved popular with the city's affluent. Warren Delano, grandfather of Franklin Delano Roosevelt, New York Governor

All nine original Greek Revival houses are pictured in this print of the unified Colonnade Row. The five houses on the left-hand side, once part of the Colonnade Hotel, were torn down in 1901 and replaced by the current warehouse. *(Library of Congress)*

Edwin Morgan, and John Jacob Astor all lived here. A small wedding reception for President John Tyler and Julia Gardiner took place at number 430, the home of the bride, on June 26, 1844.

LEROY STREET

110 Leroy Street

New York City's "Roaring Twenties" mayor, James Walker, was born at this address on June 19, 1881. Jimmy's father, William, was an Irish immigrant who, like his son, was a Tammany Hall politician.

LISPENARD STREET

36 Lispenard Street at the Corner of Church Street

The home of David Ruggles once stood here. He was a free African American sailor who was an author and publisher of antislavery magazines and pamphlets.

His 1838 *Mirror of Liberty* was the first African American magazine in the United States. He opened a bookstore down the block at number 67, but a racist mob destroyed it after a year. An early promoter of the Underground Railroad for runaway slaves, he helped more than six hundred fugitives escape to freedom. One of those slaves was Frederick Douglass, who hid in this home in 1838.

LITTLE WEST 12TH STREET

Little West 12th Street at the Hudson River

The *Seneca Chief,* the first boat to travel through the Erie Canal, anchored here near Fort Gansevoort. The canal boat arrived on November 4, 1825, at 6:00 a.m. after the nine-day trip from Buffalo. The five-hundred-mile journey culminated in a ceremony in the harbor, where Governor De Witt Clinton performed the "marriage of the waters" by pouring a keg of Lake Erie water into the Atlantic Ocean. Once here at the dock, the *Seneca Chief*'s cargo—flour, whitefish, butter, potash, maple, and red cedar from western New York, Pennsylvania, Ohio, and Michigan—was unloaded. This was only the beginning of a cornucopia of goods that could now be cheaply transported to and from the city. The canal was a tremendous economic boon to New York City, which now became the nation's dominant seaport for goods to the West.

LUDLOW STREET

Ludlow Street between Grand Street and Broome Street, East Side

Ludlow Street Jail—On election day, November 5, 1872, candidate Victoria C. Woodhull, the first woman to run for the presidency, was housed in cell number eleven. She had been arrested for publishing in her *Woodhull & Claflin's Weekly* the first account of the affair between the Reverend Henry Ward Beecher and one of his parishioners. Although she lost the election to President Ulysses S. Grant, she was acquitted of the obscenity charges and released. On and off for the next five years, this jail would be home to William Marcy Tweed. Boss Tweed, the leader of Tammany Hall—the most powerful and corrupt political machine in nineteenth-century America—spent his time here in a two-room "suite" complete with servant and piano. During his twenty-year career, he and his cronies may have embezzled as much as $75 million in various schemes to loot the city trea-

"Who Stole the People's Money" is one of many Thomas Nast cartoons attacking Tammany Hall graft. In an age before widespread literacy, his cartoons were instrumental in educating the public about government corruption. Boss William Tweed with a diamond stickpin is on the left. *(Harper's Weekly, August 19, 1871)*

sury. The beginning of the collapse of the "Tweed Ring" was on July 8, 1871, when *The New York Times* started publishing its exposé. The *Times* articles and Thomas Nast's scathing cartoons in *Harper's Weekly* ultimately lead to Tweed's 1873 conviction on misappropriation of public funds. Several trials, an escape to Spain, and failing health took their toll on the overweight, once-powerful boss. He died on April 12, 1878, here in the jail, which he as a member of the Board of Supervisors had authorized to be built in 1859.

MACDOUGAL ALLEY

19* MacDougal Alley

In 1907 Gertrude Vanderbilt Whitney, heiress cum sculptor, converted this vacant stable into her art studio. Whitney was a late convert to this artist's enclave; Frederick Triebel had moved into number 6 in 1902 and was soon followed by three additional sculptors, Henry Kirke Bush-Brown, Daniel Chester French, and James D. Fraser. By 1917, people in the art world were calling the block "Art Alley de Luxe."

MACDOUGAL STREET

93* MacDougal Street

San Remo Bar—This corner bar was the epicenter of the Beat Generation in the late forties and early fifties. The regulars were Larry Rivers, Merce Cunningham, Paul Goodman, and James Agee. Allan Ginsberg referred to the patrons as the "subterraneans," the term Jack Kerouac used as the title of his novel about the scene. After the uptown gawkers discovered the place, the beats moved on to other quarters.

113* MacDougal Street

This building was the birthplace of *Reader's Digest* in February of 1922. DeWitt Wallace founded and worked on early issues of the popular magazine while in this basement under a speakeasy.

133 MacDougal Street

Provincetown Playhouse—Eugene O'Neill's play *Emperor Jones* was first produced in this theater in 1920. The production was considered radical for the time because an African American actor was in the cast. Twenty-one-year-old Bette Davis made her New York acting debut at this theater in 1929. The first home of the playhouse in 1916–17 was down the block at 139 MacDougal.

137 MacDougal Street

Liberal Club—In 1913 a splinter group from an earlier club moved to this address, once the home of Nathaniel Currier of Currier and Ives lithography fame. The group became an influential meeting ground for Village left-wingers and intellectuals. Members like Lincoln Steffens, Margaret Sanger, Sherwood Anderson, Max Eastman, and Emma Goldman passionately discussed all possible topics, including eugenics, women's rights, free love, free verse, and Sigmund Freud. A year later the club gave birth to the Washington Square Players, a group of theater amateurs, including Lawrence Langer and Helen Westley. The Players, who later changed their name to the Theater Guild, helped encourage more intellectual and artistic theatrical productions in the city. Polly's Restaurant on the ground floor was the like-minded eatery where the participants would go to continue their discussions. The club lasted until 1919 after Polly's moved around the block.

MADISON STREET

Madison Street between Clinton Street and Montgomery Street, East Side

Rutgers Female Institute—This school for women opened in 1839. It was later affiliated with Rutgers University in New Jersey.

MONROE STREET

10 Monroe Street

Knickerbocker Village*—While in his top-floor apartment, Julius Rosenberg was arrested by the FBI on July 17, 1950. Rosenberg and his wife, Ethel, were later convicted for their alleged part in passing atomic secrets to the Soviet Union. In spite of massive protests, they were each put to death in the electric chair in Sing Sing prison on June 19, 1953. The couple were the only American civilians ever to be executed for espionage.

MONTGOMERY STREET

58 Montgomery Street

This site was the birthplace of editor and novelist Manuel Komroff on September 7, 1890.

MULBERRY STREET

39½ Mulberry Street

A gap between these two lots was once the infamous alley "Bandits' Roost" immortalized in a Jacob Riis photograph of 1888. This hazy image forever captures the steely gaze of the criminals that stare back at the camera. Riis used this and other documentary photographs, along with his writings, as instruments of social change to improve the conditions of the poor. In an effort lead by Riis, all the buildings on this side of the street were demolished in 1897 to create Mulberry Bend Park, now called Columbus Park.

Jacob Riis wrote of this photograph, "Bandits' Roost, Bottle Alley, were names synonymous with robbery and red-handed outrage. By night, in its worst days, I have gone poking about the shuddering haunts with a policeman on the beat and came away in a ferment of anger and disgust." *(Museum City of New York)*

247* Mulberry Street

Ravenite Social Club—This clubhouse was a popular stronghold with the Gambino crime family. The FBI secretly bugged the back room of the club and an apartment two floors above in the late 1980s. The taped conversations became the basis of the government's evidence used to finally convict the country's leading Mafia head John Gotti during his fourth racketeering trial. It was here in the club-house that John Gotti and his under-boss Salvatore "The Bull" Gravano, who later turned key government witness, were arrested on December 11, 1990. The U.S. Marshals Service seized the property and sold it in 1998.

260–64 Mulberry Street

Old Saint Patrick's Cathedral*—Begun one year after Pope Pius VII established the Roman Catholic Diocese of New York in 1809, the original building was one of the earliest Gothic Revival churches in America. The barricade-like surrounding walls were built as protection against anti-Catholic Nativist attacks in the 1830s and 1840s. It served as the Roman Catholic cathedral for the archdiocese until a fire damaged the structure and was replaced by the larger uptown St. Patrick's. Rebuilt and remodeled, the building was demoted to a neighborhood parish church. It was here on April 27, 1875, that John McCloskey was invested as the first American cardinal. A year later, on April 16, 1876, Emperor Dom Pedro II of Brazil attended Mass here, while on a visit to the United States to attend the Centennial Exposition.

300 Mulberry Street

Police Headquarters—While Theodore Roosevelt was president of the Board of Police Commissioners from 1895 to 1897, he had an office in this building, the department's first headquarters. Roosevelt introduced several innovations to the force: training for new recruits, the bicycle squad, and his policy that every officer be polite to the public.

OLIVER STREET

25* Oliver Street

Now a national historic landmark, this Greek Revival house was the home of Alfred E. Smith from 1909 until 1924. While living here he rose from member of the New York State Assembly to governor of the state.

President of the New York City Board of Police Commissioners Theodore Roosevelt in his office at 300 Mulberry Street. One of the changes Roosevelt initiated during his two-year tenure was to redesign the police uniform to resemble that of the London bobby. *(Theodore Roosevelt Collection, Harvard College Library)*

ORCHARD STREET

97 Orchard Street

Orchard Street Tenement Museum *—This museum is now a living memorial to the seven thousand immigrants who lived here from 1863 to 1939. Reconditioned to look very much as it did, the tenement helps illustrate how several generations of newcomers lived, contributed to, and assimilated into the American experience. One resident of this building, the actor Sam Jaffe, was born here on March 10, 1891.

PARK ROW

Park Row between Duane Street and Pearl Street, North Side
Chatham Street Chapel—An abolitionist meeting in this former theater on October 2, 1833, touched off a riot. Twenty-eight-year-old radical William Lloyd Garrison was one of the organizers.

Park Row and Pearl Street
On Sunday, July 16, 1854, Elizabeth Jennings, an African American public-school teacher, stepped aboard a Third Avenue horse-drawn streetcar reserved for whites. She was on her way to the First Colored American Congregational Church where she was the organist. After the conductor demanded she get off and she refused, he ejected her with force. Jennings, with the support of the African American community and Frederick Douglass, who printed an account of the episode in the African American newspaper called the *North Star,* sued the privately owned company and won. Her twenty-four-year-old attorney was Chester A. Arthur, a recent law-school graduate and future president of the United States. Jennings was awarded a settlement of $250, and as a result of her case, all New York City streetcars were desegregated.

Park Row near Worth Street
Tea Water Pump—The freshwater spring that once flowed near this present-day intersection was prominent in the early history and growth of the city. The water from this pump, considered the best for making tea, was carted around the city in casks and sold. This and other neighborhood pumps, plus backyard cisterns, supplied the city's population, then about ten thousand people, with water until the development of the Manhattan Company Reservoir on Chambers Street in 1799.

201–5 Park Row
Chatham Theater—Also known as the National Theater, this was the scene of New York City's first performance of *Uncle Tom's Cabin* on August 24, 1852. The play, hastily written by Charley Taylor and minus the characters Topsy and Eva, was put into production to take advantage of the uproar caused by Harriet Beecher Stowe's novel. The play was very popular and ran almost uninterruptedly until May of 1853.

PARK STREET

61 Park Street

The Old Brewery—This one-time brewery was a notorious flophouse, cache for stolen goods, and gang hangout that even the police shunned. It was a five-story dilapidated eighteenth-century building with a dirt basement sometimes used for sudden and secretive burials. The upper floors were a labyrinth of many chambers, the largest one called the "Den of Thieves," where more than seventy-five men, women, and children lived in appalling poverty. As early as the 1820s it had the reputation for being the most dangerous spot in the city. For many years, it was said, a murder was committed here nearly every night. Out of sheer frustration, the Ladies Home Missionary Society had the building razed and replaced by a mission in 1853. This mission lasted well into the twentieth century and was then leveled for the present New York Courthouse.

PATCHIN PLACE

4* Patchin Place

The poet e. e. cummings lived at this address, a cul-de-sac hidden off West 10th Street, for more than forty years until his death in 1962. He first moved to the top floor of this three-story 1848 house in 1923 with his new wife, fashion model Marion Morehouse.

PERRY STREET

4* Perry Street

Margaret Sanger was living in this townhouse in 1914 when she founded the National Birth Control League. She opened America's first birth-control clinic in Brooklyn on October 16, 1916.

Perry Street and the Block Bounded by Charles, West 4th, and Bleecker Streets

Sir Peter Warren's Mansion—This block was once the site of Sir Peter Warren's hilltop home, the country seat of his three hundred–acre estate. One of the largest landowners in Greenwich Village, he owned property extending from present-day Fifth Avenue to the old Hudson River shore, today's Washington Street, north to West 21st Street, and south to Christopher Street. Warren, who arrived in the city in 1728, was a vice admiral of the British Navy and commander of its fleet in the colony. He was also a pirate, which, in addition to his 1731 marriage to Susannah de Lancey of an old New York family, accounted for his ability to buy so much land. After his return to England in 1747, he was knighted and served in Parliament. He is buried in Westminster Abbey. His house, complete with widow's walk, lasted until 1865, when it was replaced by the current townhouses.

106* Perry Street

Dawn Powell, novelist and New York City chronicler, lived at this address from 1926 until 1934.

Reduced to a billiard hall and carpenter shop, this once-proud Federal-style home at Prince and Lafayette was the site of President James Monroe's death on the Fourth of July, 1831. A campaign to save this house failed, and it was razed. *(FPG)*

PRINCE STREET

Prince Street and Lafayette Street, Northwest Corner

In a small two-story brick house that once stood on this corner, former president James Monroe died on July 4, 1831. After his wife had died the year before, the ailing seventy-three-year-old Monroe moved here from Virginia to live with his daughter, Maria, and her husband, Samuel L. Gouverneur, postmaster of New York City. Five years earlier, on July 4, 1826, two other ex-presidents, John Adams and Thomas Jefferson, died on the same day.

113* Prince Street

This address was the home of six-year-old Etan Patz. On May 25, 1979, Etan left his home to catch a school bus and has not been seen since. The publicity surrounding his haunting disappearance helped create a national awareness of the missing-children problem.

READE STREET

Reade Street between Broadway and Center Street

Negroes Burial Ground*—Present-day Reade Street runs roughly through the middle of a graveyard that occupied this site from 1755 to 1790 on land that was then the outskirts of the city. A burial ground for slaves and free African Americans, it was also a potter's field for paupers, criminals, and American prisoners of the British who died during the Revolutionary War. Uncovered in September of 1991 during construction of the Federal Office Building, the hundreds of graves and skeletons proved a great find to archaeologists and historians hoping to learn more about the lives and conditions of African Americans during the Colonial Period. What they did not find was interesting too: almost no worldly goods—leading the archaeologists to believe these were very poor people, indeed. David Dinkins, the city's first African American mayor, observed, "Two centuries ago, not only could African Americans not hope to govern New York City, they could not even hope to be buried within its boundaries." The Landmarks Preservation Commission voted to make the site and the surrounding blocks as far south as the tip of City Hall Park a historic district two years later in 1993.

SAINT JAMES PLACE

55–57 Saint James Place
First Shearith Israel Graveyard—Members of Shearith Israel, the first Jewish congregation in North America, arrived in New York City in 1654. They were Spanish and Portuguese Jews who had fled from Recife, Brazil, during the Inquisition. Not permitted to worship freely by the Dutch, they were nonetheless given a small plot of consecrated burial ground outside the city limits in 1656. The site of this original graveyard has been lost to history. What today is known as the First Shearith Israel Graveyard dates from 1683. This triangular graveyard, which once covered the entire square, is the oldest Jewish cemetery in the United States and has the distinction of being the oldest remaining European landmark in Manhattan. The renowned Rabbi Gershom Mendez Seixas, a leader of Shearith Israel and a clergyman at George Washington's inauguration, is buried here, along with eighteen Revolutionary patriots, all members of the congregation.

SAINT LUKE'S PLACE

6* Saint Luke's Place
This address was the childhood home of Mayor James Walker and became the mayor's official residence in 1925. "Jimmy" Walker, a successful songwriter, was stylish, urbane, and perfectly suited to the extravagance and follies of the "Jazz Age." His Honor loved the Broadway nightlife and often didn't arrive at City Hall until late in the afternoon, and only a couple of days a week at that. The demands of the job finally did catch up to the mayor, though. In 1932 he was forced to resign after Judge Samuel Seabury's investigation discovered city-wide corruption in his administration. This townhouse is still adorned with a pair of ornamental lanterns marking it as a mayor's residence.

14* Saint Luke's Place
The poet Marianne Moore lived in the basement apartment of this townhouse with her mother from 1918 until 1929. For one year, 1922, she had literary neighbors on both sides: Sherwood Anderson lived at number 12, and Theodore Dreiser lived at number 16.

SAINT MARK'S PLACE

8 Saint Mark's Place
Innovative teacher and reformer Juliet Corson opened the first cooking school in the United States, the New York Cooking School, here in her home in November of 1876. Tuition was based on the ability to pay. She often held her classes at public markets to teach quality, freshness, and price. In addition to writing food columns for both *Harper's Bazaar* and the New York *Tribune,* she was the author of several cookbooks and handbooks on household management.

77* Saint Mark's Place
This building was home to the poet W. H. Auden. He lived in a four-room apartment on the second floor from 1953 until 1972. Another famous tenant, revolutionary Leon Trotsky, lived in the basement in 1917.

SPRING STREET

29–31* Spring Street
Once a private sanatorium, this twenty-room building was home and studio to sculptor Louise Nevelson. The fifty-nine-year-old Ukraine-born artist used the space to create her large-scale wooden sculptures. She lived here from 1959 until her death on April 17, 1988.

53* Spring Street
The first pizzeria in New York City, and perhaps the country, opened at this address in 1905. The restaurant was a combination Italian social club, grocery, and bakery run by Gennaro Lombardi, an immigrant from Naples.

91 Spring Street
Eighty-nine-year-old Lorenzo da Ponte died here in his home on August 17, 1838. Da Ponte, the librettist of Mozart's *Marriage of Figaro* and *Don Giovanni,* was a man of many talents: an ordained Catholic priest, a poet, a scholar, and a scoundrel who left many debts and lovers behind in Europe. He was also the guiding force in building the city's first opera house.

STANTON STREET

85 Stanton Street
U.S. Senator Jacob Javits was born in this tenement on May 18, 1904. His father worked here as a janitor.

STUYVESANT STREET

21 Stuyvesant Street
Stuyvesant-Fish Home*—Seemingly out of sync with the neighboring right-angled streets, Stuyvesant Street is the only true east-west street in Manhattan. It served as the approach to the Dutch Governor Peter Stuyvesant's country home from the old Bowery road. The house at number 21 Stuyvesant Street was built in 1804. It was a wedding present for Governor Stuyvesant's great-great-grand-daughter Elizabeth Stuyvesant and her husband, Nicholas Fish, from the bride's father. Nicholas Fish was a colonel during the American Revolutionary War. Their son, Hamilton, born here on August 3, 1808, served as governor of New York and U.S. senator. General Lafayette, a friend of the family, visited this house on September 10, 1824, during his second visit to the United States.

Stuyvesant Street and East 10th Street
The country home of the last Dutch governor, Peter Stuyvesant, stood just south of this intersection until it burned down in 1778. Here were signed the Articles of Capitulation that delivered New Amsterdam over to the British on September 6, 1664. The story of the end of Dutch rule began earlier, when King Charles II of England gave his brother, James, the Duke of York, a grant in America covering the Dutch holdings. Shortly after, Col. Richard Nicolls, the first deputy-governor of the duke's territories, quickly set sail with four warships for the city and forced the Dutch to surrender. Colonel Nicolls immediately renamed the city and the province "New York," in honor of the duke.

SULLIVAN STREET

177 Sullivan Street
This address was the birthplace of Mayor Fiorello La Guardia on December 11, 1882. The colorful future mayor spent the first three years of his life here. The build-

ing collapsed while undergoing renovation on November 11, 1987. A thirteen-month-old child was killed.

THOMAS STREET

41 Thomas Street

A brothel at this address on April 10, 1836, was the scene of the grisly ax murder of the beautiful and renowned prostitute Helen Jewett. Her lover, Richard Robinson, the last person to see her alive, was arrested. The "penny press," the new mass circulation daily newspapers competing for readership, extensively covered his murder trial. Robinson was acquitted by a jury who felt, as did the press, that he did the community a service by killing this celebrated sinner.

TOMPKINS SQUARE PARK*

On the sub-zero-degree morning of January 13, 1874, about seven thousand unemployed workers and their families filled this park to demonstrate for jobs in the midst of a financial panic. They were waiting to hear Mayor William F. Havemeyer, who never appeared. The police declared the rally illegal, and a melee broke out. The mounted officers charged the crowd and clubbed the protesters. The park has continued to be a lightning rod for opposing forces: the hippies versus the establishment in the 1960s and the homeless versus the gentrification of the neighborhood in the 1980s.

UNIVERSITY PLACE

24 University Place

Cedar Tavern—Once the epicenter of the "New York School" of painting, this bar was a popular 1950s watering hole for painters Jackson Pollock, Willem de Kooning, and Franz Kline. The bar was as famous for its marathon boozing and brawling as for its intense discussions of the nature of art. It was also popular with the literary crowd of the period: Frank O'Hara, Allen Ginsberg, Gregory Corso, and Jack Kerouac. The bar regulars discouraged the management from remodeling the rather drab decor, hoping to prevent "uptown types" from dropping in. The bar left this address in 1963 and moved up the street.

University Place and East 11th Street, Southeast Corner

*Albert Hotel**—Now an apartment house, this one-time hotel was owned by the brother of the artist Albert Pinkham Ryder and named in his honor. The romantic painter had a studio here for a short time. The hotel room of Robert Louis Stevenson also served as an artist's studio. It was here that the ailing and bed-ridden author sat for his portrait medallion created by the sculptor Augustus Saint-Gaudens. Two other famous writers have also stayed here: Leo Tolstoy and Thomas Wolfe.

WASHINGTON MEWS

14A* Washington Mews

This building, tucked between numbers 14 and 15 Washington Mews, was the first-floor home of John Dos Passos. He wrote *Manhattan Transfer* while living here in 1922.

58–60* Washington Mews

These two connected carriage houses were home to Gertrude Vanderbilt Whitney from early 1940 until her death in 1942.

WASHINGTON PLACE

10 Washington Place

The last home of Cornelius Vanderbilt once stood at this address. A modest townhouse, it hid an extensive stable and a small racetrack in the back. The "Commodore" died here on January 4, 1877. At the age of sixteen, he had bought a sailing ship and started a ferryboat service between Staten Island and Manhattan. At his death at age eighty-two he was the richest man in the United States, worth more than $100 million. His death, like that of other American millionaires of the period, was well publicized and made an example of how hard work is rewarded.

14* Washington Place

A twelfth-floor apartment, with bullet-proof windows, in this building was home to Edward Koch from 1965 until 1989. Even while he was mayor for twelve years and had the use of Gracie Mansion, he refused to give up his lease on this $479.49-a-month rent-controlled one-bedroom apartment. He did give up his lease after losing the Democratic primary to David Dinkins. He spent his last night of office in Gracie Mansion on December 31, 1989, and then moved to his new home at 2 Fifth Avenue.

23* Washington Place

On March 25, 1911, a fire at this location killed 146 workers, most of whom were

Firefighters hosing water at the upper floors during the Triangle Shirtwaist Company fire of March 25, 1911. The building is still here at the northwest corner of Washington Place and Greene Street. *(FPG)*

poor Italian and Jewish women and girls. The Triangle Shirtwaist Company was located on the top three floors of this building. Trapped because many of the exits were locked and the rear fire escape had collapsed, some of the victims chose to jump to their deaths rather than be burned alive. The company ran an all-too-common garment-worker sweatshop. The immigrant laborers worked long hours under horrendous conditions for low wages, not only here but in more than ten thousand similar shops, mainly in the Village and the Lower East Side, sewing mass-produced clothing for the thriving fashion industry. The company owners were acquitted of any wrongdoing, but the tragedy increased support for the Ladies Garment Workers Union. In addition, the New York State Legislature passed thirty-six laws improving safety in the work place.

27 Washington Place

This address was the birthplace of author Henry James on April 15, 1843. James, a great chronicler of the Washington Square social scene, lived at this address only six months before his family visited Europe. But the author and his future psychologist brother did spend time visiting their grandmother, Elizabeth Walsh, at her home at 18 Washington Square North, the setting for Henry's *Washington Square.*

82* Washington Place

This building was home to Willa Cather from 1908 until 1913. Another author, Richard Wright, also lived here, in a third-floor apartment, for several months in 1945.

WASHINGTON SQUARE EAST

80 Washington Square East

Tuckerman Building*—Still standing, this building was once home to the artist Albert Pinkham Ryder, who lived here for more than ten years, beginning in 1880.

Washington Square East between Washington Place and Waverly Place

New York University Old Main—Construction of this building, considered a replica of King's College Chapel in Cambridge, England, prompted New York's first labor demonstration, which escalated into the four-day "Stone-cutter's Riot" in August of 1834. The building contractor had hoped to save costs by using convicts from Sing Sing prison. The stone-cutter's guild protested, and eventually the National Guard had to be called in to keep the peace. Old Main also supplied housing for New York University faculty and others. It was here that professor of fine arts Samuel F. B. Morse invented the telegraph. Samuel Colt developed the "six-shooter" revolver, and John William Draper experimented with the daguerreotype photography process. Chemistry professor Draper snapped one of the earliest photos of a human face while on this roof. The March of 1840 sunlit portrait is of his sister Dorothy Catherine Draper in a flowered bonnet. Other famous lodgers were poet Walt Whitman, architects Alexander Jackson Davis and William Morris Hunt, and painters Eastman Johnson and Winslow Homer. Old Main was replaced in 1894.

WASHINGTON SQUARE NORTH

2* Washington Square North

One of his generation's finest architects, Richard Morris Hunt lived here between 1887 and 1895. Hunt was the first American architect trained at the Ecole des Beaux-Arts in Paris and the founding president of the American Institute of Architects.

3* Washington Square North

For more than fifty years this was the home and studio of artist Edward Hopper. He died here while working in his fourth-floor studio on May 15, 1967. Other artists who lived here were Thomas W. Dewing, William Glackens, Ernest Lawson, and Rockwell Kent. The building now houses New York University's School of Social Work.

12* Washington Square North

Edward Cooper lived at this address from 1879 until his death in 1905. The son of Peter Cooper, Edward was an industrialist and a political reformer. He served as mayor from 1878 until 1880. His brother-in-law and business partner Abram S. Hewitt was also a mayor.

WASHINGTON SQUARE PARK

Originally a marsh fed by the Minetta Brook, which still flows underneath, the area was a favored colonial hunting ground. Purchased by the city in 1793, it was drained and filled for a much-needed potter's field. More than 22,000 victims of the yellow fever epidemics that afflicted lower Manhattan in the early years of the nineteenth century were buried here. The cemetery also served as a public hanging ground. The Revolutionary War hero General Marquis de Lafayette was reported to have been a guest at the execution of twenty highwaymen during his American tour in 1824. On the Fourth of July of 1828, the anniversary of the signing of the Declaration of Independence, the "Washington Military Parade Ground" was officially opened as a public park. Governor De Witt Clinton hosted the celebration with a public barbecue. The pastoral setting attracted the wealthy, who built homes on streets that lined the park. The city grew around Greenwich Village and the park, leaving the Village's street pattern intact—which helped keep passing traffic out and ensured the quiet village atmosphere. This eight-acre rectangle of green is the heart of Greenwich Village and the unofficial campus for New York University.

Frozen in time, Dorothy Catherine Draper sat still for fifteen minutes in front of her brother's early camera for an 1840 portrait. Professor Draper also used the roof of New York University's Old Main on Washington Square East to capture the first photographic image of the moon. (FPG)

WASHINGTON SQUARE SOUTH

42 Washington Square South

Once a rooming house, this site was home to muckraking journalist Lincoln Steffens in 1912. His friend and fellow writer John Reed lived in the room one floor below. Reed made the house famous in his farcical poem "A Day in Bohemia: Or, Life Among the Artists." This address was also home to Eugene O'Neill in 1916 and to the sculptor Jacques Lipchitz, who lived here in the early 1940s after fleeing France during World War II.

55 Washington Square South

Judson Memorial Baptist Church*—Built in honor of the first American foreign missionary to Burma, Adoniram Judson, this church was devoted to improving the lives of the large immigrant population south of Washington Square at the end of the nineteenth century. Always progressive, the church took an even sharper philosophical left turn in 1956, when Howard Moody was appointed minister. A self-proclaimed "Christian atheist," he led the congregation in reform politics and civil rights. In 1961 the church won the hearts of the neighborhood by helping to overturn the police ban on folksinging in the park. It was a center of early 1960s avant-garde art, particularly in theater and dance. The church has continued its activist role to the present day, fighting to protect the environment and protesting against indifference to the AIDS epidemic.

58 Washington Square South

A small wooden house that once stood on this corner was the home of Daniel Megie. Mr. Megie was the hangman for the state prison on Washington Street. He didn't have far to walk to work. The public hangings were performed on the large elm tree, one of the city's oldest, in the northwest corner of Washington Square Park.

In 1913 Guido Bruno moved into the second floor of this house. An original and true Greenwich Village bohemian, he was a native of Czechoslovakia and a patron of the arts. He promoted and published Hart Crane and Djuna Barnes.

61 Washington Square South

Until its demolition in 1948, the "House of Genius" stood at this location. A four-story boardinghouse, it was run by Swiss-born Mrs. Branchard, who favored writers as tenants. As the nickname implies, there were several gifted boarders:

Before it was a place to buy candy and cigars, this tiny corner shop at Washington Square South and Thompson Street was once the home to state prison hangman Daniel Megie. *(FPG)*

Stephen Crane, Frank Norris, and poet Alan Seeger. Artistic license and time have added numerous artists to the roster, but most of these were just visitors.

WASHINGTON SQUARE WEST

29* Washington Square West

Eleanor Roosevelt moved to an apartment in this building in 1945. She and President Roosevelt had planned to retire to New York City after the completion of his third presidential term in 1944, but he won a fourth term and died in office the following year. She lived here until 1953.

WASHINGTON STREET

Washington Street between Christopher and Perry Streets

State Prison—New York State's first prison opened on this once bucolic site along the shore on November 28, 1797. The prison, one of the first reform penitentiaries in the country, was viewed as a model of rehabilitation, with separate quarters for women, bathing areas, and workshops for teaching the inmates a trade. As the neighborhood grew more residential and security became more of a problem, it was relocated "up the river" to the town of Ossining as Sing Sing Prison in 1829.

Washington Street and Little West 12th Street

Fort Gansevoort—A small fort, nicknamed the White Fort, was erected near this corner in 1811. The fort was designed to help protect the city against the British in the War of 1812. It was leveled in 1849 as part of a landfill project to extend the present shoreline one block west.

835* Washington Street

The Mineshaft—An earlier gay dance club, called the Fawn, was here in the mid-1960s, but later this location was home to the notorious gay bar and sex club The Mineshaft. The club opened in September of 1976 and flourished along with the sexual revolution. But by the mid-1980s this club, along with others, became the center of a heated debate over the spread of AIDS. The city shut down The Mineshaft in 1985.

WATER STREET

616 Water Street

This address was listed in the 1825 city directory as a "Fresh Provision Store." It was also home to Ezra Daggett and his son-in-law Thomas Kensett, who introduced canning to America. On January 19, 1825, they were the first to obtain a patent to "preserve animal substances in tin." Salmon, lobster meat, and oysters were the first to be packed in tin cans.

WAVERLY PLACE

112* Waverly Place

In 1911 this was the home and studio of the painter Everett Shinn. Shinn, a realist painter and member of "The Eight," was also an amateur playwright. His Waverly Place Players performed their humorous satires on a backyard stage.

116 Waverly Place

In 1845 a house at this address was the setting for America's earliest literary salon. Hosted by Anne Charlotte Lynch, these weekly gatherings were attended by the leading writers of the time: William Cullen Bryant, Herman Melville, Horace Greeley, Margaret Fuller, and Bayard Taylor. It was here that Edgar Allan Poe gave the first public reading of his greatest poem, "The Raven." Later the wife of Professor Vincenzo Botta, Lynch moved her home several times farther uptown, each time faithfully followed by her literati friends and guests.

137* Waverly Place

This house was once the home of the artist John Trumbull. Later, in 1837, it was home to Edgar Allan Poe and his new bride and cousin, Virginia Clemm, who was only fourteen years old.

WEST STREET

507 West Street

In December of 1866 author Herman Melville began work here as a custom agent for the Port of New York. For nineteen dull years, despite administration changes, blatant corruption, and cronyism, Melville toiled honestly and faithfully as Inspector 75. He was often assigned duties on the nearby wharves at the foot of Gansevoort Street, named after his maternal grandfather, Revolutionary War Gen. Peter Gansevoort.

WESTSIDE HIGHWAY

Westside Highway between Little West 12th Street and Gansevoort Street

On December 15, 1973, a dump truck and passenger car fell through the north-bound lane of the elevated highway. The truck was carrying ten tons of asphalt to repair this part of the decrepit artery. Both drivers suffered minor injuries, but the consequences were to last for more than twenty years. The accident was a prelude for the ill-fated $1.1 billion boondoggle called Westway, a totally new roadway from the Battery to West 42nd Street, half to be tunneled through new landfill. Every politician up to President Ronald Reagan took a stand, sometimes several

On October 27, 1930, Borough President Julius Miller of Manhattan tightens the final bolt on the tablet marking the completion of the Westside Highway. Forty years later, Westway, the replacement for the aged elevated highway, became a testament to how community opposition and litigation can eventually stop unpopular public projects. *(FPG)*

over the years, on Westway, but the mega-scheme died a slow death from local opposition and environmental concerns. The replacement surface-road compromise is under construction.

WORTH STREET

Worth Street at Baxter Street and Park Street

This intersection, now gone, was once the infamous "Five Points," so named because of the meeting of these three streets. This was the heart of the nation's most notorious slum for much of the nineteenth century. The run-down buildings were homes to newly arrived and destitute immigrants, the poorest of the poor, and the city's toughest gangs. The slum became a daytime tourist stop for Victorians anxious to learn about the plight of the urban poor. Charles Dickens, on one such tour, described the scene: "...all that is loathsome, drooping and decayed is here." Today much of the neighborhood is gone. It was leveled to build the U.S. Courthouse on Foley Square.

SECOND AVENUE

Second Avenue and East 6th Street, Northwest Corner

Fillmore East*—On June 27, 1971, this one-time movie palace was the site of the "last" rock-and-roll concert. The Allman Brothers, Edgar Winter, the Beach Boys, and Country Joe McDonald performed this swan-song show. Music promoter Bill Graham had only created this concert hall shrine to rock three years earlier. In the early 1980s the interior was remodeled into the Saint, a disco and center of gay nightlife. Famous for its "Black and White" parties, the club had a dance floor that was covered with a huge dome. Much of the structure was torn down in 1997 and replaced by an apartment house. The old lobby was converted into a bank.

149 Second Avenue

Le Metro Cafe—This coffeeshop was a popular hangout with the beat poets of the 1950s. Poets Allen Ginsberg and Jack Kerouac gave readings here. The cover charge was twenty-five cents, for a cup of coffee.

What are now Worth and Baxter Streets converge in this lively rendering of the dangerous "Five Points" slum in 1827. Much of this neighborhood was condemned and removed by the end of the nineteenth century. *(Author's collection)*

Second Avenue between East 2nd Street and East 3rd Street

New York Marble Cemetery*—This spot marks the entrance to the cemetery centered in the block bounded by Second Avenue and the Bowery and East 2nd and East 3rd Streets. Opened on July 13, 1830, this cemetery was Manhattan's first nonsectarian burial ground open to the public. Among those buried here are James Lenox and the Kips family of Kips Bay.

Second Avenue and East 10th Street, Northwest Corner

St. Mark's-in-the-Bowery Church*—This location has been used continually for houses of worship for more than three hundred years—longer than any other religious site in the city. The present church, which dates from 1799, was erected on the site of a 1660 Dutch chapel built here by Peter Stuyvesant on his estate. Grave robbers took the remains of A. T. Stewart, the "Merchant Prince," from the family vault in the churchyard. The body, stolen on November 7, 1878, was returned two years later after his widow paid a $20,000 ransom. The remains were reburied in Westchester. Two famous New Yorkers still buried here are Peter Stuyvesant and Philip Hone.

Women medical students listening to a lecture at the New York Medical College for Women, at Second Avenue and East 12th Street. Dr. Elizabeth Blackwell, the first woman graduate from an American medical school, founded the school. *(Frank Leslie's, April 16, 1870)*

Second Avenue and East 12th Street, Southeast Corner

New York Medical College for Women—Dr. Elizabeth Blackwell and her sister Emily, also a doctor, opened this medical college for women in 1868. Dr. Blackwell, who had been rejected by twenty-nine medical colleges before being accepted, wanted to help other women enter the medical field. She had also earlier established the nation's first nursing school, to train nurses for the Union Army during the Civil War.

THIRD AVENUE

Third Avenue between East 6th Street and East 7th Street, East Side

Seventh Regimental Armory—On April 19, 1861, just five days after the bombardment of Fort Sumter, the men of the Seventh Regiment, NYSM, were given a rousing farewell as they marched down Broadway on their way to defend Washington, D.C., for the Union cause. The regiment, established for the War of 1812 and famous for its service during the nearby Astor Place riots in 1849, was the first regiment selected from New York for Civil War duty. Their arrival six days later in Washington, D.C., earned them the sobriquet "the regiment that saved the capital." The armory, with a market on street level and drilling rooms on the floor above, was home to the Seventh before it moved uptown to its present location on Park Avenue at 69th Street in 1881.

97 Third Avenue

Maxwell Bodenheim and his wife were discovered murdered at this address on February 7, 1954. Bodenheim, a once-successful poet and novelist of the 1920s, was living in this unheated furnished room that rented for $5 a week.

Third Avenue and East 13th Street, Northeast Corner

From 1647 until 1867 a pear tree, which had been planted by Governor Peter Stuyvesant, grew at this corner, which was once his orchard. Originally imported from Holland, the tree flourished, bearing fruit for more than two hundred years before becoming a victim of a traffic accident between two wagons.

FOURTH AVENUE

61* Fourth Avenue between East 9th Street and East 10th Street

The Reuben Gallery—A venue for new and experimental work, this art gallery is regarded as the birthplace of "Happenings." Happenings of the 1960s were part art show and part performance art with audience participation. The first was Allan Kaprow's "18 Happenings in 6 Parts" held on October 4 and 6–10, 1959, when the gallery was arranged into three rooms with transparent partitions and multicolored lights. Tape recorders and slide projectors were also used, along with the one hundred some guests, who were part of the action.

103 Fourth Avenue

In September of 1848 Herman Melville and his new bride, Elizabeth Knapp Shaw, moved into a house at this site. They shared the house with Melville's also recently married brother and his wife, along with the author's mother and four of his unmarried sisters. It was here that Melville wrote *Mardi, Redburn,* and *White-Jacket.*

145 Fourth Avenue

Once called "Bookseller's Row," this portion of Fourth Avenue was part of the city's used-book store district in the early decades of the twentieth century. The shop at number 145, owned by Jacob Abrahams, also traded in secrets. It was used by German spies during World War I to pass messages.

FIFTH AVENUE

Fifth Avenue and Washington Square North

Washington Arch*—A wooden arch covered with plaster spanning Fifth Avenue was built at this site in 1889 to commemorate the centennial of George Washington's inauguration as president. Popular with Village residents, Stanford White was asked to design a permanent marble monument. Set back into the park, it was completed in 1895. The arch has long been a symbol of Greenwich Village and the subject of countless paintings. As such, it was fitting that the roof of the arch was the place to declare Greenwich Village a free and independent state. This act of rebellion was performed in January of 1917 by Gertrude Drick and several other artistic types, including John Sloan and Marcel Duchamp.

A formal inspection team surveys the process during the construction of the Washington Arch in 1892. Finished later that year, the arch was not formally dedicated until May 4, 1895. *(Collection of the New-York Historical Society)*

1 Fifth Avenue

This address was once the site of the Misses Green's School. These two Massachusetts sisters ran a fashionable school for young ladies of the upper classes around the time of the Civil War. Here Jennie Jerome, mother of British Prime Minister Winston Churchill, was once a student, and Elihu Root and John Bigelow were once teachers. The current apartment house was home to poet Sara Teasdale, who committed suicide by taking an overdose of sedatives here on January 29, 1933.

3 Fifth Avenue

"A Club"—A fund-raising banquet for the Russian Revolutionary movement sponsored by Mark Twain, William Dean Howells, and Jane Addams was held at this literary club on the night of April 11, 1906. The guest of honor was writer Maxim Gorky, who was touring America to speak out against the Czarist government. In an effort to discredit Gorky, the Russian embassy leaked to the press that his female companion was not his wife. Within days, the scandalized management at the Hotel Belleclaire on Broadway and 77th Street, where he was staying, asked the writer to leave. Refused at several other hotels, Gorky and his companion were forced to take refuge here at the club.

Fifth Avenue and West 8th Street, Southwest Corner

John Taylor Johnston built the first marble house in the city at this corner in 1856. He converted the stables behind the house into an art gallery, which he opened to the public every Thursday. Johnston later became a founder and first president of the Metropolitan Museum of Art.

Fifth Avenue and East 8th Street, Northeast Corner

Hotel Brevoort—The first female of royal lineage to visit the United States, Emma, dowager queen of the Sandwich Islands, was a guest here, on August 8, 1866. The hotel, the first to be built on Fifth Avenue, was a Village landmark well into the 1920s. Its basement café was popular with avant-garde personalities in the arts, including Charles Demuth, Isadora Duncan, Eugene O'Neill, and John Reed. The Brevoort was also a landmark in the history of fashion. Henri Gretchen, the hotel's barber, is credited with inventing the daring and liberating "bob" haircut for dancer Irene Castle and her flapper followers. Another celebrity of the 1920s, Charles A. Lindbergh, was honored here for his solo nonstop flight to Paris. A breakfast was held on June 17, 1927, to present the "Lone Eagle" with a $25,000 prize, offered by Raymond Orteig, the owner of the hotel. The Brevoort was razed in 1954.

14 Fifth Avenue

Isaac Merritt Singer once lived in a house that stood at this address. He was a partner in the invention of the modern sewing machine, in the 1860s.

Fifth Avenue and East 9th Street, Northeast Corner

In 1851 the architect James Renwick Jr., a cousin of Henry Brevoort, his neighbor across the street, designed a three-story Italianate house for his own home. He created a special study for his friend the author Washington Irving, who wrote here while visiting the city. Another author, Mark Twain, lived in this house from 1904 through 1908. He wrote "The Mysterious Stranger" while at this address.

Named after an early Greenwich Village family, the Hotel Brevoort at Fifth Avenue and East 8th Street was bought by French-born Raymond Orteig, who also owned the Parisian-flavored Lafayette on University Place. Both hotels were popular with Village bohemians. *(FPG)*

This James Renwick Jr.-designed townhouse at the corner of Fifth Avenue and East 9th Street was the last New York City home of Mark Twain. The house was replaced by the Brevoort apartment building in the 1950s. *(FPG)*

Fifth Avenue and West 9th Street, Northwest Corner

This corner was once the home of Henry Brevoort. Completed in 1834, this was the first great mansion built on Fifth Avenue. The Greek Revival home, attributed to the architect Alexander Jackson Davis, was the enchanted scene of one of the city's first costume balls on February 24, 1840. One of the guests, Matilda Barclay, the daughter of the British consul to New York, used her disguise as a Persian princess in order to meet her American boyfriend, Captain Burgwyne, of whom her parents did not approve. At 4:00 in the morning, the lovers slipped out of the party, found a preacher, and were married before dawn, all while in costume. Society was aghast and blamed the affair on the masquerade party. No New York hostess dared give another costume ball for fourteen years.

23 Fifth Avenue

No longer here, the townhouse at this address was the home of the extraordinary Daniel Sickles. A U.S. representative, he shot and killed Philip Barton Key, the son of Francis Scott Key, because of Key's attention to Mrs. Sickles. At his trial, he was the first person acquitted on a plea of temporary insanity in the United States. He subsequently became a major general during the Civil War and lost a leg at the Battle of Gettysburg. In 1912 he rented his second floor to equally colorful Mabel Dodge and her estranged second husband, the architect Edwin Dodge. Mrs. Dodge's famous weekly soirées attracted intellectuals, artists, and celebrities of the period. Her involvement with radical causes led to her meeting with John Reed, who later became her lover. Rounding out this cast of characters was William Sulzer, who lived on the top floor. He was governor of New York for about a year until he was impeached in 1913. Sickles died here at the ripe old age of ninety-one on May 3, 1914.

36–38 Fifth Avenue

Church of the Ascension*—Erected in 1840, this was the first church on Fifth Avenue. President John Tyler, a widower with seven children, married Julia Gardiner here in a secret ceremony on June 26, 1844. The country's first lady was a local beauty who was thirty years younger than the president. The president had first met his bride only four months earlier under tragic circumstances. Julia and her father, David Gardiner, were aboard the warship USS Princeton as guests of the president on a cruise on the Potomac River. One of the ship's guns exploded, and several passengers, including Mr. Gardiner, were killed. The president was very kind to Julia in her grief. They fell in love and decided to wed. She bore him seven more children, the last one when Tyler was seventy years old.

40* Fifth Avenue

New York Supreme Court Judge Joseph F. Crater, "the missingest man in New York," once lived in a fourth-floor two-bedroom apartment of this building at the corner of 11th Street. In January of 1931, almost five months after he vanished and after several police searches, three envelopes with cash, insurance policies, and the judge's will mysteriously turned up in the bedroom. These items, most likely placed after his disappearance, offered no clues to his whereabouts. Judge Crater was declared legally dead in 1937.

Before the current building, number 40 was the brownstone home of Cyrus McCormick from 1866 until 1871.

53 Fifth Avenue

From 1845 until 1869 this address was home to the eccentric bibliophile James

Widely circulated throughout the country, this is the New York City Police's missing poster for Joseph F. Crater. His disappearance is still a total mystery today. Crater lived with his wife in an apartment at 40 Fifth Avenue. *(Daily News L.P. Photo)*

DETECTIVE DIVISION
CIRCULAR No. 9
SEPTEMBER 8, 1930

POLICE DEPARTMENT
CITY OF NEW YORK

BE SURE TO FILE
THIS CIRCULAR
FOR REFERENCE

Police Authorities are Requested to Post this Circular for the Information of Police Officers and File a Copy of it for Future Reference.

MISSING SINCE AUGUST 6, 1930

HONORABLE JOSEPH FORCE CRATER,
JUSTICE OF THE SUPREME COURT, STATE OF NEW YORK

DESCRIPTION—Born in the United States—Age, 41 years; height, 6 feet; weight, 185 pounds; mixed grey hair, originally dark brown, thin at top, parted in middle "slicked" down; complexion, medium dark, considerably tanned; brown eyes; false teeth, upper and lower jaw, good physical and mental condition at time of disappearance. Tip of right index finger somewhat mutilated, due to having been recently crushed.

Wore brown sack coat and trousers, narrow green stripe, no vest; either a Panama or soft brown hat worn at rakish angle, size 6⅞, unusual size for his height and weight. Clothes made by Vroom. Affected colored shirts, size 14 collar, probably bow tie. Wore tortoise-shell glasses for reading. Yellow gold Masonic ring, somewhat worn; may be wearing a yellow gold, square-shaped wrist watch with leather strap.

COMMUNICATE with CHIEF INSPECTOR, POLICE DEPARTMENT, 18th Division, (Missing Persons Bureau), New York City. T⬛⬛⬛⬛ring 3100.

Lenox, who was one of the richest men in the city. He gave land and his book collection to establish the Lenox Library, which later became part of the New York Public Library.

65 Fifth Avenue
Edison Electric Light Company—Thomas Edison leased this four-story brownstone early in 1881 as headquarters and showplace for his new company. On April 4, 1881, one hundred lights came on and this building became the first to be lighted exclusively by electricity.

SIXTH AVENUE

Sixth Avenue and West 4th Street, Southeast Corner

The Golden Swan—Another haunt and source of inspiration to playwright Eugene O'Neill, this was the site of an Irish saloon known to regulars as "The Hell-Hole." The nickname fit, in spite of such pretensions as a 4th Street "family entrance" and a front room restricted to men. It was also subject matter for artists John Sloan and Charles Demuth. The building was demolished for the subway in 1928.

Sixth Avenue and Washington Place

On June 28, 1970, one year to the day after the Stonewall Rebellion, a group of several thousand proud marchers gathered here to begin the first New York Gay Pride March. The march up Sixth Avenue grew in numbers and strength as normally indifferent New Yorkers offered restrained support to the column of gay men and lesbians who were marching into the mainstream of American consciousness. The parade was only one of several events that week to celebrate the historic riot at the Stonewall bar, where gay patrons refused to be harassed by the police. The parade ended in typical 1960s fashion in Central Park's Sheep's Meadow with a "Gay-In."

368 Sixth Avenue

William Dunlap rented a home at this address in 1832. Dunlap, sometimes called the "Father of American Drama," supplemented his playwrighting by painting and writing books on the theater and design.

425 Sixth Avenue

Jefferson Market Library*—This exuberant example of Victorian Gothic architecture was built in 1877 as a combination police and civil courthouse, produce market, and volunteer fire station, complete with fire lookout. The courtroom on the second floor was the site of the Harry K. Thaw murder trial, which opened on January 23, 1907. Thaw, a mentally unstable millionaire, shot and killed the architect Stanford White, who had had a torrid affair years earlier with Thaw's wife, Evelyn Nesbit, before their marriage. The trial ended in a hung jury. A second jury found Thaw not guilty by reason of insanity, and he was sent to an asylum until his release in 1915. By the 1950s the courthouse was considered an architectural monstrosity and was threatened with demolition. A tenacious group of admirers,

The high Victorian Gothic-style Jefferson Market Courthouse was the height of fashion when completed in 1877. By the early 1960s it took a determined grassroots campaign to save it from being razed. The world's first session of night court was held here on September 1, 1907. *(Author's collection)*

in the days before any Landmarks Preservation Commission, convinced the city to save the building and turn it into a branch library in 1967.

522–24 Sixth Avenue

This was the first address of R. H. Macy's "fancy dry goods store" in 1858. Former Nantucket sea captain Rowland Hussey Macy opened his small shop selling ribbons, laces, and handkerchiefs. On opening day, October 27, 1858, the proceeds were a modest $11.06, but the business grew, and by the 1870s the store occupied the entire block from 13th to 14th Streets.

EAST 1ST STREET

51 East 1st Street

Justus Schwab's Saloon—Once at this address, this saloon was the favored hangout where anarchists and literati mixed and argued during the last decade of the nineteenth century. Stocked with books, it was frequented by Johann Most and Emma Goldman.

EAST 2ND STREET

52–74 East 2nd Street

New York City Marble Cemetery*—In 1831 President James Monroe was one of the first persons to be interred in this cemetery, which was then on the outskirts of town. But in 1858 his remains were exhumed and moved to his native Virginia. Another famous man once buried here and then exhumed was John Ericsson, the builder of the Ironclad *Monitor,* who died in 1889. His remains were returned to Sweden the following year. Still here are members of the Kips, Fish, and Roosevelt families.

55 East 3rd Street

*Mary House**—Dorothy Day died on November 29, 1980, here, at this Roman Catholic settlement house, one of the "Houses of Hospitality" she founded. The eighty-three-year-old Day, the co-founder of the Catholic Worker movement, was a revered radical activist devoted to helping the poor.

112–38 East 3rd Street

*First Houses**—This block of tenements was remodeled during the depths of the Great Depression as the first municipal housing project of the New York City Housing Authority. Inaugurated on December 3, 1935, by Governor Herbert Lehman, Mayor Fiorello La Guardia, and First Lady Eleanor Roosevelt, this venture was also the nation's first public low-income housing project. After advertisements touting one-bedroom apartments with private bathrooms for only $4.40 per week appeared, four thousand families applied for the 122 available apartments.

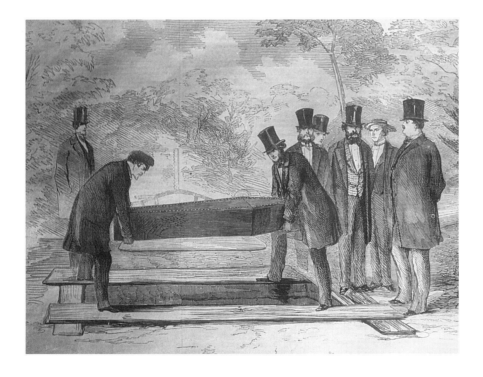

At dawn on July 2, 1858, former president James Monroe's body began its journey to Richmond, Virginia, for reburial. New York City Marble Cemetery, entered from East Second Street, is now surrounded by neighboring buildings. *(Author's collection)*

East 3rd Street at the East River

3rd Street Pier—The *General Slocum*, a triple-decked paddle-wheeler, left for an outing to Locust Grove on Long Island Sound at 9:40 a.m. on June 15, 1904, from this site. Filled with more than 1,330 happy picnickers, mainly mothers and children, the boat headed upriver in a brisk wind. Less than a half hour later, the *Slocum* caught fire. Capt. William Van Schaick increased the boat's speed, hoping to reach North Brother Island, but only succeeded in fanning the flames. The charred wreck came to rest on a sandbar opposite 145th Street in the Bronx. The final death toll was 1,021 people, making it the worst disaster in the city's history. A memorial in Tompkins Square Park honors those lost that day.

EAST 4TH STREET

64* East 4th Street

Labor Lyceum—It was here, in this now-abandoned building, that the International Ladies Garment Workers Union was founded on June 3, 1900.

The bodies of the dead from the *General Slocum* tragedy are laid out on the grass on North Brother Island. Thirty minutes after the fire was first discovered by a small boy, the wooden side-wheeler ship was almost completely consumed. *(FPG)*

66–68* East 4th Street

Turn Hall—On August 18, 1882, this German fraternal and gymnastic society was the site of the first professional performance of a Yiddish play in the United States. Boris Thomasshefsy, a choir singer in an East Side synagogue, presented Avrom Goldfaden's play *The Witch*. Nearby Second Avenue would later become known as "the Jewish Rialto" in the early years of the twentieth century, when the avenue was lined with close to twenty theaters staging Yiddish plays.

329 East 4th Street

This address was the birthplace of George Cukor, the motion-picture director, on July 14, 1899.

390 East 4th Street

This address was the birthplace of novelist Jerome Weidman. The author of *I Can Get It for You Wholesale* was born here on April 4, 1913.

11* West 4th Street

Gerde's Folk City—This popular cabaret was an essential stop for all folksingers hoping to make a name for themselves. On April 11, 1961, Bob Dylan, opening for John Lee Hooker, made his debut as a paid performer. The club also hosted the debut of Simon and Garfunkel.

147* West 4th Street

Finding this setting more conducive than his nearby Patchin Place home, John Reed in 1918 completed the articles that became *Ten Days that Shook the World*, his personal account of the Bolshevik Revolution. This diminutive house was also the home of the Whitney Studio Club, which offered art classes and exhibitions, and was for a time the second home to the popular eatery Polly's Restaurant.

EAST 5TH STREET

210* East 5th Street

Beethoven Hall—To revive declining interest in the sport of bowling, stigmatized as a betting sport, the American Bowling Congress (ABC) was formed here on September 9, 1895. This organization established the modern game by standardizing rules and equipment and in 1901 sponsored the first national championship games.

EAST 6TH STREET

325* East 6th Street

St. Mark's Lutheran Church—This Lutheran congregation was the spiritual heart of "Kleindeutschland," or Little Germany, an immigrant neighborhood. On Wednesday morning, June 15, 1904, the Reverend George Haas and his parishioners from this church left for a Sunday school outing. They boarded the doomed *General Slocum,* chartered for the church's annual excursion, and set off for Long Island Sound. By nightfall, more than one thousand people, including the reverend's wife and daughter, were dead as a result of the fire that swept the ship. The disaster was also the death knell for the German community here, as many families moved uptown to Yorkville and other sections of the city to escape painful memories. As more Jews moved into the area, the church became a synagogue in 1940.

EAST 7TH STREET

15 East 7th Street

McSorley's Old Ale House*—One of the city's oldest saloons still in operation, it was opened in 1854 by John McSorley, an Irish immigrant. The bar was open to Presidents Franklin D. Roosevelt and John F. Kennedy, but not to women. Not until August 10, 1970, 116 years after the opening, were women permitted entrance and then only after a court order. In 1912 the bar was immortalized in a painting by John Sloan that now hangs in the Detroit Institute of Arts.

207 East 7th Street

In 1853 this was the site of a dispensary for women opened by Dr. Elizabeth Blackwell, the first woman to be licensed as a physician in the United States. This one-room facility was established "to provide for poor women the medical advice of competent physicians of their own sex." She later opened the first hospital for women.

EAST 8TH STREET

35 and 39 East 8th Street

Friday night symposia on modern art were held here in 1948. The group included artists Robert Motherwell, Mark Rothko, Adolph Gottlieb, and Willem de Kooning. By 1949 some of this group spilled over to 39 East 8th Street, a small rented loft, and became known as "The Club." Lectures and panel discussions on a wide range of aesthetic topics were presented, especially abstract expressionism. Membership grew to include the major artists of the period, such as Franz Kline, Helen Frankenthaler, and Robert Rauschenberg.

46 East 8th Street

Artist Jackson Pollock lived and worked here beginning in 1933, joined by his future wife, Lee Krasner, in the early 1940s. Peggy Guggenheim, his patron, commissioned a work for her townhouse. The mural, more than nineteen feet long, was the largest work he ever painted and required knocking out a wall here to complete it. Pollock and Krasner stayed until 1945 and then moved to East Hampton.

WEST 8TH STREET

5* West 8th Street

Marlton House Hotel—The future president of Ecuador, Galo Plaza, was born in this building on February 17, 1906. His father was a minister to the United States at the time.

8* West 8th Street

Whitney Museum of American Art—Gertrude Vanderbilt Whitney leased this address, once the studio for sculptor Daniel Chester French, for additional space because it was directly behind her studio at 19 MacDougal Alley. Whitney, a prominent sculptor, was the granddaughter of Cornelius Vanderbilt and the wife of the financier Harry Payne Whitney. In 1929 she decided to donate her collection of American art to the Metropolitan Museum of Art. The Metropolitan director, Dr. Robinson, declined the offer, saying, "What will we do with them, my dear lady? We have a cellar of those things already." That refusal precipitated the opening at this address and the three adjoining townhouses of the Whitney Museum of American Art on November 18, 1931.

18 West 8th Street

Randolph Bourne, the philosopher and critic, died at this address on December 22, 1918. Severely handicapped by a birth defect and childhood spinal tuberculosis, the gifted writer was only thirty-two years old when he succumbed to the flu epidemic of 1918.

52 West 8th Street

Electric Lady Studios*—Hans Hofmann, the German-born abstract-expressionist painter and teacher, had his art school from 1938 to 1958 on the floor above an avant-garde movie theater in this building. Considered a major figure in the development of modern and abstract art, Hofmann inspired a new generation of American artists. Some of his students were Helen Frankenthaler, Lee Krasner, Red Grooms, Allan Kaprow, and Larry Rivers.

In 1970 the rock musician Jimi Hendrix converted the theater space into his Electric Lady recording studio. He left America for the last time on the day it formally opened. He died soon after in Europe, but the space has continued to be used by many renowned musicians, including Stevie Wonder, Diana Ross, Led Zeppelin, and the Rolling Stones.

EAST 9TH STREET

52 East 9th Street

An eighteen-year-old Lillian Russell lived here with her mother in 1879. The painter Franz Kline also lived at this address from 1944 until the building was torn down in 1953.

60 East 9th Street

Once a vacant barber shop, the storefront that once stood here was transformed into an art gallery for an early showing of the abstract expressionists. The "Ninth Street Show," which began on May 21, 1951, was the public's early exposure to this emotional nonfigurative movement. Sixty-one artists, including Robert Rauschenberg, Jackson Pollock, Robert Motherwell, and Franz Kline, were permitted to submit one work each.

WEST 9TH STREET

10* West 9th Street

The painter William Glackens lived in this house for more than twenty years, until his death in 1938.

12* West 9th Street

Henry Jarvis Raymond lived here from 1860 until 1867. Raymond was a founder and first editor of the *New York Times* and the first editor of *Harper's Magazine.*

He was later a lieutenant governor of New York and a member of the U.S. House of Representatives.

35* West 9th Street

Marianne Moore died here at the age of eighty-four on February 5, 1972. She had lived here in apartment 7B since 1966.

EAST 10TH STREET

90 East 10th Street

Tanager Gallery—When this address was the second home of Tanager Gallery, this was an important stepping-stone to public recognition for artists of the 1950s. This once low-rent block and surrounding area, casually referred to as "Tenth Street," was the place to see daring and innovative American art. By 1956 this block between Third and Fourth Avenues was home to the studios of more than a dozen artists: Michael Goldberg, Philip Guston, Willem de Kooning, Milton Resnick, and Esteban Vicente. It was also home to the Camino, Brata, Area, and March Galleries.

118 East 10th Street

Stanford White, the Gilded Age's most famous architect, was born at this address on November 9, 1853. His father was Richard Grant White, the music and drama critic.

269 East 10th Street

In late 1883 this was the home of Edward H. Johnson, an associate of Thomas Edison. The holiday trimmings were very special this year, as the Johnson Christmas tree was the first in the world to be decorated with electric lights.

The first Christmas tree lighted with incandescent bulbs in December of 1882. This was the home of Edward H. Johnson, vice president of the Edison Electric Light Company on East 10th Street. *(Edison National Historic Site)*

WEST 10TH STREET

14* West 10th Street

Mark Twain lived in this house shortly after returning from Europe in 1900.

Sadly, this house also has a tragic history, for it was here that Joel Steinberg fatally beat to death his six-year-old illegally adopted daughter, Lisa. Steinberg was found guilty of first-degree manslaughter on January 30, 1989. Damaging testimony by Hedda Nussbaum, Steinberg's lover, helped convict the defendant. The shocking details of the couple's life in this building drew nationwide attention to the problem of child abuse.

20* West 10th Street

Frederick MacMonnies had a studio at this address in the 1930s. The sculptor created several public works in the city, among them the controversial statue *Civic Virtue*, which once stood in front of City Hall. *Civic Virtue*, a male chauvinist allegory of "good" government pictured as a male figure standing atop "evil" female forces, was banished to the Queens Borough Hall in the 1940s. Later, the painter Louis Bouche also lived here.

23 West 10th Street

*Marshall Chess Club**—In 1915 Frank J. Marshall, the U.S. champion between 1909 and 1936, founded this chess club. The club's most famous member was Marcel Duchamp, the Dada artist. In 1949 he won every game in the Class A Section of the New York State Chess Association Tournament. A lifetime aficionado of the game, he lived in the late 1950s down the block at 28 West 10th Street just to be near his club. He was quoted as saying chess had "all the beauty of art—and much more."

40* West 10th Street

The sculptor Charles Keck lived in this carriage house from 1923 until his death in 1951. This same address had been his studio since 1911. Charles Keck was the sculptor of the *Father Duffy* statue in Times Square.

51–55 West 10th Street

Studio Building—This building, designed by the architect Richard Morris Hunt, was built especially for artists' studios. When opened in 1858, it soon became the center of late-nineteenth-century artistic activity in the city. Painters Frederick

Church, Emanuel Leutze, William Merritt Chase, Winslow Homer, Albert Bierstadt, and Eastman Johnson all had studios here, as did sculptors Augustus Saint-Gaudens and A. Stirling Calder, father of mobile creator Alexander Calder. Each studio was connected to its neighbor by large doors, which were kept open during receptions and art shows. Hunt was justifiably proud of his building—his first large commission in New York—and established his own studio and office here. The poet Kahlil Gibran, who was also a painter, had an apartment here for twenty years beginning in 1911. The building was razed in 1956.

58 ¹/₂ West 10th Street

A small building at the back of this lot on a courtyard was the home of artist Francis Hopkinson Smith. It also served as the headquarters for the celebrated Tile Club in the 1880s. Among the members of this male supper/artist club were Stanford White, Sanford Gifford, Winslow Homer, William Merritt Chase, and Augustus Saint-Gaudens.

West 10th Street at the Hudson River

Robert Fulton invited forty guests to witness his first public trial of his steamboat on August 17, 1807. After a false start and a slightly embarrassing delay, the ship lurched forward, to the cheers of the crowd and the passengers. The ship was most likely called the *North River Steam Boat,* or simply the *North River.* It wasn't generally called the *Clermont* until 1810. The historic journey up the Hudson to Albany took about thirty hours at five miles per hour. The *North River* was not the first steamboat but was the first one built and operated at a cost that promised fair profits to its investors.

EAST 11TH STREET

125 East 11th Street

Webster Hall*—Nicknamed "The Devil's Playhouse," this building, still operating as a club, was a popular place for many avant-garde parties as well as left-wing political rallies. On the night of May 25, 1917, it was the site of the fancy dress "Blind Man's Ball," attended by artists Marcel Duchamp, Joseph Stella, Man Ray, and Francis Picabia. Inspired by the Dada art movement balls in Paris, this party was a protest against the Society of Independent Artists' recent exhibition, which had refused to display Marcel Duchamp's entry, *Fountain.* Submitted as a test of the society's rather lax rules, Duchamp's "ready-made" porcelain urinal was signed with the pseudonym "R. Mutt." Branded as "non-art" by the show judges, it has since become an icon in the history of modern art.

318* East 11th Street

Abraham Goldfaden, the "Father of Yiddish Theater," died here in his home on January 9, 1908. More than seventy-five thousand mourners lined the route of his funeral cortege to his burial in Brooklyn.

WEST 11TH STREET

18 West 11th Street

A powerful explosion destroyed a Greek Revival–style townhouse, once occupied by the novelist Walter D. Edmonds, here on March 6, 1970. The 1960s revolutionary group the Weather Underground was using the building's basement as a bomb factory. Three died in the blast. Cathlyn Wilkerson, one of the survivors who fled the scene, went underground for ten years. At her subsequent trial in 1980 she was sentenced to three years for illegal possession of dynamite.

West 11th Street between Sixth and Seventh Avenues

*St. Vincent's Hospital**—The poet Kahlil Gibran died here on April 10, 1931. The author of *The Prophet* had lived in the village since 1914.

EAST 12TH STREET

234 East 12th Street

According to a detailed Pinkerton National Detective memorandum recording the whereabouts of Butch Cassidy and the Sundance Kid, the two outlaws were living at this address in early 1901. Robert Parker (a.k.a. Butch Cassidy) and Harry Longabaugh (a.k.a. Sundance) were staying here at Mrs. Taylor's boardinghouse.

WEST 12TH STREET

14 West 12th Street

The sculptor John Rogers used this address as his studio and home from 1890 to 1895. The artist was best known for his statuette groups, which he successfully marketed to the American middle class hungry for culture. Called "Rogers Groups," these reasonably priced mass-produced plaster reproductions depicted Civil War scenes, literary figures, and sentimental genre scenes.

24* West 12th Street
Built in 1851, this brownstone was a gift to "Old Fuss and Feathers" Winfield Scott from a group of admirers headed by U.S. Senator Hamilton Fish. Another admirer, the Prince of Wales, the future King Edward VII, visited the war hero here on October 13, 1860.

37 West 12th Street
This address was the home of Daniel E. Butterfield, the Union general and composer of "Taps," the bugle call. The current apartment house was named after him.

212 West 12th Street
George Clemenceau, the future premier of France, lived in the United States from 1865 until 1869. Trained as a physician, he taught French and was a Civil War cor-

This was the New York City home of George Clemenceau and his American wife, Mary Plummer, at 212 West 12th Street. The photograph was taken about 1917, when he was the premier of France. (FPG)

respondent for the French newspaper *Paris Temps*. While in New York City he lived at this address.

247* West 12th Street

Manufacturers Transit Company—This building, once a warehouse for flammable chemicals and whiskey, exploded on July 18, 1922. Nicknamed the "Greenwich Village Volcano," the fire smoldered and burned for four days. Seventy people were hurt and two thousand neighbors were forced to evacuate their homes. The building is now condominium apartments.

EAST 13TH STREET

208* East 13th Street

Political radical Emma Goldman lived in a two-room apartment in this tenement from 1903 until 1912. In 1906 her long-term lover and fellow revolutionary Alexander Berkman was released from prison for his attempted assassination of industrialist Henry Clay Frick. He often joined her here, writing together on her anarchist journal *Mother Earth*. They were both deported and sent to the Soviet Union in 1919.

WEST 13TH STREET

8* West 13th Street

Two famous muralists lived in this building in the 1930s. Diego Rivera was working on his controversial murals at Rockefeller Center. Thomas Hart Benton was working on his mural at the New School.

215* West 13th Street

Anaïs Nin lived in the top-floor studio of this building from 1940 through the 1960s.

421 West 13th Street

Delamater Iron Works—The engine for the famed Civil War ironclad ship *Monitor* was made here in the 1860s. A hundred years later this address was the site of one of the earliest gay "members only" after-hours bars, called the Zoo.

West 13th Street at the Hudson River

Cunard Piers—On April 18, 1912, at 9 a.m., the ship *Carpathia* docked here at Pier 54 with the survivors from the "unsinkable" *Titanic*. The newest luxury liner in Britain's White Star Fleet, the *Titanic* had hit an iceberg on her maiden voyage to New York and sank, killing 1,493 passengers and crew. The rescue ship, the *Carpathia*, picked up the SOS signal and rushed to the scene but didn't arrive until about two hours after the magnificent ship had slipped beneath the waves. The *Carpathia* took on board as many dazed survivors from the too-few lifeboats as it could find and headed for New York. More than seven hundred victims of the disaster arrived here, where many were taken to St. Vincent's Hospital in Greenwich Village for treatment.

The Cunard Line piers were also the scene of the last sailing of the *Lusitania*, another ill-fated British luxury liner, on Saturday, May 1, 1915, at 12:28 p.m. A German U-boat sank this ship a week later on May 7 while she was en route to Liverpool during World War I; 1,198 passengers and crew, including 128 Americans, lost their lives. American indignation over the sinking contributed to the U.S. entry into the war against Germany two years later.

The *Lusitania* docked at the West 13th Street pier soon after her maiden voyage to New York. When the *Lusitania* left this pier for the last time on May 1, 1915, the German embassy ran ads in the morning newspapers, warning passengers of a "war zone." Six days later, German submarine *U-20* torpedoed and sank the ship off the coast of Ireland. *(Museum City of New York)*

EAST 14TH STREET

11 East 14th Street

Cunard Mansion—In 1906 a Victorian brownstone at this address was the second home to the early motion picture studio the American Mutoscope and Biograph Company. The old ballroom served as a studio for many of the fledgling silent films that were first made in New York City. D. W. Griffith directed his first movie, *The Adventures of Dollie,* here in 1908. Many of the silent screen's greatest stars—Mary Pickford, Lionel Barrymore, Lillian and Dorothy Gish, Mabel Normand, and director Mack Sennett—began their careers here.

109–11 East 14th Street

Steinway Hall—This concert hall, opened after the Civil War, was the site of performances by renowned pianists Anton Rubinstein, Rafael Joseffy, and Moriz Rosenthal. Operatic soprano Adelina Patti also gave a series of concerts here in 1881. The building was demolished in 1916.

110 East 14th Street

Luchow's Restaurant—This famed German eatery, established in 1882, was popular with writers H. L. Mencken, George Jean Nathan, and Theodore Dreiser. Luchow's had the distinction of receiving the first restaurant liquor license after the repeal of Prohibition on December 1, 1933. This was four days before the Utah state legislature voted for repeal, officially ending Prohibition. The restaurant lasted until the 1980s at this address, then moved uptown, but closed shortly thereafter. The building burned and was later replaced by New York University student housing.

116 East 14th Street

Gramercy Gym—Cus D'Amato, one of the greatest boxing trainers, ran this gym for more than forty years. D'Amato, who died in 1985, trained three world champions here. Both Floyd Patterson, the youngest heavyweight champion ever, and José Torres, the light-heavyweight champ in 1965, were his pupils. But his greatest student and virtually adopted son was Mike Tyson. The building is now gone, torn down in 1993, but this stretch of 14th Street has been named "Cus D'Amato Way."

East 14th Street and Irving Place, Northeast Corner

Academy of Music—On the night of October 12, 1860, the imposing theater, which once stood on this corner, was converted into a huge ballroom for a party

in honor of the Prince of Wales. The nineteen-year-old prince, later King Edward VII, was given the royal treatment by New York City society eager to impress the first member of British royalty to visit this former colony. Even the collapse of the temporary dance floor—dumping two hundred well-heeled guests—was unable to dim the excitement. A few months later, on February 20, 1861, Abraham Lincoln saw his first and only opera, Verdi's *Masked Ball,* here. The president-elect was in the city on a stopover on his way to his inauguration in Washington. Another opera, *Aida,* had its U.S. premier at this theater on November 26, 1873.

145–47 East 14th Street

Tammany Hall—The once powerful Tammany organization was built here, on the former site of the first New York University Medical School, in 1866. The hall officially opened for the Democratic National Convention on the Fourth of July in 1868. Delegates from thirty-seven states nominated a reluctant Horatio

The highlight of the Prince of Wales's New York City visit in October of 1860 was a gala at the Academy of Music on East 14th Street. The teenaged son of Queen Victoria and future king of England reportedly had a grand time dancing and left at 4:30 in the morning. *(Harper's Weekly, October 20, 1860)*

In a niche on the roof is the statue of Tamanend, the Delaware chief and symbol of Tammany Hall, the political organization that ran the city for most of the nineteenth century and the early part of the twentieth. The hall at 145 East 14th Street was also home to Tony Pastor's new 14th Street Theater. Tammany Hall and its neighbor, the Academy of Music, left, were both replaced by the Consolidated Gas Company, the current Consolidated Edison Company Headquarters. (FPG)

Seymour, an ex-governor of New York, for president on the twenty-second ballot. For his running mate they chose Civil War hero and former Republican Congressman Francis P. Blair Jr. of Missouri. This mismatched ticket lost in November to Ulysses S. Grant and the Republicans. Tony Pastor moved his successful vaudeville theater into the building in 1881.

WEST 14TH STREET

36 West 14th Street
This address was the childhood home of poet Emma Lazarus in the years before the Civil War.

128 West 14th Street
The Douglas mansion was the second home of the Metropolitan Museum of Art from 1873 until the present Central Park building was completed in 1879.

142 West 14th Street
Church of the Annunciation—On July 2, 1858, the body of former president James Monroe lay in state at a church that once stood on this site. Monroe had died July 4, 1831, twenty-seven years earlier, and had been buried in New York City Marble Cemetery on East 2nd Street. The body was taken to Richmond, Virginia, for reburial.

210* West 14th Street
Dada artist Marcel Duchamp rented a fourth-floor walk-up studio here in early 1943. His rent was only $25 a month, but he was still unable to afford a telephone. His friends had to reach him by letter or telegram.

242* West 14th Street
The second floor of this building was the studio of artist Franz Kline from 1957 until his death in 1962.

St. Patrick's Cathedral outlined with electric lights. *(Author's collection)*

MIDTOWN

BEEKMAN PLACE

1* Beekman Place

This large apartment house has been home to the novelist John P. Marquand and actors Noel Coward and Gertrude Lawrence.

2* Beekman Place

Mary McCarthy lived in this building from 1933 to 1936. Another writer, Antoine de Saint-Exupéry, also lived here in 1941.

17* Beekman Place

This townhouse was the last home of Irving Berlin. The 101-year-old dean of American popular music died here on September 22, 1989. In 1911 he wrote his first hit, "Alexander's Ragtime Band," and continued writing songs well into the 1960s. Some of his best known are "Always," "White Christmas," and "There's No Business Like Show Business."

23* Beekman Place

From 1921 to 1951 this was the home of actress Katharine Cornell and her husband, director Guthrie McClintic.

BROADWAY

Broadway and West 14th Street to West 26th Street

"...the bright white jets along Broadway began to flame out like stars emerging from the darkness." This poetic line from a *New York Times* article described the moment, 5:27 P.M. on December 20, 1880, when the first electric streetlights were turned on in New York City. The invention of Charles Francis Bruch, the electric arc lights stood on tall poles marching uptown from Union Square.

857* Broadway

The realist painter Isabel Bishop worked here in her fourth-floor studio for more than forty-four years until 1978.

932 Broadway

The Pearsall Brothers opened the first velocipede riding school on December 5, 1868. "Velocipede" was an early name for the bicycle.

Abbey's Park Theater—Lillie Langtry was to have made her American debut at this theater. But on opening night, October 30, 1882, the theater caught fire and burned. "The Jersey Lily," as she was known, watched the blaze through opera glasses from her hotel window at the Albemarle on Broadway at 24th Street. The greatly altered and present building was built a year later as Brooks Brothers store.

1107 Broadway

Albemarle Hotel—Sarah Bernhardt was a guest at this hotel while on her first visit to the United States on October 27, 1880. She stayed in a second-story suite with a balcony over the main entrance. Henry Abbey, her New York producer, had it redecorated to remind her of her Parisian home. Two years later, on October 23, 1882, Abbey booked the same suite for another foreign theatrical star making her U.S. debut, Lily Langtry. The arrival of the "Divine Sarah" in New York may been as tumultuous as Langtry's, but only the "Jersey Lily" was welcomed to the United States by a brass band playing "God Save the Queen" and by her friend and compatriot Oscar Wilde dressed in a cowboy hat, direct from his tour of the American West.

1115–17 Broadway

Hoffman House—This popular Victorian hotel was the home to the kitschy nude painting *Nymphs and Satyrs* by Adolphe Bouguereau, which hung in the male-only hotel bar. Widely advertised by savvy management, this painting became a mustsee tourist attraction at the turn of the century. So great was the demand from art lovers that one day a week was set aside for ladies to view the masterpiece. This was the first New York City home of publisher William Randolph Hearst in 1895.

1133 Broadway

St. James Building*—The future Israeli Prime Minister Golda Meir worked for the Pioneer Women's Organization for Palestine in 1932 for two years at this address. This Zionist group was concerned with feminine participation in the building of Palestine.

1157* Broadway

The ground floor of this building was the Holland Brothers' Kinetoscope Parlor. This first home of Thomas Edison's new invention, the kinetoscope, was opened on April 6, 1894. The hand-cranked machine allowed the viewer to see true moving pictures. One of these short clips exhibited the rippling muscles of Eugene

Sandow, the celebrated strongman. The kinetoscope and the many parlors opened all over the country were made obsolete just two years later by another Edison invention, the Vitascope, the first motion-picture projector. Earlier, this same address had been the studio of John Rogers, the Victorian genre-scene sculptor.

1200* Broadway—Northeast Corner of West 29th Street

Gilsey House Hotel—This hotel replaced the Anderson Cottage, the last surviving farmhouse in midtown off Broadway. It was also the first hotel in the United States to offer telephone service to guests. Originally painted white when it opened on April 15, 1871, this cast-iron creation looked like a giant tiered wedding cake. It closed in December of 1904, and it was converted into offices. In the 1970s it was again converted, this time into a co-operative apartment house.

Broadway between West 29th and West 30th Streets, West Side

Wood's Museum—In spite of the highbrow name, this theater was one of the earliest homes to burlesque, or the "girlie show." In 1868 it was on this stage that "Lydia Thompson and her British Blondes" appeared. The act was a song-and-dance skit performed in form-fitting tights, a common Victorian guise to reveal women's figures.

1271 Broadway

This address was once the site of Albert Bierstadt's studio during the 1890s. This once immensely popular painter continued working here in near obscurity. He had become a victim of the changing taste in art, and at this time his monumental landscapes were considered unfashionable.

1275* Broadway

Gimbel Brothers Department Store—On October 29, 1945, the first practical ballpoint pen went on sale at this now-closed department store. Developed earlier that year by Milton B. Reynolds, the pens were an instant hit, and their remarkable first-day sales have become part of business legend. More than ten thousand were sold on that day, particularly surprising since they were priced at an extravagant $12.50 apiece.

1410 Broadway

Casino Theater—This corner lot was the site of the renowned Casino Theater, the first theater illuminated entirely with electricity and the first with a roof garden.

The Florodora sextet appeared at the Casino Theater on Broadway and 39th Street in 1900. They were performing in the play *Florodora,* dancing their famous number "Tell Me Pretty Maiden." *(FPG)*

On January 18, 1896, the first X-ray machine was publicly exhibited here. The machine's medical benefits remained undeveloped, and it was treated as just a sideshow attraction. It was billed as the "Parisian Sensation," and the curious were charged twenty-five cents to see it. Another revealing innovation introduced at this theater four years later was the Florodora Girls, the earliest Broadway chorus line.

Broadway between West 39th Street and West 40th Street

Metropolitan Opera House—This block of Manhattan real estate marked the final battleground between old New York society and the robber barons. The robber barons won. By the "Gilded Age" of the 1880s, the Academy of Music on East 14th Street had become too small to accommodate the growing number of rich businessmen eager to flaunt their new wealth and status. After the Old Guard had refused to vacate or allow any new boxes to be built at the academy, William K. Vanderbilt and other members of the nouveau riche decided to build their own larger and more opulent opera house. The Metropolitan Opera company was formed. It wasn't long before owning a plush red box here became the ultimate symbol of social success. The new company's opening night was on October 22, 1883. *Faust* was performed, starring Italo Campanini. There were many more momentous nights at the opera: November 23, 1903, Enrico Caruso's American debut; December 10, 1910, the world premier of Giacomo Puccini's *La Fanciulla del West* with the composer seated in the audience; and April 12, 1916, dancer Vaslav Nijinsky's American debut. On its final night, April 16, 1966, conductor Leopold Stokowski said to the audience, "I beg you to help save this magnificent house." But it was not to be. Efforts to preserve the grande dame failed, and the building was razed the following year. The opera moved to its new home in Lincoln Center.

Broadway and West 40th Street

The sculptor Karl Bitter and his wife were both hit by an automobile at this intersection after leaving the Metropolitan Opera House on April 9, 1915. Mrs. Bitter was not seriously hurt, but her husband was fatally injured. He had been working on the Pulitzer Fountain in front of the Plaza Hotel at Grand Army Plaza at the time.

Josiah Cleaveland Cady designed the Metropolitan Opera Company's new home on Broadway at West 38th Street. The much maligned exterior is having construction work on the entrance in this photograph from about 1889. *(Author's collection)*

1466* Broadway

Knickerbocker Hotel—Opening in 1906, the Beaux-Arts Knickerbocker was a fashionable hotel for the theater crowd attracted to burgeoning Times Square. In addition to 556 guest rooms, its multiple dining rooms and bars seated more than 2,000 people a night. It was also home to opera great Enrico Caruso from 1908 until 1920. In 1919 his daughter Gloria was born here in their fourteen-room suite on the ninth floor. Also a favorite with George M. Cohan, the hotel was converted into an office building in the 1920s. It was home to *Newsweek* for twenty years.

Broadway and West 42nd Street, Northwest Corner

Times Tower*—Once home to the *New York Times,* namesake of Times Square, this tower was stripped of its frilly terra-cotta ornamentation during a 1966 renovation. The building's opening on December 31, 1904, began the tradition of welcoming in New Year's Eve en masse in Times Square. Midnight fireworks marked that evening's first observance. When the city later tightened the regulations on fireworks above crowds, the *Times* ushered in the annual celebration, in 1907, with the lowering of the familiar lighted rooftop ball. The ball has dropped right on time every year since—except for 1943 and 1944, when it was feared the lights might attract an Axis air attack. The tower, now called One Times Square, is still home to the world's first "moving sign." This wraparound sign began on November 6, 1928, by flashing the results of the presidential election: Herbert Hoover over New York Governor Al Smith. This same sign touched off one of the city's largest and most joyous celebrations at 7:03 P.M. on August 14, 1945. The message—"Official—Truman announces Japanese surrender"—was a godsend to the thousands of New Yorkers packed in nearby streets, signaling the end of World War II. The *New York Times* reported the next day that a thunderous roar from the crowd lasted for twenty minutes after the announcement.

Broadway and West 43rd Street, Northeast Corner

Barrett House Hotel—This hotel, now gone, in the heart of the theater district, was a fitting birthplace for America's greatest playwright. Eugene O'Neill was born in room 236 on October 16, 1888, while his actor father was in town on tour in the play *The Count of Monte Cristo.*

Broadway between West 43rd and West 44th Streets, East Side

Rector's—The famous "lobster palace" restaurant that once occupied the middle of this block was a favorite with "Gay Nineties" society and the theatrical crowd.

Thousands streamed into Times Square to enjoy VE Day, Victory in Europe, on May 7, 1945. This gathering proved to be just a warm-up party for the colossal celebration on VJ Day, Victory in Japan, August 14, 1945, which ended World War II. The replica of the Statue of Liberty was visiting Times Square to help sell war bonds. *(FPG)*

Bon vivant James Buchanan "Diamond Jim" Brady with his legendary appetite was a favored diner. Owner Charles Rector referred to him as "the best twenty-five customers I have." The front entrance had New York's first revolving door installed about 1899. The restaurant was torn down in 1910 to build the Hotel Rector, which later became the Claridge.

Broadway and West 44th Street, Southeast Corner

Hotel Claridge—ASCAP, the American Society of Composers, Authors, and Publishers, was born here on February 13, 1914. The group was founded to ensure that songwriters and music publishers would be fairly compensated for public performances of their works. Music publisher George Maxwell was elected president of the new organization, whose first members included composers Irving Berlin, John Philip Sousa, and Victor Herbert.

The hotel also served as the home for the fondly remembered Camel cigarette sign that blew giant smoke rings. Put up in 1941, the smoking billboard was an imaginative answer to the World War II blackout ban of outdoor lighting. The sign blew its last puff in 1966.

By the time this photograph was taken in 1947, the Camel billboard smoker had returned to wearing civilian clothes. The tireless chain-smoker on the side of the Hotel Claridge blew smoke rings into Times Square for twenty-five years. *(FPG)*

1505 Broadway

Paramount Building*—Built in 1926 as the New York headquarters for Paramount Motion Pictures, this office building was also home to the Paramount Theater, a 3,900-seat movie palace famous for its live stage shows. It was a favorite with the Big Bands of the thirties and forties. Frank "The Voice" Sinatra, the first of the teenage idols, made a solo appearance on its stage on December 30, 1942, in a program headlined by Benny Goodman and his orchestra. Sinatra's concerts were the scenes of near riots and mass hysteria among his "bobby-soxer" fans. At another frenzied return engagement, on October 12, 1944, more than thirty thousand fans mobbed Times Square. These public exhibitions of devotion helped launch the singer's career but provoked outcries from authorities and parents worried about wartime frivolity and truancy from school. The theater was converted into additional office space in the 1950s.

Broadway between East 44th and East 45th Streets, East Side

Olympia Theater—Oscar Hammerstein, grandfather of Broadway lyricist Oscar Hammerstein II and unofficial grandfather of "Times Square," opened here on November 25, 1895, the first theater above 42nd Street on what was then called Long Acre Square. The block-long complex was actually three theaters seating six thousand patrons, all under one glass-enclosed roof garden. This roof-top attraction, the Jardin de Paris, was the first home of Florenz Ziegfeld's "Follies" in 1907. The Olympia was too large, too soon, and was never very successful this far uptown. Hammerstein was forced to sell, and it was divided into three separately managed theaters. The building was demolished in 1935.

1515 Broadway

Hotel Astor—The hotel that once stood on this site was the 1916 election-night headquarters for the Republican presidential candidate Charles Evans Hughes. Believing he had won the election, he went to bed, but while he was asleep, late returns from California went to President Woodrow Wilson. When pressed by a reporter from *The World* for Mr. Hughes's reaction, a valet told him, "The President has retired." "When he wakes up," the reporter replied, "tell him he is no longer the President."

Concluding an all-day Conference of Major Industries held at Columbia University on October 24, 1928, two thousand people attended the Industrial Pioneers of America dinner in the grand ballroom at the hotel. The guests of honor were Thomas Edison, Henry Ford, Harvey S. Firestone, Charles M. Schwab, George Eastman, Julius Rosenwald, and Orville Wright.

Will Rogers and Arturo Toscanini both lived at the Hotel Astor at various times.

1537 Broadway, Northwest Corner of West 45th Street

Astor Theater—Baseball's Babe Ruth made his last public appearance at this movie theater for the premier of the film *The Babe Ruth* Story on July 26, 1948, official "Babe Ruth Day" in New York City. "The Sultan of Swat" was so weak that he had to leave halfway through the film. He died less than a month later on August 16, 1948.

1557* Broadway

Horn and Hardart's opened their first New York City automat at this location in 1913. The automat, a modern marvel thoroughly identified with New York, was not a native. The proprietors were from Philadelphia, where the first coin-operated automatic restaurant had opened eleven years earlier. This restaurant with a seemingly endless supply of tempting food behind little glass doors was a hit. The novelty eateries peaked by the 1920s and eventually succumbed to the fast-food chains. The last automat closed on April 9, 1991, at 200 East 42nd Street.

1564 Broadway

Palace Theater—Before this famed theater was built, this site was once the brownstone home of America's greatest theatrical family, the Barrymores. Lionel, age eleven, Ethel, age ten, and John Barrymore, age seven, lived here in 1889. The Palace was built in 1913 and quickly became the career destination of every vaudevillian, whose dream it was "to play the Palace." America's most celebrated performers have played this stage: Eddie Cantor, Fanny Brice, Kate Smith, W. C. Fields, Will Rogers, and the Marx Brothers. Sophie Tucker, another popular alumna, prevented panic during her act after a fire broke out backstage. Her cool performance saved lives and earned her the next day's tabloid headline tribute "RED-HOT MAMA BURNS UP PALACE THEATER."

When vaudeville started to fade, the theater reluctantly turned to movies to fill the house. One of those movies was Orson Welles's *Citizen Kane,* believed by many to be the greatest movie ever made, which premiered here on May 1, 1944. The director had been unable to find any theater willing to show his classic because RKO studio and William Randolph Hearst, the veiled subject of the picture, had tried to block the film. It was only after Wells threatened to sue RKO that the studio agreed to release his masterpiece.

On November 28, 1947, the funeral procession for Bill "Bonjangles" Robinson stopped here for a final tribute. The crowd of mourners for the "King of Tap" along Broadway and the rest of the route to Evergreen Cemetery in Brooklyn numbered more than half a million.

The Palace is forever linked in most people's minds with Judy Garland's triumphal engagement beginning on October 16, 1951. Garland's nineteen-week run broke the theater's all-time long-run record. Today's Palace, once again presenting Broadway shows, is entirely encased in a slick new skyscraper.

Broadway and the Block Bounded by Seventh Avenue and West 47th and West 48th Streets

This small trapezoid block, now the Ramada Renaissance Times Square Hotel, has been home to some of Manhattan's greatest nightclubs, starting in the 1920s when it was the Palais Royal, where bandleader Paul Whiteman made his debut. From 1936 to 1940 it was the legendary Cotton Club, transplanted from Harlem. The club's headliners were Duke Ellington, Cab Calloway, Ethel Waters, Lena Horne, and Louis Armstrong. Next came the Latin Quarter in 1942, where the entertainment was supplied by stars like Ted Lewis, Sophie Tucker, Frank Sinatra, and Milton Berle. The Latin Quarter lasted until 1969. Then changing tastes and a changing neighborhood contributed to a slow decline of this showplace block.

Broadway at West 50th Street

While in the city to address the United Nations, Soviet leader Mikhail Gorbachev showed some personal *glasnost* by stepping out of his limousine to greet American well-wishers near this intersection on December 7, 1988. Manhattan traffic came to a virtual halt during the leader's motorcade sightseeing trips.

1645 Broadway, Southwest Corner of West 51st Street

Capitol Theater—A lavish movie theater, the Capitol was used for early radio broadcasts such as *Major Bowes' Original Amateur Hour*. This show, first broadcast coast to coast on March 24, 1935, was a cultural phenomenon. "Around and around she goes, and where she stops, nobody knows," the show's opening line, was a siren call for Depression-weary listeners and hopeful contestants. The amateurs, with varying degrees of talent—including one New Jersey singer, Frank Sinatra—flocked to New York to appear on the show and be discovered. Travelers Aid and the Salvation Army had to care for the overflow of hopefuls, who often used the last of their savings to get here. *Newsweek* reported that in only one month in 1935, 1,200 contestants had applied for emergency food and shelter.

On August 17, 1939, the East Coast premier of the film *The Wizard of Oz* took place here. The star, Judy Garland, and her partner in later films, Mickey Rooney, appeared five times daily for sold-out live stage shows between showings of the film.

1658 Broadway

Roseland Ballroom—This was one of the largest ballrooms in the city from the 1920s through the 1940s, and the expression "taxi dancing" is said to have originated here. Male patrons bought their ten-cent tickets, allowing them to dance with a hostess, whose income depended on the tickets she earned. The hostess was likened to a taxi driver who worked for hire. A later, 1956 incarnation of Roseland is on West 52nd Street.

1662 Broadway

Warner's Theater—The first feature-length "talking" picture, *The Jazz Singer* staring Al Jolson, premiered at this theater on October 6, 1927. This picture was the first to feature singing and a few lines of dialogue. In addition to being a milestone in the history of the movies, *The Jazz Singer* also introduced some great songs: "Waiting for the Robert E. Lee," "Blue Skies," and "Toot, Toot, Tootsie, Goodbye." The first "all-talking" picture also premiered at this same theater a year later on July 7, 1928. *The Lights of New York* was advertised by Warner Brothers as "100% Talking." The review in *Variety* was far less kind: it called the picture "100% Crude."

1678* Broadway

Birdland—Headliner and namesake Charlie "Bird" Parker opened this legendary jazz cabaret on December 15, 1949. Also appearing were several caged parakeets, who within weeks succumbed to all the smoke and the air conditioning. Parker made his final public appearance here on March 4, 1955; he died eight days later. Revered by jazz lovers, the club had its own theme song, "Lullaby of Birdland," composed by George Shearing.

1685* Broadway

Colony Theater—This theater, now a stage theater called the Broadway, was originally built as a motion-picture theater in 1924. It was here on November 18, 1928, that the world's first talking cartoon with sound, Walt Disney's *Steamboat Willie*, debuted, with Walt himself providing the voice of the film's star, Mickey Mouse.

1697 Broadway

The Ed Sullivan Theater*—Originally named Hammerstein's Theater, this playhouse was built in 1927 by Arthur Hammerstein as a monument to his father, Oscar, the opera impresario. The versatile auditorium has been used for film, radio, and Broadway productions. In the 1930s it even served as a mob-connected nightclub. Beginning in the late 1940s and lasting until today, the theater has been home to several television shows, including *The Honeymooners* and *The Merv Griffin Show*. It was renamed in honor of television variety host Ed Sullivan, whose long-running show was broadcast from here. His most famous guests, the Beatles, appeared live on this stage and on millions of American television screens on February 9, 1964. It is now home to *Late Night with David Letterman*.

1721 Broadway
Hotsy Totsy Club—Gangster Jack "Legs" Diamond was a silent partner at this notorious second-floor speakeasy, in a building long since replaced. It was from here that he directed his illegal activities and rackets. It was also the murder site of a

The Beatles, rehearsing for their appearance on the Ed Sullivan Show in what is now called the Ed Sullivan Theater at 1697 Broadway. Leaders in the first wave of the British invasion, the musical group revolutionized popular music. *(FPG)*

hoodlum named Red Cassidy on Friday, July 13, 1929. Legs and his crony Charles Entratta were the police's prime suspects. However, the case against the two was eventually dropped when all the known witnesses, by some counts eight people, died or mysteriously disappeared.

Broadway and West 55th Street, Northwest Corner

The small IRT subway exit on this corner was the primary escape route for injured riders in one of the city's worst transit accidents on January 6, 1915. During the morning rush hour, three downtown subway cars stalled due to a short circuit between the Columbus Circle and the 50th Street stations. Heavy smoke resulting from the electrical fire slowly filled the tunnel. Stranded and in the dark, the passengers panicked at the smell of smoke. It took rescuers hours to get almost 2,500 terrified passengers to street level. Two people died and 172 were injured. Many of the injured suffered from smoke inhalation, but most of those who were hurt were injured during the panic.

1790* Broadway

National Headquarters of the National Association for the Advancement of Colored People—An emotional press conference with Clarence Norris, the sole surviving member of the "Scottsboro Boys," was held here to announce that Norris had been given a "full and unconditional" pardon by Alabama Governor George Wallace on October 25, 1976. In 1931 Norris and eight other African American youths were ordered off a train and accused of raping two white women. They were found guilty, and eight were sentenced to death at a trial the following year. The celebrated case, a symbol of racial injustice before the Civil Rights Movement, eventually reached the U.S. Supreme Court and became an international cause. Norris spent fifteen years in prison, five on death row, and thirty years as a fugitive for violating an earlier Alabama parole and leaving the state to ultimately live in New York City.

BRYANT PARK

Cleared by the city with convict labor, this land was used as a potter's field in 1823. It was the site of America's first world's fair, the "Exhibition of the Industry of All Nations" which was opened on July 14, 1853, by President Franklin Pierce. The centerpiece of the fair was an enormous yet delicate iron and glass hall, the Crystal Palace, which held four thousand exhibitors from around the world. More than a

Designed for the Exhibition of 1853 in today's Bryant Park, the Crystal Palace was a marvel of modern architecture. New technological advances, such as the iron frame and prefabricated parts, enabled the builders to cover a vast space. *(Author's collection)*

million visitors came to marvel at the displays of machinery and the new consumer goods available as America entered the Industrial Age. The Crystal Palace remained as a showplace for exhibits and fine art after the fair but burned to the ground in about an hour on the night of October 5, 1858. A few years later Union troops used the site as a camp during the Civil War.

Declared a park in 1871, it was later named for the poet William Cullen Bryant, a major advocate of public parks in the city. On August 26, 1970, the park was the site of an early and enthusiastic women's-liberation rally. Ten thousand demonstrators marched down Fifth Avenue to the park to celebrate the fiftieth anniversary of American women's right to vote and to mark "Women's Strike for Equality Day." Gloria Steinem, Kate Millett, and Betty Friedan spoke to the crowd. After work on the huge underground storage area for book stacks was finished in the early 1990s, the park was beautifully restored and reclaimed from the drug dealers who often considered it their own turf.

CENTRAL PARK SOUTH

36 Central Park South
Park Lane Hotel*—Shortly after midnight on April 15, 1992, Leona Helmsley tried to sneak out of her duplex penthouse apartment atop this hotel she also owns. She

was hoping to avoid the reporters waiting for her out front. The self-proclaimed hotel "queen" was off to federal prison near Lexington, Kentucky, guilty of tax evasion and fraud. Helmsley, who had to face trial and prison alone because her husband, Harry, was deemed too ill, was ordered to begin serving her four-year sentence on that fateful day, April 15, the day Americans pay their income taxes. She returned here on November 26, 1993, to finish the remainder of her reduced sentence in "house confinement."

50 Central Park South
St. Moritz*—This hotel was the first U.S. home of Marc Chagall. The painter, who had been living in France, arrived in this country on June 23, 1941, the same day the Nazis invaded his native Russia. It was also the long-time home of gossip columnist Walter Winchell and baseball star Mickey Mantle.

240* Central Park South
This address was home to author and aviator Antoine de Saint-Exupéry beginning in early 1941. The exiled Frenchman lived here during the German occupation of France. He used the upper-floor apartment as a laboratory to ponder some possible military options for the Allied invasion of France. The airman sailed paper helicopters out the windows into Central Park to simulate an airborne attack and used the bathtub for wave studies for a water attack. He wrote *The Little Prince* here and in a summer house on Long Island.

GRAMERCY PARK
This handsome forty-two-acre private park was once part of a farm owned by James Duane, the city's first mayor, after the American Revolution. He had purchased the land from the descendants of Peter Stuyvesant. The land was already called Gramercy Seat—from the original Dutch *krom moerasje,* meaning, roughly, "crooked little swamp." In 1831 Samuel B. Ruggles, a lawyer and developer, created the park as an added attraction to selling the surrounding sixty-six property lots.

GRAMERCY PARK EAST

34* Gramercy Park East
Built in 1883, this Queen Anne–style apartment building is one of the earliest co-operatives in the city. The nine-story structure had the distinction of having one of

the oldest direct plunger elevators, installed by Otis Elevator when the building was constructed. Two large water tanks, one on the roof and one in the basement, contained the water that drove the five-story-high piston assembly up and down. The 111-year-old elevator was replaced in 1994. The building is popular with actors, and owners have included Margaret Hamilton and James Cagney.

36* Gramercy Park East
This address has been home to circus impresario John Ringling, actor John Barrymore, and sculptor Daniel Chester French.

GRAMERCY PARK NORTH

52* Gramercy Park North
Gramercy Park Hotel—The current hotel, built in 1923, replaced the corner townhouse of Stanford White, the beaux-arts architect, and the townhouse, two doors west, of Robert G. Ingersoll, noted agnostic lecturer. The hotel was home to eleven-year-old John F. Kennedy, who lived on the second floor for a few months in 1928. The Kennedy family was living here temporarily before moving to London, where father Joseph had recently been appointed U.S. ambassador. The humorist Sidney Perelman also lived here from 1972 until his death in 1979.

60 Gramercy Park North
This address, replaced in 1929 by the Gramercy Park Hotel Annex, was home to George Templeton Strong. Strong, a great chronicler of mid-nineteenth-century New York City life, was married to Ellen Ruggles, the daughter of Gramercy Park developer Samuel B. Ruggles. Strong was one of the leading supporters and treasurer of the Civil War Sanitation Commission, created to aid the Union cause. Shortly after the war, the man of the hour, Gen. Ulysses S. Grant, showed his appreciation by accepting a dinner invitation to this house on November 18, 1865.

GRAMERCY PARK SOUTH

10* Gramercy Park South
This was the home and studio of Robert Henri from 1909 until 1919. It was here on the top floor that Tuesday evenings were set aside for an open house. At these gatherings, Henri, other painters, and his students met to discuss art and liberal politics.

11* Gramercy Park South

This townhouse, constructed in 1856, was home for fifty years until 1971 of the composer Samuel L. M. Barlow.

15* Gramercy Park South

National Arts Club—Samuel J. Tilden, the governor of New York, purchased this townhouse in 1863; later, he purchased the house next door at number 14. In 1881 he asked Calvert Vaux, of Central Park design fame, to combine the two structures with a unified Gothic Revival façade. Tilden, a political reformer who made some enemies, was concerned with his personal safety. His remodeling plans included a secret escape tunnel to East 19th Street. After his death in 1886 his estate was combined with the Lenox and Astor libraries to create the New York Public Library. The National Arts Club bought the double-sized house in 1906. The club, founded eight years earlier, was the first arts' club to have both women and men as members. The membership included nonartists, too; both Theodore Roosevelt and Woodrow Wilson were active in club activities. It was here that member Paul Manship, the sculptor of *Prometheus* at Rockefeller Center, died of a heart attack on January 31, 1966.

16* Gramercy Park South

The Players Club—In 1888 the great thespian Edwin Booth bought this townhouse and had it remodeled by Stanford White as a clubhouse for actors and other friends of drama. Booth founded The Players Club in the hopes of creating a cultured atmosphere for his fellow actors, who were considered coarse bohemians by much of society. Appropriately theatrical, Booth died here in his room on June 7, 1893, during a tempestuous thunderstorm that had blacked out the entire club. This bedroom has been preserved just as it was that night. Club members, all male until as late as May 31, 1989, have included Mark Twain, Booth Tarkington, Sir Laurence Olivier, and Irving Berlin.

17* Gramercy Park South

Publisher Joseph Pulitzer leased this house in 1883 for two years. This was his first New York address. He had recently moved from St. Louis to take ownership of the *New York World.*

19* Gramercy Park South

Purchased in 1887 by Stuyvesant Fish and his wife, Mamie, this corner townhouse was a major battleground in nineteenth-century society wars. The flamboyant Mrs.

Still at 15 Gramercy Park South, this townhouse was the home of New York Governor Samuel J. Tilden. An early successful corporate lawyer before entering politics, he spent lavishly on his home and book collection. Many of the interior rooms are still decorated in the exotic Aesthetic style of the 1880s. *(FPG)*

Fish was determined to unseat the stodgy aristocratic Mrs. William Waldorf Astor as New York's reigning society hostess. She nearly succeeded. She gave lively and less formal parties and is credited with shortening the traditional ten-course dinner to a mere fifty minutes. By the turn of the century, both Mrs. Astor and Mrs. Fish had moved up to more fashionable digs on the Upper East Side.

In the 1950s and 1960s this house again became a society mecca when it was the home of Benjamin Sonnenberg Sr., the public-relations wizard. It was Sonnenberg who thought up the idea of having John D. Rockefeller give away dimes to kids. He lavishly entertained his clients and celebrity, artist, and politician friends in this house.

21* Gramercy Park South

This house was the winter home of the writer and diplomat John Bigelow, from 1881 until his death in 1911. Bigelow, who was the U.S. minister to France during the Civil War, persuaded the French government not to recognize the Confederacy.

25 Gramercy Park South

Thomas Edison and his family took a two-year lease on this $400-a-month townhouse in September of 1882. They lived here for two years before moving to West Orange, New Jersey.

32* Gramercy Park South

A steam main buried in the middle of the street outside this co-operative apartment house burst on August 19, 1989, at 6:30 P.M. The explosion and resulting eighteen-story geyser of scalding steam killed two Con Edison repairmen who were working on the scene and a woman who lived on the third floor of this building. Hundreds of nearby residents were forced to evacuate their homes. In addition to suffering the devastation caused by the blast, residents were later informed of the risk of asbestos contamination. Asbestos, a carcinogen covering the steam pipes, had been sprayed by the steam over the surrounding neighborhood.

GRAMERCY PARK WEST

1* Gramercy Park West

This townhouse was once the home of Dr. Valentine Mott, a famous surgeon during the Civil War, who helped to reorganize Bellevue Hospital.

2* Gramercy Park West

The wedding reception for ex-president Benjamin Harrison and his bride, Mrs. Mary Scott Dimmick, was held here at the home of Mr. Gifford Pinchot, America's first professional forester, on April 6, 1896. Mrs. Dimmick was the young widowed niece of Harrison's first wife.

3* Gramercy Park West

Actor John Garfield died of a heart attack in this home of a friend on May 21, 1952. Garfield was only thirty-nine years old.

4* Gramercy Park West

James Harper Sr. bought this house in 1847. Harper was the eldest of the four brothers who founded Harper and Brothers in 1817, now Harper and Row Publishers. He moved in with his second wife shortly after finishing a term as the sixty-fifth mayor of the city. The two iron street lamps still mark the home as a mayoral residence.

IRVING PLACE

22 Irving Place

Elihu Root, secretary of war and later secretary of state under President Theodore Roosevelt, lived on this site from 1871 until 1878.

24 Irving Place

The Italian patriot Guiseppe Garibaldi was a house guest of Michele Pastacaldi in August of 1850. He stayed at this address about two months before moving on to Staten Island, where he worked as a candlemaker. He became a naturalized citizen and stayed in the United States until 1854. Returning to Italy, he was instrumental in the unification of the country.

46 Irving Place

This was once the home of Helena Petrovna Blavatsky, an author and visionary who was instrumental in introducing Eastern religion and spiritual thinking into Western culture. It was here on the evening of September 8, 1875, that HPB, as she was often called, along with Henry Steel Olcott and William Q. Judge, founded the Theosophical Society.

55* Irving Place

Author O. Henry lived in this house from 1903 to 1907. Legend has it that it was here that the deadline-pressed O. Henry wrote the classic Christmas tale "The Gift of the Magi" in a three-hour drunken haze.

71* Irving Place

Norman Thomas, the socialist politician and thinker, lived here in 1945. His wife, Violet, owned the building and opened a tearoom here ten years before they moved upstairs. Thomas was the Socialist Party candidate for president of the United States in every election from 1928 to 1948.

LEXINGTON AVENUE

1 Lexington Avenue

Cyrus Field built and lived in a brownstone that once stood at this corner in 1851. Mr. Field was a financier who dedicated his life and fortune to laying the first submarine telegraph cable between America and Europe. Despite the loss of his personal fortune in the depression of 1857, he found the needed capital to complete the project in 1858. He was also instrumental in building the elevated railroad system in New York City in the late 1870s.

9 Lexington Avenue

One of the most influential figures in New York during the nineteenth century was Peter Cooper. His home stood on this site. He designed and built the first successful American steam locomotive, *Tom Thumb,* and produced the first steel rails. Because of his invention, he became very wealthy and used his fortune to improve the lives of working-class citizens. His greatest gift was the founding of Cooper Union for the Advancement of Science and Art. After he died here on April 4, 1883, his son-in-law Abram S. Hewitt and his family lived in the house. Hewitt, a reform mayor of New York City from 1887 to 1888 and U.S. representative, was instrumental in overthrowing the Tweed Ring's control of the city's government. He also spearheaded the fight for New York City's subway system.

Hewitt's daughters, Eleanor and Sarah, began collecting and storing examples of decorative arts in this house as teenagers. Their collection of lace, glass, buttons, drawings and prints, furniture, and countless forms of decoration and ornament became the core of the Cooper-Hewitt Museum. It was first displayed at their grandfather's Cooper Union and moved uptown to Andrew Carnegie's mansion in 1967.

Lexington Avenue and East 23rd Street, Southeast Corner

The Free Academy—One hundred and forty-nine teenage boys attended their first day of school here on January 29, 1849. Chartered by the state legislature just a year and a half earlier, this was the first municipal system created for higher education in the United States. The Free Academy, renamed the College of the City of New York in 1866, was the beginning of the City University of New York. In 1907 it moved to the main campus at West 138th Street.

68 Lexington Avenue

69th Regiment Armory*—The famous Armory Show, officially called the International Exhibition of Modern Art, opened here on February 17 and ran until March 15, 1913. Some 1,300 works of art were displayed in the great drill hall of this building. The best-known and most influential exhibition in the United States, it introduced a provincial American public to modern art. In addition to the impressionists, post-impressionists, Fauves, and cubists from Europe, half the show was made up of works by America's emerging modernists. Fueled by the popular

James Renwick Jr. designed the first home of the Free Academy at Lexington and East 23rd Street in 1848. Baruch College, part of the City University of New York (CUNY) system, now occupies the corner site. *(Author's collection)*

press, close to seventy thousand visitors came to view and judge the controversial works. Caricatured and praised, the most talked about painting of the show was Marcel Duchamp's cubist/futurist *Nude Descending a Staircase, No. 2.*

123* Lexington Avenue

Vice President Chester A. Arthur took the oath of office as president of the United States in this modest brownstone on September 20, 1881, at 2:00 A.M. upon learning of the death of President Garfield. The oath was administered by New York Supreme Court Justice John R. Brady. Other than George Washington, Arthur was the only president to take the oath in New York City. He later died at this house on November 18, 1886, a year after leaving Washington, D.C. Another famous resident of this house was William Randolph Hearst, from 1900 until 1903.

405 Lexington Avenue

Chrysler Building—Everyone's favorite Art Deco skyscraper was the tallest building in the world for a few months in late 1930 before the completion of the Empire State Building. But this 1,048-foot-high spire has another claim to fame: it was from here that the first color television broadcast in history was transmitted. CBS station W2XAB held a press preview for its high-definition, electronically scanned color broadcast on September 3, 1940.

480 Lexington Avenue

Grand Central Palace—No longer here, this hall was the site of the "First Annual Exhibition of the Society of Independent Artists," from April 10 to May 6, 1917. Organized by the avant-garde artists of the day, the show was championed as a challenge to the art establishment. Another challenge came in the form of a lecture on Modern Art by the colorful art critic and Dadaist Arthur Cravan. An hour late and totally drunk, Craven staggered to the podium to address an audience of wealthy and socially prominent ladies. Not long into his discourse, he started undressing and shouting obscenities and insults at the shocked art lovers. At this point the police ended his lecture and took him to the station. Later, this building served as the major New York City–area induction center for World War II draftees. It was torn down in the mid-1960s and replaced by the forty-seven-story office tower, 245 Park Avenue.

525 Lexington Avenue

Shelton Tower Hotel—The tallest hotel in the world when built, it was home to Alfred Stieglitz and Georgia O'Keeffe from 1925 to 1935. Their thirtieth-floor view

New York City was an important center in the invention of television. The circled antenna atop the Chrysler Building in 1940 identifies an important event in its history, the transmission of early color television signals. The Columbia Broadcast System used this antenna and a corresponding one on the north side of the roof to develop and refine color broadcasting. *(FPG)*

was subject matter for his photographs and her paintings. Another famous art couple also lived here in 1941, Peggy Guggenheim and Max Ernst.

New York Marriott East Side*—In a second-floor conference room of this hotel on November 5, 1990, Rabbi Meir Kahane was assassinated shortly after addressing a group of his supporters. The Brooklyn-born rabbi was the founder of the Jewish Defense League and a leader of a militant anti-Arab movement in Israel. El-Sayyid A. Nosair was acquitted of the murder charges but was convicted on a lesser charge and imprisoned. Several of Mr. Nosair's followers were later implicated in the 1993 World Trade Center bombing and terrorist plot to blow up the United Nations and the Holland and Lincoln Tunnels.

MADISON AVENUE

Madison Avenue and East 24th Street, Southeast Corner

Madison Square Presbyterian Church—Nicknamed "Dr. Parkhurst's Church" after its fiery minister, the Reverend Charles H. Parkhurst, this church was the scene of his blistering 1892 St. Valentine's Day sermon against citywide crime and police corruption. The city's Tammany Hall politicians denied his allegations, and the reverend was accused of making unsubstantiated accusations to a grand jury. At this point the good doctor, along with a detective, took it upon himself to make a personal excursion into the city's underworld. This unlikely duo visited the worst gambling dens, saloons, and brothels and learned of the police payoffs that kept them in business. Now armed with proof, Parkhurst reported back to his congregation and to the press. This time, his revelations resulted in another grand-jury investigation and the appointment of Theodore Roosevelt to the Board of Commissioners. The reverend's guide that night, the detective Charles W. Gardner, later wrote his account of the underworld visit, called *The Doctor and the Devil, or the Midnight Adventures of Dr. Parkhurst.*

Madison Avenue and East 26th Street

This southwest corner site was once the home of Leonard Jerome, the financier and society leader. He built his palatial six-story Second Empire–style mansion here in 1859. The huge second-floor ballroom was the scene of many of the era's most elegant parties. Around the corner on 26th Street, Jerome built a six-hundred-seat private theater for his guests. Jennie Jerome, his daughter who lived in this house from 1860 to 1867, married Randolph Churchill and was the mother of British Prime

Minister Winston Churchill. In 1868 it became the home of the Union League Club, which had been formed to help raise troops for the Union Army in the early years of the Civil War. The house was razed in 1967.

Madison Avenue between East 26th and East 27th Streets, East Side

Madison Square Garden—This lavish exhibition hall was erected on the site of the original terminal of the New York and Harlem Railroad, the Union Depot, and an even earlier version of a hall called Gilmore Gardens. Designed by Stanford White in 1890, the structure contained a huge amphitheater, two theaters, and a 332-foot tower topped with the scandalous nude statue *Diana* by Augustus Saint-Gaudens. It was on the roof garden cabaret on the night of June 25, 1906, that Stanford White was fatally shot by Harry K. Thaw, husband of showgirl Eve-

Two notable buildings of architect Stanford White are visible in this aerial view of Madison Square Park of about 1920. The Madison Square Presbyterian Church, the domed structure on the right, and Madison Square Garden, the tall tower in the center, have both been destroyed. *(FPG)*

Dubbed the "Horseless Horse Show," the nation's first automobile show took place in the second Madison Square Garden at Madison Avenue at East 26th Street. Thirty automobile manufacturers displayed their latest models in the huge amphitheater on November 3, 1900. *(FPG)*

lyn Nesbit, the architect's former mistress. Madison Square Garden was the site of the country's first auto show on November 3, 1900, and the Paterson Strike Pageant on June 7, 1913. The Democrats met here for their longest national convention on June 24, 1924, and stayed for seventeen days until they agreed on John W. Davis for president and Charles W. Bryan for vice president. As the hotels and restaurants moved uptown, the Garden, which was never very successful, had an even harder time attracting crowds and making a profit. The advent of legalized professional boxing in New York State helped extend the life of the complex until it was demolished in 1925 to build the current headquarters for The New York Life Insurance Company.

Madison Avenue and East 27th Street

Although there are many myths about the origins of baseball, it is well documented that New York City played an important role in the evolution of a child's ball game called rounders into organized baseball as early as the spring or summer of 1842. These first games, just as later baseball, were played on a diamond-shaped infield with two teams, one "at bat" and the other "in the field." A pioneer in the development of the "New York game," as it was called, was the Knickerbocker Base Ball Club, which played games in a lot near this intersection. The club was formally established on September 23, 1845, with twenty-eight young men who played the game "for health and recreation merely" but did set about improving and standardizing the rules. Their first organized game using the modern rules took place across the Hudson River at Elysian Fields in Hoboken, New Jersey, on June 19, 1846.

Madison Avenue and East 29th Street

In the early 1850s the Honeymoon Gang made this intersection a favorite site for their muggings. This gang, one of the city's most brutal, tyrannized the neighborhood. Hapless pedestrians were blatantly robbed until a new police precinct captain, George W. Walling, formed in 1853 the city's first Strong Arm Squad to drive gang members out of business.

219 Madison Avenue

The nation's most famous banker, John Pierpont Morgan, bought a brownstone at this site in 1882. An early financial backer of Thomas Edison, Morgan soon commissioned the inventor to install his new invention, electric lighting, in his home. In spite of some mishaps, Morgan was pleased, and this residence was the first in the world to be electrically lighted throughout. A specially built generator located in a cellar under his stable supplied the power. Morgan built his famous library to house his art and rare books, next door, on East 36th Street in 1906. After his death, his house was torn down in 1928 to build an extension for the library.

251 Madison Avenue

This address was the birthplace of writer Clarence Day on November 18, 1874. He also lived farther up the street at 420 Madison, where he described his childhood in his book *Life with Father*.

Pedestrians and reporters watching guests arrive at the old Ritz Carlton Hotel on Madison Avenue for Brenda Frazier's debutante party, the social event of 1938. Frazier and other society debutantes were well-publicized celebrities of the Depression. *(FPG)*

Madison Avenue between East 46th and East 47th Streets, West Side

Ritz-Carlton Hotel—This hotel, popular with New York society, was the location of "Castle House," a dancing school run by Vernon and Irene Castle in the years before World War I. The Castles, America's favorite dancing team, were the originators of the one-step and the Castle Walk. Two of Café Society's biggest coming-out parties were held here in the Depression-racked 1930s. "Poor Little Rich Girl" Barbara Hutton, granddaughter of dime-store king Frank Woolworth, had her $60,000 gala on December 21, 1930. Brenda Frazier, "Glamour Girl Number One," came out on December 27, 1938. The hotel that gave us the slang terms "ritzy" and "puttin' on the Ritz" was razed and passed into memory in 1957.

451 Madison Avenue

Villard Houses*—The Whitelaw Reid mansion was the site of an art show organized by exiled European artists for the benefit of French Relief. "First Papers of Surrealism" was held here from October 14 to November 7, 1942. The title of the show was an allusion to the first papers of immigrants to the United States. Marcel Duchamp, the designer of the show, used more than sixteen miles of string to create a giant web covering the galleries. He wanted "to force the viewer to involve himself with his surroundings."

485* Madison Avenue

Once called the Columbia Broadcasting Building, this was home to CBS from 1929 until 1965. On the top five floors were the early radio studios where Lowell Thomas, Edward R. Murrow, and Eric Sevareid broadcast the news and set the standards for broadcast journalism. It was also from here that Orson Welles broadcast his famous and frightening adaptation of H. G. Wells's *War of the Worlds* Halloween program on October 30, 1938. The show, which realistically "documented" a Martian invasion, provoked hundreds of calls to local police and radio stations. These same studios were also landmarks in the history of television, beginning with the inauguration of the first regular schedule of TV broadcasting in the country. These daily test broadcasts from 2:00 to 6:00 and from 8:00 to 11:00 P.M. on station W2XAB were largely without sound. The first of these telecasts was on July 21, 1931. It was hosted by Mayor Jimmy Walker and featured Kate Smith, George Gershwin, and the "Columbia Television Girl."

Madison Avenue and East 54th Street

Club Monte Carlo—On December 10, 1946, real-estate developer William Zeckendorf Sr. and his wife were celebrating their wedding anniversary. At 2:00 A.M. his party was interrupted by a visit from Wallace Harrison, his architect. Harrison had come to ask if Zeckendorf would sell a piece of property along the East River at East 42nd Street to John D. Rockefeller Jr., who in turn would give the land to the fledgling United Nations. The developer agreed to the $8.5 million deal on the spot. Four days later the U.N. General Assembly voted to accept the offer and stay in New York. This late-night negotiation and Rockefeller's generosity kept the U.N. in town.

625* Madison Avenue

Jacqueline Kennedy Onassis reported here at Viking Press for work in September of 1975. Not surprisingly, her foray into the workaday world as a consulting editor was a media circus. The former first lady's previous job was as the "Inquiring Camera Girl" in 1953.

647 Madison Avenue

This was the last home of William M. Tweed. On December 4, 1875, while on a furlough from jail to visit his sick wife, he escaped from his guard. He slipped out the front door of this house after dark. The disgraced former political boss fled to Cuba and then sailed for Spain, where he was arrested upon arrival the following

September. The fugitive was identified by means of one of his old nemesis Thomas Nast's political cartoons from *Harper's Weekly*. He was extradited to the United States the following year.

MADISON SQUARE PARK

As was often the case with New York City parks, this land was first used as a potter's field. In 1807 the U.S. Arsenal was built to defend the city at this strategic junction of the Eastern Post Road and Bloomingdale Road—now Broadway. By 1824 the arsenal was converted into the "House of Refuge of the Society for the Reformation of Juvenile Delinquents," the nation's first institution for delinquent children that separated them from adult criminals. Named in honor of President James Madison, the park was opened in the 1840s. On November 11, 1877, the forty-two-foot-high right arm of the *Statue of Liberty* holding her torch was forlornly planted here, where it remained for seven years as a scheme to help raise money for the pedestal in the harbor.

PARK AVENUE

Park Avenue between East 32nd and East 33rd Streets, West Side

"The Woman's Home"—Opened on April 2, 1878, this lavish hotel was built with funds bequeathed by the late merchant prince A. T. Stewart as a social experiment. It was intended to provide a supervised, wholesome environment for the new emerging class of urban female workers. The strict house rules did not permit gentlemen visitors, pets, sewing machines, pianos, or personal memorabilia. The home closed after only two months; it proved to be too expensive and too restrictive even for Victorian women of the times. It reopened shortly as the Park Avenue Hotel and supplied rooms for both sexes. The hotel was torn down in 1927 for the present office building.

91 Park Avenue

This address was once the home of Andrew Haswell Green, who was called the "Father of Greater New York" because of his work on the commission to consolidate the city's boroughs in the 1890s. Green, a city comptroller, was also a major force in establishing Central Park, the Metropolitan Museum of Art, and the New York Public Library. He was shot three times and killed by an insane man here on the sidewalk on November 13, 1903. The killer and his victim did not know each other.

112 Park Avenue

Murray Hill Hotel—Now gone, the hotel that stood at this address for sixty-three years was popular with Presidents Grover Cleveland and William McKinley. The red brick pile also served as national election headquarters for two losing candidates for the presidency: James Blaine in the 1884 campaign and Alfred Landon in the 1936 campaign.

The Park Avenue Hotel at East 32nd Street rises above its rustic neighbors in this photograph from about 1890. *(Author's collection)*

Dwarfed by the cavernous tunnel, two workers pose during the construction of the subway about 1910. Both on railroad tracks, the small railroad car, left, was used to remove rubble dug out by the huge shovel, right. *(FPG)*

Park Avenue and East 41st Street

On January 27, 1902, the roar of the city was humbled by a blast the equivalent of several bombs at the construction site for the new subway stop at this intersection. Moses Epps, a workman for the subway, had foolishly lit a candle to warm his hands, within a few feet of 548 pounds of dynamite. The dynamite, used to help dig the tunnels, exploded with a thunderous blast. The blast blew out the clocks in Grand Central Station and shattered glass for blocks. Epps managed to survive with just a few scratches, but 5 people died and 180 were injured. Most of those injured were guests at the Murrary Hill Hotel.

200* Park Avenue

Pan Am Building—The fifty-nine-story rooftop heliport was the site of a tragic accident on May 16, 1977. An idling helicopter keeled over, killing four people on the landing pad and a woman walking on Madison Avenue, who was hit by a piece of the rotor blade. The building was renamed by the new owners, The Metropolitan Life Insurance Company, after the airline went out of business.

301 Park Avenue

Waldorf-Astoria Hotel*—This second address of the famous hotel was once the site of the Women's Hospital, a 150-bed institution opened just after the Civil War. When the hotel opened on September 30, 1931, the first meal was served to the king of Siam. The first Tony Awards ceremony took place in the Grand Ballroom on Easter Sunday, April 6, 1947. The awards, presented by the American Theater Wing, were created to recognize distinguished achievements in the American theater. Among those first winners were Helen Hays, José Ferrer, and Fredric March. The hotel has been host to every U.S. president since Franklin D. Roosevelt, who arrived by private railroad car on the tracks buried beneath Park Avenue. The hotel was the meeting place between President Lyndon Johnson and the first pope to travel to America, Pope Paul VI, on October 4, 1965.

Park Avenue between East 50th and 51st Streets

Saint Bartholomew's Church*—Beginning in 1983, this church was the focus of a protracted legal battle over whether owners of landmarked property could overturn their protected status in the face of financial hardship. The church wanted to demolish their community house and sell the land to an office developer. Refused twice by the Landmarks Preservation Commission, the case reached the U.S. Supreme Court, which upheld the commission's denial in March of 1991.

390 Park Avenue

Lever House*—Completed in 1952, this international-style skyscraper was the first building to break the "street wall" of Park Avenue. The Lever House marked the transformation of the avenue as a residential block to the premier address for postwar corporate America. Sleek, airy, and dramatic, this building presented a striking contrast to its old-fashioned stone neighbors. Threatened with the wrecker's ball, it was saved just in time when it became eligible for landmark status on its thirtieth birthday. It was designated an official landmark on November 9, 1982.

Park Avenue and East 56th Street

The railroad tunnel leading to Grand Central Terminal beneath this intersection was the scene of one of the city's worst train accidents. At 8:20 A.M. on January 8, 1902, a commuter train's steam engine rammed into the last car of another standing commuter train. The crash, which killed fifteen passengers on the standing train, was the result of poor visibility in the tunnel, which was filled with steam,

Before it was covered over and renamed Park Avenue, this was the view of the exposed Fourth Avenue railroad tracks north of the old Grand Central Depot at West 42nd Street. After the current Grand Central Station was built in 1912 and the underground trains were electrified, Park Avenue was transformed into one of the city's most prestigious addresses. *(Author's collection)*

fog, and smoke. The accident prompted legislation prohibiting steam-powered trains on the island of Manhattan, which led to the exclusive use of cleaner electric locomotives. Without the soot and fumes, Park Avenue developed into a very desirable residential district, lined with apartment houses for the wealthy. Since World War II office buildings have replaced all but one apartment house below 59th Street.

450 Park Avenue

Jerome Kern collapsed on the sidewalk at this address at noon on November 5, 1945, the victim of a cerebral hemorrhage. The composer of "Ol' Man River" died six days later at Doctor's Hospital.

PARK AVENUE SOUTH

201 Park Avenue South

*Guardian Life Building**—Theodore Dreiser rented an office in this office tower to finish his novel *An American Tragedy* in 1925.

213* Park Avenue South

Max's Kansas City—This building once housed a bar and restaurant that was a hangout for Andy Warhol and his "mod" entourage in 1966. The back room became a meeting place for his rock band, "The Velvet Underground," and his underground-movie-star and artist friends. Patti Smith, Bruce Springsteen, and the band Devo also performed here.

Park Avenue South and East 18th Street, Southeast Corner

Clarendon Hotel—This hotel, now gone, was the site of a meeting in March of 1854 of Cyrus Field, Peter Cooper, and other investors to raise money for the transatlantic underwater telegraph cable. In 1871 Grand Duke Alexis Aleksandrovich of Russia, the first member of the czar's family to visit the United States, was a guest here. The grand duke had stopped in New York on his way to hunt bison on the frontier.

Park Avenue South and East 19th Street, Southwest Corner

Parker Building*—In 1907 Lee De Forest, a pioneer and inventor in the field of early radio, began fairly regular radio broadcasts from his top-floor laboratory. De Forest promoted and expanded the idea of public broadcasting.

287 Park Avenue South, Northeast Corner of East 22nd Street

United Charities Building*—In hopes of improving race relations, the National Negro Conference and W. E. B. Du Bois's Niagara Movement Group met here on May 31, 1909. They joined together to form the National Association for the Advancement of Colored People (NAACP), in this the year of the one hundredth anniversary of the birth of Abraham Lincoln. The conference passed resolutions calling for equal civil, political, and educational rights and demanded the enforcement of the Fourteenth and Fifteenth Amendments to the Constitution.

Park Avenue South and East 26th Street, Southeast Corner*

Now a cooperative apartment complex, these three nineteenth-century buildings were once the headquarters of Louis Comfort Tiffany. Tiffany, the son of the jewelry founder, was a master of late-nineteenth-century design. His firm designed and manufactured his opulent stained-glass windows, mosaics, and glasswork here from 1881 to 1905.

Park Avenue South and East 28th Street

28th Street IRT Subway Station*—On opening day of the new subway, October 27, 1904, Henry Barrett entered this station and rode on one of the first trains. Shortly into his ride, he looked down and realized his $500 diamond horseshoe stickpin was missing. Mr. Barrett became the first recorded subway-crime victim.

ROCKEFELLER PLAZA

30 Rockefeller Plaza

RCA Building*—The focal point of Rockefeller Center and its highest building is the seventy-story RCA Building, home of the National Broadcasting Company. This art-deco landmark was home to many milestones in the history of radio and television. Arturo Toscanini and the NBC Symphony Orchestra radio broadcasts originated from studio 8-H on Christmas Day, 1937. Early television broadcasting began from studio 3-H in 1935. Studio 6-B, beginning on September 21, 1948, was home to Milton Berle's *Texaco Star Theater,* the media's first smash hit. As the show's popularity skyrocketed, so did the sales of television sets. When his comedy variety show first aired, there were about five hundred thousand sets in the country; within two years, the number reached six million.

The studio for the show *Twenty-One,* the focal point of the quiz-show scandals and a low point in the history of television, was also located here. On the December 5, 1956, show, contestant professor Charles Van Doren beat Herbert Stempel. This show, watched by millions, set in motion the public's eventual realization that this extremely popular quiz program and others had been rigged by supplying the contestants with the correct answers.

The famous Christmas trees out front in the plaza predate the completed complex. The first one, in 1931, was put up and decorated by construction workers grateful to have a job in the Depression.

50 Rockefeller Plaza

Associated Press Building*—Antiwar and civil-rights activist Allard K. Lowenstein was shot at his law office in this building on March 14, 1980. Lowenstein, a former one-term U.S. representative from Long Island, was shot by a long-time acquaintance, Dennis Sweeney, who was deemed mentally ill. Lowenstein died later that evening at St. Clair's Hospital.

On December 10, 1991, Terry Anderson, the Associated Press's chief Middle East correspondent and America's longest-held hostage, returned home for a sentimental visit. A quick tour to the fourth-floor newsroom was a highlight of Anderson's first day back in the United States. Showered with yellow rose petals from his emotional colleagues, the understandably crowd-shy Anderson had been given a hero's welcome from the time of his arrival at Kennedy Airport earlier in the day. The last of America's eighteen hostages held in the Middle East, he was released after 2,455 days, almost seven years, in captivity.

RUTHERFORD PLACE

Rutherford Place and East 16th Street, Northwest Corner

St. George's Church*—Nicknamed "Morgan's Church," this church built with contributions from financier John Pierpont Morgan was the site of his funeral on April 14, 1913. He had been a member of the vestry since 1868. His son John Pierpont Morgan Jr. escaped an assassination attempt here on Sunday, April 18, 1920. Thomas W. Simpkin, an escaped mental patient, missed Morgan but shot Dr. James Markoe, who was the Morgans' family friend and physician. The doctor had treated

Milton Berle, affectionately known as "Uncle Miltie," was television's first star. His Tuesday night Texaco Star Theater show, broadcast from 30 Rockefeller Plaza, was the model for later comedy/variety programs. *(FPG)*

Morgan the elder when he himself was the victim of an earlier assassination attempt. The dying Markoe was rushed to the Lying-In Hospital across the park. The hospital, built by Morgan at Dr. Markoe's urging, was where the doctor died.

SUTTON PLACE

3* Sutton Place
The Official Residence of the Secretary General of the United Nations—This house was once the home of Anne Morgan, a society maverick and daughter of John Pierpont Morgan. She helped establish this wealthy enclave in the 1930s when the only proper home for the rich was either Park or Fifth Avenues.

13* Sutton Place
Seventy-seven-year-old Elizabeth Marbury died here in her home of a heart attack on January 22, 1933. The unconventional Miss Marbury, who was the American literary agent for Oscar Wilde and George Bernard Shaw, was also the lesbian lover of Elsie de Wolfe, a society trendsetter and a National Democratic Committeewoman.

SUTTON PLACE SOUTH

1* Sutton Place South
The penthouse of this seventeen-story apartment house was the rented home of oil billionaire Jean Paul Getty from 1936 until 1942.

25 Sutton Place South
This was the home of Robert Sherwood, the noted playwright and author who won four Pulitzer Prizes. He lived here from 1937 until his death in 1955.

SUTTON SQUARE

14* Sutton Square
Robert Henri, the artist, moved into this four-story house after he returned from Europe in 1900. The river views from these windows became the subject of several of his paintings.

UNION SQUARE EAST

18 Union Square East

Union Square Hotel—Henry George, the economist who formulated the single-tax theory, died on October 29, 1897, at the hotel that used to stand at this address. He was campaigning for the office of mayor of New York City at the time.

Union Square East between East 15th and East 16th Streets

On August 28, 1991, at ten minutes after midnight, the tunnel under this block became the horrifying scene of the subway system's worst accident in sixty-three years. The crash occurred two hundred feet north of Union Square Station when the drunken motorman Robert E. Ray fell asleep and rammed the speeding train into a dozen steel beams supporting the tunnel. The accident killed five riders and injured two hundred others. It took six days to remove the wreckage of the train and repair the damaged station. Mass transit was in chaos as thousands of commuters were unable to use Manhattan's only East Side subway. The accident focused attention on safety advocates' calls for drug and alcohol testing for transportation workers.

Union Square East and East 17th Street, Southeast Corner

Westmoreland Apartments—The uncompromising abolitionist and publisher of the *Liberator* for thirty-five years, William Lloyd Garrison, died here at the home of his daughter on May 24, 1879.

UNION SQUARE PARK

At what was then just a crossing of two country roads, Gen. George Washington assembled a military unit and a committee of citizens to accompany him on his march into the city to take formal possession of New York from the British after the Revolutionary War. The equestrian statue of Washington, now near the center of the park, used to stand on the small traffic island at the intersection of Fourth Avenue and 14th Street. This was said to be the exact spot where grateful New Yorkers welcomed Washington. That date, November 25, 1783, later called Evacuation Day, was annually observed as a major city holiday well into the twentieth century.

Laid out as a residential square in 1831, the park became the focal point of the emerging theatrical district after the Academy of Music opened in 1854. The park became the place to mark the triumphs and tragedies of the Civil War. On April 20, 1861, the first huge rally to support the Union cause was held shortly after the bombing of Fort Sumter. Almost four years to the day, on April 25, 1865, it was the site of President Abraham Lincoln's funeral. He was assassinated just three days after the war ended.

The park continued to be a popular location for rallies and protests, particularly labor demonstrations, well into the 1940s. On August 22, 1927, five thousand people converged on the square to demonstrate and keep vigil until the time of Sacco and Vanzetti's execution. The immigrant pair were put to death after what most agreed was an unfair trial.

It is fitting that Union Square is linked with the formation of another holiday, this one commemorating America's work force. On September 5, 1882, the park was the final destination of ten thousand marchers who left City Hall on what

This orderly procession around Union Square Park on September 5, 1882, marked the nation's first Labor Day celebration. Originator of the holiday, Peter J. McGuire envisioned a parade to "show the strength and esprit de corps of the trade and labor organizations." *(Frank Leslie's, September 16, 1882)*

would be known as the country's first observation of Labor Day, twelve years before Congress made it a national holiday in 1894. Peter J. Maguire, founder of the new Brotherhood of Carpenters and Joiners, devised and promoted the idea of the holiday to acknowledge the contributions of the American worker.

UNION SQUARE WEST

33* Union Square West
Artist Andy Warhol moved his "factory" to the sixth floor of this building in early 1968. It was here on June 3, 1968, that he was shot by Valerie Solanis, the founder and sole member of S.C.U.M. (Society for Cutting Up Men). A disgruntled hanger-on, Solanis had wanted Warhol to film a screenplay of hers. Warhol survived the attack but became even more remote and lost his interest in making movies.

FIRST AVENUE

First Avenue and East 18th Street
Meyer London, three-term congressman from New York, was struck by an automobile while crossing First Avenue on the afternoon of June 6, 1926. London, a founder of the Socialist Party in America, died later that day at Bellevue Hospital.

First Avenue between West 42nd and West 48th Streets
United Nations Headquarters*—Even before the U.N. had its permanent headquarters along the East River, delegates were already meeting at several locations around the city to plan the development of the new international organization. John D. Rockefeller Jr. donated the First Avenue site to help keep the organization from moving to either San Francisco or Philadelphia. For the last half of the twentieth century leaders from every nation have used the United Nations as a stage to capture the world's attention. And none more colorful than Soviet Premier Nikita Khrushchev, who gave his shoe-thumping tirade in September of 1960. Issues concerning diplomacy and egos were compounded during the visit of more than two hundred world leaders on October 24, 1995, to celebrate the organization's fiftieth birthday.

The United Nations General Assembly meets to commemorate the organization's fourth anniversary and to dedicate the cornerstone for their permanent headquarters at First Avenue and 42nd Street. President Harry S. Truman, on the podium, addresses the assembled diplomats on October 24, 1949. *(United Nations)*

SECOND AVENUE

231 Second Avenue

This address was the birthplace of Maxwell Perkins, legendary editor at Charles Scribner's Sons, on September 20, 1884. He worked with the writers F. Scott Fitzgerald, Ernest Hemingway, and Thomas Wolfe.

Second Avenue and East 18th Street, Southeast Corner

William Makepeace Thackeray spent time here at the brownstone home of the George Baxter family while visiting New York in late 1852. Mr. Baxter had attended one of the writer's lectures and invited him home. They formed a life-long friendship. Thackeray was very taken with Baxter's beautiful daughter Sally.

THIRD AVENUE

Third Avenue and East 46th Street, Northeast Corner

U.S. Provost Marshal's Office—The infamous New York City Draft Riots began on this spot when a mob burned down this building on July 13, 1863. Two days earlier on Saturday, the first names in the military draft lottery had been chosen under Congress's recent Conscription Act ordering compulsory military service in the Union Army during the Civil War. The draft was especially unpopular with the working class and Irish immigrants who were indignant over the stipulation that a $300 payment or the procurement of a substitute enabled the wealthy to escape service. The riot spread from this corner and engulfed much of the city. The violence and destruction lasted for three days. President Lincoln ordered Union troops back from the recent engagement at Gettysburg to quell the anarchy. The number of dead has never been known exactly, but it has been estimated that the number of killed and wounded reached over a thousand. Known abolitionists and African Americans were the preferred targets. As many as seventy African Americans were lynched or otherwise viciously murdered.

The Civil War draft lottery began on July 11, 1863, at the Provost Marshal's office on Third Avenue and East 46th Street. This site was the flash point for the worst riot in New York City history. The first American conscripted into the Union Army was New Yorker William Jones. *(Author's collection)*

922* Third Avenue

Clancy's Bar—On June 25, 1983, federal agents captured Joseph "Joe" Patrick Thomas Doherty while he was tending bar here. Doherty, a one-time Irish Republican Army guerrilla, was wanted in Britain for his part in killing a British soldier in Belfast in 1980. He escaped from a British prison while on trial and fled to New York. Doherty and his eight-year legal struggle in this country to prevent his extradition to Britain had become a cause célèbre for opponents to British rule of Northern Ireland. After a U.S. Supreme Court ruling, he was eventually deported on February 19, 1992, and returned to Britain.

938 Third Avenue

This address was the first home of Bloomingdale's Department Store. On opening day in April of 1872, the sales total was a paltry $3.68.

FIFTH AVENUE

Fifth Avenue and East 14th Street, Northeast Corner

On February 20, 1861, President-elect Abraham Lincoln had a breakfast meeting here at the home of Moses Hicks Grinnell, a Republican supporter, with one hundred prosperous merchants. This same house became the third home of Delmonico's restaurant. The Sorosis Club, the first organized women's club, held its first official meeting on April 20, 1868, in a private dining room here. The club's founders included Phoebe Cary, Ann Lynch Botta, and Jenny June. Famous banquets were held for S. F. Morse in honor of his inventing the telegraph, Grand Duke Alexis Aleksandrovich of Russia, and Charles Dickens.

79 Fifth Avenue

This address was once the home of Mayor George Opdyke. During the four days of the Draft Riots in July of 1863, his house was attacked twice. The house was saved, the first time, by about fifty neighbors who helped turn back a mob intent on burning it down. The second time, the city police kept the rioters at bay.

Fifth Avenue and West 15th Street, Northwest Corner

Carlo Tresca, radical writer and leader, was assassinated on this corner on January 11, 1943, at 9:40 P.M. in the darkness of the wartime blackout. He had just left the offices at 96 Fifth Avenue of the Italian anti-Fascist newspaper *Il Martello* ("The

Hammer") where he was the editor. Tresca, a friend of Mayor La Guardia, had many enemies across the political spectrum. His killer was never captured.

Fifth Avenue and East 16th Street, Northeast Corner

The home of Levi Parson Morton once stood at this corner. Morton, who was a New York congressman and New York governor, lived here for three years until he was elected vice president under President Benjamin Harrison and moved to Washington, D.C., in 1889.

Fifth Avenue and East 18th Street, Northeast Corner

August Belmont's elegant mansion and art gallery stood on this corner site in the second half of the nineteenth century. This house was the first in the city to have a private ballroom. Belmont, a society leader, was a leading financier in the development of the subways.

110 Fifth Avenue

Judge Building*—This lovingly restored structure was designed by McKim, Mead and White in 1888 as the offices for *Frank Leslie's Illustrated Newspapers* and *Judge,* a nineteenth-century humor magazine.

130 Fifth Avenue

Chickering Hall—An auditorium, named for the piano makers, was once at this site. It was here on May 17, 1877, that Alexander Graham Bell made the first interstate telephone call over telegraph wires to Thomas Watson in New Brunswick, New Jersey. The attentive listeners heard Watson not only speak but also sing. On January 9, 1882, Oscar Wilde gave his first American lecture titled "The English Renaissance" to a sold-out, standing-room audience. Another Englishman, Matthew Arnold, made his debut at this hall a year later. In addition to writers, Chickering was also a showplace for music: the Russian pianist Vladimir de Pachmann performed for his first American audience here.

149 Fifth Avenue

Lotos Club—A reception was given here in honor of the newly arrived team of Gilbert and Sullivan, the composers of light opera, on November 8, 1879. Somewhat later, this club held a dinner for Henry Morton Stanley in honor of his successful search for Dr. David Livingstone in Africa.

160 Fifth Avenue

*Mohawk Building**—The offices of the architectural firm of McKim, Mead and White were on the fifth floor of this building from 1895 until 1913. The firm at this time was at the height of its influence in American architecture. The partners had been a driving force in the design of the Columbian Exposition of 1893. This exposition, held in Chicago, established the neoclassical as the only "proper" style for architecture for the next forty years.

162 Fifth Avenue

Union Club—The front steps of this club served as the stage for James Gordon Bennett Jr.'s fall from grace from New York society on January 2, 1877. Bennett, heir of the founder and editor of the New York *Herald* James Bennett Sr., was, like his father, a brilliant newspaperman. He was a great sportsman and a celebrated drunk. He had appeared to be on the road to reform after he fell in love and became engaged to the socialite Caroline May, but he regressed and embarrassed his future in-laws by publicly urinating in their fireplace at a New Year's Day reception. The next day, at high noon, Caroline's brother Frederick horsewhipped Bennett here at the Union Club. Bennett challenged the other man to a duel, but no one was injured. This scandal destroyed Bennett's reputation, and he left the country for France, where he established the *Paris Herald.*

Fifth Avenue between East 22nd Street and East 23rd Street

St. Germain Hotel—The first flicker of the Great White Way can be traced to an early electric sign on the Madison Square Park side of this hotel in July of 1892. It was a manually synchronized flashing sign in blue, green, red, and frosted white lights. The sole function of this primitive spectacle was an advertisement for new homes at Manhattan Beach on Long Island. This same block would become home to the Flatiron Building.

*Flatiron Building**—Even before the innovative steel cage frame had reached the full twenty-one stories, many New Yorkers were convinced that a strong wind would bring down this early skyscraper. Their fears and jokes about the high-rise were tragically reinforced by a real-life accident only a year after the building was completed. On the evening of February 5, 1903, a powerful wind from a thunderstorm blew John McTaggart into Fifth Avenue, where he was run over by an automobile. The fourteen-year-old messenger from Brooklyn was on his third attempt to round the corner of the building when he was swept up by the powerful blast. He died that night of internal bleeding.

Fifth Avenue and 23rd Street

On April 19, 1866, at this intersection, Henry Bergh reprimanded and threatened to arrest a wagon driver for beating his exhausted horse. Bergh, the guiding spirit of the Society for the Prevention of Cruelty to Animals, informed the man that a new law, which he fathered and which had passed earlier that day in the state legislature, now prohibited cruelty to animals. He was also instrumental in establishing the Society for the Prevention of Cruelty to Children in 1875.

200 Fifth Avenue, between West 23rd Street and West 24th Street

Franconi's Hippodrome—This corner was the site of the Hippodrome, a huge two-story brick amphitheater with a tented roof, that had replaced a long-popular tavern called Madison Cottage. The highly publicized arena opened on May 2, 1853, to the largest crowd yet gathered in the city. In spite of rather daring and innovative performances, including chariot races and gladiatorial contests, among other fare, the arena was a complete financial failure and was abandoned within two years.

Fifth Avenue Hotel—This hotel, the next structure on the site, opened on August 23, 1859. It was famous for its early elevator, described as a "perpendicular railway intersecting each story," and as a gathering place for political power brokers of the era. Plans for making Ulysses S. Grant president were conceived here. The hotel dining room was the setting for an infamous Republican campaign dinner for James Blaine on October 30, 1884. A partisan speaker described the Democrats as the party of "rum, Romanism, and rebellion." Candidate Blaine's failure to disavow this insult cost

The Fuller Building, aptly nicknamed the Flatiron, during construction on Broadway at 23rd Street in 1902. Like an elegant ship sailing uptown, the Flatiron was a favorite subject of photographers Edward Steichen and Alfred Stieglitz. *(Collection of the New-York Historical Society)*

For much of the nineteenth century, the Fifth Avenue Hotel was the most fashionable hotel in New York. Located on the northwest corner of Fifth Avenue and West 23rd Street, it was in the heart of the entertainment district centered on Madison Square Park. *(Harper's Weekly, October 1, 1859)*

him needed Irish votes in the city. Five days later, the Democrat, Grover Cleveland, carried New York State and won the election.

Toy Center*—The current office building replaced the hotel in 1909. It was in a fifth-floor showroom of Mattel Toys that the first "fashion doll" Barbie was introduced to the world during the Annual Toy Fair on March 9, 1959. Ruth Handler, whose husband, Elliott, had started Mattel, created Barbie, naming her after their daughter Barbara. Still popular forthy years later, Barbie had sales of more than 172,000 last year.

Fifth Avenue between 24th Street and 25th Street

A massive wood-and-plaster triumphal arch once spanned Fifth Avenue at this spot. The arch was built to commemorate Adm. George Dewey's victory over the Spanish fleet in Manila Bay during the Spanish-American War. On September 30, 1899, the returning hero was received with a huge procession that passed beneath this arch. Another tribute from the city was a sign hung from the Brooklyn Bridge, written out in electric lights, "Welcome Dewey." Dewey's fame was almost as short lived as his decisive naval victory. Within a few months, as the full-scale model arch began to crumble, plans for a permanent marble version were abandoned due to a lack of interest and donations.

Topped with a statue of Victory, this was the Dewey Arch that stood at Fifth Avenue at West 24th Street in 1899. A national hero on his return from the Spanish-American War, Admiral George Dewey was so popular that there was talk of his running for president of the United States. These aspirations were quickly dismissed after several embarrassing statements by the admiral. *(FPG)*

Fifth Avenue and West 24th Street

On May 15, 1920, at the annual Police Parade, dignitaries and honored guests seated on a reviewing platform, here at this traffic island shared with the Worth Monument, were embarrassed by an interloper in their parade. Waving to assembled leaders of New York's finest was Nicky Arnstein, a small-time gambler and wanted fugitive. He was also the husband of Fanny Brice, the comedian and

Ziegfeld Follies star, who was with him during his surprise appearance. The couple and their lawyer had joined the parade and drove past on their way downtown to surrender to the assistant district attorney. Arnstein had disappeared three months earlier and was wanted for his part in a plot to steal Wall Street bonds. He was later convicted and sent to jail. Fanny, after much soul-searching, divorced him.

Fifth Avenue and West 27th Street, Southwest Corner

Victoria Hotel—This hotel was the New York home of President Grover Cleveland during his terms in the White House. In August of 1909 Carry Nation, the hatchet-wielding temperance and moral leader, brought her crusade to the city. Shortly after registering here as "Carry Nation, your loving home defender, Kansas," she demanded the hotel remove a nude statue of Diana in the lobby. The management responded by placing some cheesecloth over the "offensive" statue.

237 Fifth Avenue

This house was the first home, in 1892, of the Macbeth Gallery, one of the earliest galleries dealing solely with American art. The top floor was the studio of painter Arthur B. Davies, an artist represented by William Macbeth.

Fifth Avenue and 28th Street

Underworld crime figure Louis "Lepke" Buchalter surrendered to FBI Chief J. Edgar Hoover and columnist Walter Winchell in a parked car at this intersection on August 24, 1939. "Lepke," the head of Murder, Inc., the syndicate's professional hit squad, was wanted on narcotic charges. He believed he would get more lenient treatment from the federal authorities than from the Manhattan DA Thomas E. Dewey, who was also looking for him. As it turned out, he was convicted on federal narcotic charges, and then in a later trial Dewey won another conviction on murder charges. "Lepke" was executed in the electric chair on March 4, 1944.

Fifth Avenue and West 29th Street, Northwest Corner

Marble Collegiate Church*—On August 20, 1918, opera tenor Enrico Caruso married his American bride, Dorothy Benjamin, here. This church later became the pulpit for the influential Rev. Dr. Norman Vincent Peale in 1932 until his retirement more than fifty years later. It was here that he refined and preached his message that a proper state of mind, induced by simple prayer, could produce spiritual and material success on earth, ideas he presented in his best-selling book *The Power of Positive Thinking*. Richard Nixon was a member of this congregation and a follower of Dr. Peale. The reverend officiated at the wedding, here, of President-elect Nixon's daughter Julie and Dwight David Eisenhower II, only grandson of President Eisenhower, on December 22, 1968.

Fifth Avenue and West 30th Street, Southwest Corner

Holland House—Thomas Gainsborough's masterpiece *The Duchess of Devonshire,* the most famous stolen painting of its time, spent the night of March 29, 1901, at this hotel before returning to England and its rightful owners. The painting, recovered the day before, had been stolen by American-born Adam Worth in London in 1876. Worth was the greatest criminal mastermind of the nineteenth century and the prototype for the villain Professor Moriarty in the Sherlock Holmes mysteries. Frustrated in negotiations to ransom the painting, Worth kept it for more than twenty-five years, often carrying it in the false bottom of his luggage or rolled up in an umbrella.

291 and 293 Fifth Avenue

The Little Galleries of the Photo-Secession—Both these addresses served as an innovative art and photography gallery founded by Alfred Stieglitz and Edward J. Steichen in 1905. Henri Mattisse was first shown in American in 1908 at "291," as the gallery was later named: so were Henri Rousseau and Paul Cézanne in 1910, and Pablo Picasso in 1911. The Photo-Secession, a group of avant-garde photographers, was exhibited here. It was also the headquarters for *Camera Work,* the journal founded by Stieglitz to showcase the new photography.

322 Fifth Avenue

Hudson River School painter Albert Bierstadt died here at his home on February 18, 1902.

Fifth Avenue between West 33rd Street and West 34th Street

On the southwest corner of Fifth Avenue and West 34th Street was the mansion of the Mrs. William Astor, the leading society hostess of the Gilded Age. It was here at her annual party in the ballroom where Caroline Astor presided over New York society. Shortly before the ball in 1892, her publicist Ward McAllister released to the press the list of the invited guests, the celebrated "Four Hundred." This privileged clique took up the physical capacity of Mrs. Astor's ballroom. Next door to the south her nephew William Waldorf Astor tore down his mansion in 1893 to build an eleven-story hotel, the Waldorf.

Waldorf-Astoria Hotel—By this time Mrs. Astor decided to move uptown, and her mansion was torn down for a connecting hotel, the Astoria. The new hyphenated hotel, the Waldorf-Astoria, became an instant landmark. It was here at the hotel's inaugural dinner in 1896 that chop suey, unknown in China at the time, was invented in honor of the visiting Chinese ambassador. The Waldorf-Astoria was also the site of another famous society party, the Bradley Martin costume charity ball, reputed to be the most expensive party of modern times, held on the evening of February 10, 1897. Mrs. Martin, whose jewels were valued at more than $60,000, was dressed as Mary Queen of Scots and her husband as Louis XV. The newspapers ridiculed and satirized the extravaganza as wasteful. The hotel was the site of the National Broadcasting Company's first radio broadcast on November 15, 1926. More than two million listeners in twenty-one cities over twenty-five stations heard this historic broadcast. This was the beginning of the concept of a radio network.

Empire State Building*—The hotel gave way to the world's tallest building in 1931. A grand monument to capitalist optimism in the face of the Great

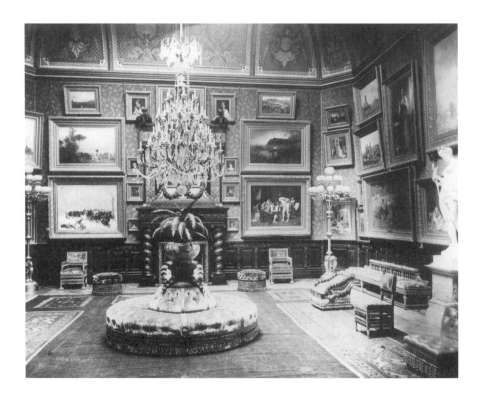

When the Victorian clutter was removed, this ballroom in William B. Astor's Fifth Avenue mansion reputedly held only the "400" of the city's social aristocracy. Mrs. Astor's ballroom was photographed about 1887. *(Collection of the New-York Historical Society)*

Depression, it was topped off with a mooring mast for the latest in air travel, dirigibles. But only one blimp ever docked, on September 16, 1931, before the idea was given up as too dangerous. The office tower was later the scene of a tragic air accident on the foggy morning of July 28, 1945. A B-25 Mitchell bomber crashed into the seventy-ninth floor on the 34th Street side. The pilot, Lt. Col. William F. Smith, his two passengers, and eight people inside the building all died.

Fifth Avenue and West 37th Street, Northwest Corner

Brick Presbyterian Church—The funeral for Mark Twain was held at this church on April 23, 1910. The beloved humorist and author spent some of the last years of his life in the city. His body was then taken to Elmira, New York, for burial.

438 Fifth Avenue

Master showman P. T. Barnum bought this house in 1868 and lived here into the next decade.

Fifth Avenue and East 39th Street, Northeast Corner

Dickel's Riding Academy—On a trip to England, Gordon Bennett Jr., the newspaper publisher, attended several polo games. Upon his return to New York, he arranged for an indoor version of the game to be played here in 1876. This was the first recorded polo game played in America and perhaps the first polo match to be played indoors. The game was a hit with Gordon and his wealthy circle. They continued to play indoors and within a few years moved their matches uptown and outside to what became known as the Polo Grounds north of Central Park. The academy lasted another three years before it was torn down to make way for the Union League Club building.

450 Fifth Avenue

Macbeth Gallery—The exhibition of "The Eight," including the painters John Sloan, Robert Henri, and Maurice Prendergast, opened on February 3, 1908, competing with the prestigious but stodgy National Academy of Design's spring show. Panned by the critics and later called the "Ash-can School," these artists painted bold and realistic portrayals of urban life. Despite the reservations of the art establishment, several works were sold and the show drew in large crowds.

Fifth Avenue between West 40th Street and West 42nd Street

Croton Reservoir—A turning point in the physical development of the city, this

Dressed in their Easter Sunday finery, these strollers are walking on Fifth Avenue at 40th Street. The Croton Reservoir, in the background, was replaced by the current New York Public Library in 1911. The Egyptian-style reservoir walls were topped with another popular place to promenade. *(FPG)*

five-acre reservoir was begun in 1837 and filled, amid great fanfare, on July 4, 1842. The entire system of reservoirs, aqueducts, and tunnels that begins forty miles north of the city was a marvel of nineteenth-century engineering. The growing city now had an abundant and potable supply of water needed to sustain a modern metropolis. Much of the system is still in use today. The thick-walled distributing reservoir rose several stories above Fifth Avenue and contained more than twenty million gallons of water. The same walls were used as the foundation for the library.

New York Public Library, Center for the Humanities*—The beaux-arts palace of knowledge that replaced the reservoir in 1898 was completed thirteen years later. The creation of the New York Public Library, one of the world's greatest, involved a consolidation of the Astor and Lenox libraries and a bequest of former New York governor Samuel J. Tilden. President William H. Taft and the library's greatest living benefactor, Andrew Carnegie, were among the famous that attended the opening ceremonies on May 23, 1911. The knowledge stored here has contributed to the birth of the Polaroid camera, the Xerox copier, the atomic bomb, *Reader's Digest*, "Ripley's Believe It or Not!" and countless other books, ideas, and inventions.

509 Fifth Avenue

A storefront shared with a milliner in 1909, this address was the first shop of Elizabeth Arden, the cosmetic entrepreneur. Arden, who changed her name from Florence Nightingale Graham, had arrived from Canada the year before. True to her given name, she studied nursing but discovered she "didn't really like looking at sick people" and turned to a career in cosmetics.

Fifth Avenue between West 43rd Street and West 44th Street

Colored Orphan Asylum—Much of the fury of the Draft Riots was directed at African Americans, who were seen as the cause of the Civil War and its hated conscription. On the first afternoon of the riot, July 13, 1863, the rioters attacked this home for about two hundred African American orphans under the age of twelve. The superintendent barricaded the front door and quickly helped her charges to

An early target of the mob during the draft riots was the Colored Orphan Asylum at Fifth Avenue and West 43rd Street. On Monday, July 13, 1863, rioters sacked and burned the orphanage and left hundreds of children homeless. A new facility was built in 1867 on West 143rd Street and Amsterdam Avenue. *(Harper's Weekly, August 1, 1863)*

safety out a back door. Once inside, the mob ravaged everything. When they found a little girl left behind and hiding under a bed, they killed her. They set fire to the home and attacked the fire fighters brave enough to try to save it. The orphanage and three other buildings on the block burned to the ground.

522* Fifth Avenue

Sherry's Hotel—Beneath three renovations is the ninety-nine-year-old core designed by McKim, Mead and White that was once the upper-crust hotel and restaurant Sherry's. It was the scene of several outrageous "Gilded Age" parties. On December 19, 1896, a bachelor's party was held here for Herbert Barnum Seeley. The evening's entertainment, a stag party standard, was the erotic dancer "Little Egypt." She managed to pop out of a cake, but the police prevented her nude "hootchy-kootchy" dance. C. K. G. Billings hosted another all-male affair on March 28, 1903, to celebrate the opening of his new stables. His guests on horseback were served by waiters dressed as jockeys. The most exorbitant was a costume party on January 31, 1905, given by James Hazen Hyde, Equitable Life Assurance's first vice president and son of its founder. This imaginative host spent more than $200,000—in policyholders' money—to recreate Versailles for his guests. His fate

"American Horse King" C. K. G. Billing held his equine dinner party at Sherry's Hotel on March 28, 1903. He had recently opened his new $200,000 trotting-horse stable on Fort Washington Avenue in what is now Fort Tryon Park. *(Museum City of New York)*

was not unlike that of the residents of Versailles. Soon after the public's indignation over the extravagance, he lost his job at the insurance company and was forced to leave the country. His party also sparked a probe of the insurance giants by the state. Chief Counsel Charles Evans Hughes, later presidential candidate and chief justice of the United States, held fifty-seven public hearings that prompted the state legislature to reform the insurance industry.

Fifth Avenue and West 45th Street, Southwest Corner

Church of the Divine Paternity—On December 4, 1872, the funeral for Horace Greeley was held at a church that once stood on this corner. Henry Ward Beecher eulogized the former editor to the illustrious mourners who included President Ulysses S. Grant, Vice President Schuyler Colfax, and Chief Justice of the U.S. Supreme Court Salmon P. Chase.

Fifth Avenue between East 46th Street and East 47th Street

Windsor Hotel—At the end of the nineteenth century this fashionable hotel was home to two of America's wealthiest capitalists, John D. Rockefeller and Andrew Carnegie, and a way station for King Kalakaua of the Sandwich Islands and authors Matthew Arnold and Oscar Wilde. But on St. Patrick's Day of 1899 it was the site of a tragic fire that took the lives of thirty-three people. Fire fighters, hin-

The debris from the still-smoldering Windsor Hotel fire on March 17, 1899. A guest started the blaze by throwing a match and igniting some lace curtains in a second-floor sitting room. *(FPG)*

dered by the parade out front, were unable to save the frantic guests, many of whom jumped from windows. One famous survivor was Isadora Duncan, who was teaching a dance class at the time of the blaze. She helped lead her young pupils to safety.

579 Fifth Avenue

The four-story corner brownstone that once stood here was the last address of the financier Jay Gould. His family had moved here in 1882 from across the street at 578 Fifth Avenue. Gould died in a second-floor bedroom here on December 2, 1892. His funeral was also held here three days later.

Now the site of Rockefeller Center at Fifth Avenue and West 49th Street, this is the scene of the 1906 Easter Parade. St. Patrick's Cathedral is on the east side of the avenue. *(National Archives)*

Fifth Avenue between East 50th and East 51st Streets

St. Patrick's Cathedral*—Begun in 1858, on Fifth Avenue, the avenue of choice for the city's Protestant ruling elite, the new St. Patrick's Cathedral of the Archdiocese of New York was a glorious symbol of the increasing Roman Catholic presence in the city in the middle of the nineteenth century. Waves of Irish immigrants, beginning in the 1830s, were changing the social fabric of the growing city and nation. By 1855 a quarter of the population of Manhattan and Brooklyn had been born in Ireland. The new cathedral, the country's largest, was a fitting stage for the emerging power of the new immigrants in American life. St. Patrick's, delayed because of the Civil War, was dedicated on May 25, 1879, and has been the center of Roman Catholic New York life ever since. Pope Paul VI, the first pontiff ever to visit the Western Hemisphere, officiated at a Mass here on October 4, 1964, the Feast Day of Saint Francis. Pope John Paul II has also made two visits. F. Scott Fitzgerald and Zelda Sayre were married here on Easter Sunday, April 3, 1920. Wakes were held for Gen. William T. Sherman on February 19, 1891; Arturo Toscanini on January 19, 1957; Governor Alfred

More than seventy-five thousand mourners line the funeral route of Babe Ruth on August 19, 1948. The revered baseball hero's body was on view at Yankee Stadium before a requiem mass at St. Patrick's Cathedral. *(FPG)*

E. Smith on October 7, 1944; Babe Ruth on August 19, 1948; and Senator Robert F. Kennedy on June 8, 1968.

626 Fifth Avenue

Merchant and avid art collector Benjamin Altman, the founder of B. Altman's Department Store, once lived in a house that stood at this address. The seventy-three-year-old bachelor died here on October 7, 1913. He had an estimated net worth of $20 million.

Fifth Avenue and East 52nd Street, Northeast Corner

This was once the site of the mansion of the city's leading abortionist, Ann Lohman, the notorious "Madame Restell." Business had been so brisk that by 1864 she had moved her practice to this fashionable address, much to the horror of her neighbors. Public opposition to abortion had curbed her practice, but she still continued to sell her "preventive powders" and pills from her basement office. She made the mistake of selling these dubious concoctions to a disguised Anthony Comstock, the moral crusader and chairman of "The Committee for the Suppression of Vice." He had her arrested and taken to The Tombs. Shortly afterward, while out on bail, she committed suicide here by slitting her throat in the bathtub on April 1, 1878, the day her trial was to begin. She left an estate of more than a million dollars.

660 Fifth Avenue

William K. and Alva Smith Vanderbilt's "Petit Château" once stood at this address. The French-styled château designed by Richard Morris Hunt set a new standard for palatial homes and started the trend for even larger "cottages" in Newport and castles on upper Fifth Avenue. A lavish house-warming costume ball was planned for March 26, 1883. More than 1,200 invitations were sent out, though none to the hostess's social rival *the* Mrs. William Astor. Mrs. Vanderbilt explained that she could not invite a total stranger to her new home. The mountain came to Mohammed. Mrs. Astor swallowed her pride and called on the social upstart to garner a coveted invitation for herself and her daughter. At the party, Alva, costumed as "The Electric Light," and Caroline Astor, dressed as a Venetian princess, jointly reigned over New York society.

Fifth Avenue and West 53rd Street, Northwest Corner

St. Thomas Church*—An earlier St. Thomas Church destroyed by fire in 1905 on this site became the place for many society weddings after the marriage here of Charles John, Ninth Duke of Marlborough, and Consuelo Vanderbilt on November 6, 1895. This unhappy union marked the peak in the rage to have New York society daughters married off to foreign nobility. Eighteen-year-old Consuelo loved another, but her mother, Alva, was determined to have a titled daughter. The duke received close to $15 million as a dowry. Former president Benjamin Harrison was also married here to Mary Scott Dimmick on April 6, 1896. Almost-president Thomas E. Dewey was married to Frances Hutt in the current church on June 16, 1928.

681 Fifth Avenue

Dodworth's Dancing Academy—The first home of the Metropolitan Museum of Art opened on February 20, 1872. The newly established museum rented space in this townhouse formerly used as one of Allen Dodworth's dancing studios.

725 Fifth Avenue

Bonwit Teller Department Store—A furious Salvador Dalí smashed the glass in a Fifth Avenue display window here on March 15, 1939. The artist was horrified that the store management had changed his surrealist window dressing without consulting him. He tipped over a bathtub filled with water. The tub crashed into the plate glass, sending thousands of pieces of glass splinters flying onto the sidewalk. He was arrested but given a suspended sentence. The incident made him a household word in America.

Trump Tower*—The department store was torn down to make room for Trump Tower. Master builder and self-promoter Donald Trump's mixed-use apartment and office building served as the honeymoon retreat for King of Pop Michael Jackson and Daughter of the King Lisa Marie Presley in the summer of 1994. The newlyweds stayed in a $10,000-a-month penthouse apartment here after their secret Dominican Republic wedding on May 26, 1994. Seemingly mismatched from the start, the couple divorced nineteen months later.

730 Fifth Avenue

Crown Building*—Originally named the Heckscher, this office building was the first home of the Museum of Modern Art in 1929. It was on the twelfth floor that the museum held its first architecture exhibit, the famed "Modern Architecture—International Exhibition," which opened on February 9, 1932. The show, curated by Philip Johnson, MOMA's first director of the Architecture and Design Department, and the architecture historian Henry-Russell Hitchcock, established the

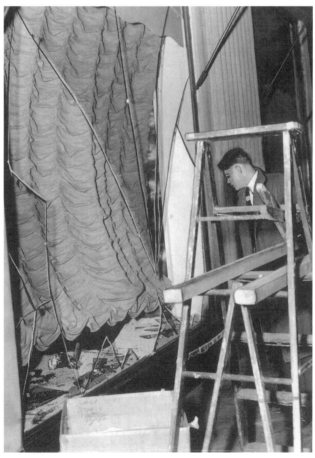

Bonwit Teller's Fifth Avenue display window on March 16, 1939, after Salvador Dalí smashed the glass in reaction to the department store's changes to his creation. Several customers had complained about the surrealist artist's use of nude manikins in a public display. *(Daily News L. P. Photo)*

"International Style" as the predominant style of architecture in America for the next forty years.

This same building was involved in years of legal battles and international intrigue when it was discovered that Ferdinand Marcos, the Philippine president, had secretly bought it in 1981. After the dictator was deposed, the Philippine government hoped to claim the profits from the sale of the building. In a compromise, the courts decided that the proceeds would be split between all the competing parties.

Fifth Avenue between West 58th Street and West 59th Street

The Plaza Hotel*—The current castle-like Plaza Hotel, which had replaced an earlier version deemed too small, opened on October 1, 1907. The occasion was marked with a round of parties, attended by the celebrities of the day—the Vanderbilts, "Diamond Jim" Brady, and Lillian Russell. The well-publicized parties proved a bonanza for the promoter of the city's first gas-driven metered taxis. He had the shining new cabs all parked in a neat little row in front of the hotel. Roughly sixty years later, the "party of the decade," Truman Capote's Black and White Ball, was held here on November 28, 1966. Truman decided to top off his recent success with his nonfiction novel *In Cold Blood* with a party for five hundred friends in honor of *Washington Post* and *Newsweek* publisher Katherine Graham. The masked ball's guest list reflected Capote's passions, mixing society (Barbara "Babe" Paley), Hollywood (Frank Sinatra and Henry Fonda), and the literary (Arthur Schlesinger).

Fifth Avenue and 59th Street

This intersection was the assembly point for ten thousand African American marchers in a silent protest down Fifth Avenue on July 28, 1917. To the accompaniment of muffled drums, three hundred children dressed in white led this country's first African American civil-rights march. The novel protest, organized under the auspices of the National Association for the Advancement of Colored People (NAACP), was prompted by recent race riots. The parade's message was communicated through placards and flyers handed out to spectators by African American boy scouts. The protesters marched to 23rd Street.

SIXTH AVENUE

616–32* Sixth Avenue

Siegel-Cooper Department Store—An estimated 150,000 people jammed this new store on Saturday night, September 12, 1896. Proclaimed "The Big Store" in

The Plaza Hotel on Fifth Avenue with a line of taxis parked at the entrance in 1915. The newly completed Pulitzer fountain is in the foreground. *(Author's collection)*

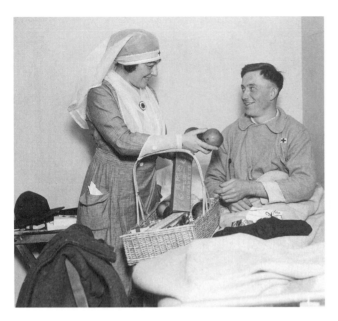

A nurse delivers Christmas gifts of cigarettes and apples to a patient at Debarkation Hospital Number Three. The closed Siegel-Cooper Department Store building, still at Sixth Avenue and West 18th Street, was converted into a veteran's hospital for wounded American soldiers returning from World War I. (FPG)

its advertising, the fifteen-and-a-half-acre building occupied the entire block. There was once a telegraph office, a nursery, a florist, a hospital, a drugstore, a bank, a photography gallery, and an aviary all inside the store. The store had "all that is between a tenpenny nail and a roast rib of beef to a diamond bracelet and a velvet cape," according to *The New York Times*. After department stores started moving uptown at the beginning of the twentieth century, Siegel-Cooper closed its doors in 1917. Shortly afterward, the federal government used the building as a U.S. Debarkation Hospital for World War I soldiers.

641–43* Sixth Avenue

Simpson, Crawford and Simpson Department Store—Here was another dinosaur of a department store left over from the turn of the century "Ladies Mile" glory days. This one, which opened in 1900, had one of the first escalators in New York City. The mammoth space came to life again in the early 1990s as Sixth Avenue again became a shopping district.

Sixth Avenue and West 23rd Street, Southeast Corner

Edwin Booth's Theater—America's great thespian Edwin Booth invested much of his own fortune in this lavish theater, which cost more than a million dollars to build. When it opened in 1869, it was declared the most beautiful playhouse in the city, in addition to being the most modern. The innovative design of the auditorium included an early use of a sunken orchestra pit to improve the view of the stage from all seats. The cost of the theater and early productions forced Booth to declare bankruptcy after just five years. He did stay on as manager and occasional star. Sarah Bernhardt made her American debut here in the play *Adrienne Lecouvreur* on November 8, 1880.

Sixth Avenue and West 43rd Street, Southwest Corner

Hanover House—In a seedy hotel room on February 23, 1940, folksinger and composer Woody Guthrie wrote his greatest hit, "This Land Is Your Land." Only in the city a few days, Guthrie had worn out his welcome with friends, including

Burl Ives, and was forced to rent a room here. The song was a parody of Irving Berlin's "God Bless America."

Sixth Avenue between West 43rd and 44th Streets, East Side

Hippodrome—New York City's answer to the Roman Coliseum, the Hippodrome, with seating for 5,697 fun seekers, was opened on April 12, 1905. Frederick Thompson and Elmer Dundy, the creators of the magical Luna Park in Coney Island, built this huge theater. Cary Grant made his American debut on this giant stage in *Good Times* on August 8, 1920. The extravaganzas presented here with hundreds in the cast became expensive and unfashionable, forcing the theater closed in 1939.

Sixth Avenue still had its "el" in this photograph of the Hippodrome about 1920. The block-wide theater was covered with forty thousand electric lights, including the balls on the top of each corner tower. *(FPG)*

Today's Rockefeller Center's Channel Gardens occupies the same location as the earlier Elgin Botanical Gardens. This engraving from about 1811 is of the greenhouse and gardens where Dr. David Hosack grew plants for possible commercial uses and herbal remedies. *(Author's collection)*

Sixth Avenue between West 47th and West 51st Streets, East Side

Elgin Botanical Gardens—Dr. David Hosack bought twelve acres of land for $4,807.36 at this site in 1802 and established his botanical garden. The doctor, a professor of botany and medicine at Columbia College, created the garden as a "repository of native plants, and as subservient to medicine, agriculture, and the arts." Unable to keep the garden up, he sold the land to New York State, which in turn gave it to Columbia University in 1814. In 1928 this same site, still owned by Columbia University, was leased and developed into a masterpiece of urban planning, Rockefeller Center. In 1985 the University finally sold the 11.7-acre plot on which the center stands to the Rockefeller Group, the family's investment company, for $400 million.

Sixth Avenue and West 50th Street

Elevated Platform of the IRT Broadway Local—On a warm Saturday afternoon, July 23, 1915, while riding the elevated train, Dr. Heinrich Albert, a German attaché, was dozing as he approached this corner, his stop. He jumped up and hurried off. Once on the platform, he realized he had left his briefcase on the train. The doctor wasn't the only person interested in that briefcase. So was Frank Burke, a Secret Service agent who had been following Albert. Burke picked up the case and took it to his superiors. Inside were details on planned German sabotage strikes against American military installations. After viewing the plans, Secretary of State Robert Lansing weighed the threat against the sensitivity of having stolen documents from a foreign diplomat. Rather than register a formal government complaint, he had the documents sent to the *New York World* newspaper. The resulting embarrassing stories helped edge the American public closer to siding with the Allies against Germany in World War I.

The wreckage of a trolley car lies in the center of a subway excavation on Seventh Avenue between West 23rd and 25th Streets. The wooden support cover collapsed after an explosion on the morning of September 22, 1915. *(FPG)*

SEVENTH AVENUE

Seventh Avenue between West 23rd and West 25th Streets

Shortly after 8:00 on the morning of September 22, 1915, this stretch of Seventh Avenue was the scene of an accident that killed twenty-five people. During work on the subway excavation for the construction of the new IRT, an explosion opened up a thirty-foot pit in the street that swallowed a crowded trolley car and a brewery truck. The death and injury toll would have been higher but for the fact that the wooden planked structure gave way slowly, allowing hundreds of people on the street to scramble to solid ground.

Seventh Avenue between West 31st and West 33rd Streets

Pennsylvania Station—These two city blocks were once the site of McKim, Mead and White's greatest masterpiece, Pennsylvania Station. The vast railroad station was modeled on the Roman Baths of Caracalla and completed in 1910. In 1963 this impressive gateway to the city was torn down in the interest of modern architecture and greed. Pennsylvania Station died so that other beautiful historical buildings might live. The loss of this monument so galvanized the public that the New York City Landmarks Preservation Commission was created within two years.

*Madison Square Garden Center**—Penn Station was replaced with a high-rise box accompanied by an equally banal hatbox for the Garden's arena, with the railroad station stashed in the basement. The arena was the site of three Democratic National Party Conventions, in 1976, 1980, and 1992. The first two nominated Jimmy Carter for president and Walter Mondale for vice president. The July of 1992 convention nominated William Clinton for president and Albert Gore Jr. for vice president.

A sad epilogue to this story of architectural loss was the death here of Louis I. Kahn. The famous architect died of a heart attack in the "new" underground station on March 17, 1974. His body was taken to the city morgue, where he remained unidentified for several days. The world learned of this loss only after his wife in Philadelphia contacted the New York police after being concerned because he was late in returning home.

McKim, Mead and White designed the General Post Office, across the street on Eighth Avenue, to compliment the original Pennsylvania Station. It is now being renovated into a railroad station, a grander addition to Penn Station.

401* Seventh Avenue

Hotel Pennsylvania—The Manhattan Room in this hotel was a favorite with the big bands of the thirties and forties. The hotel's phone number was immortalized by Glenn Miller in his song "Pennsylvania 6-5000."

Edwin H. Land publicly demonstrated his "instant" picture camera on February 21, 1947, at the winter meeting of the Optical Society of America here. The sad-eyed inventor was his own subject in an eight-by-ten-inch print developed just fifty seconds after it had been exposed.

On November 19, 1953, this hotel, now called the Statler, would be the site of a mysterious tragedy not fully explained for twenty-two years. On that night Frank Olson, a U.S. Army scientist and germ-warfare specialist, jumped through a glass window and fell ten stories to his death. It was reported as a suicide. In 1975 it was finally revealed that Olson's death was the result of a CIA experiment to study the effects of the drug LSD. The scientist, who was working on the project, code-named MKULTRA, was an unwitting guinea pig after the drug was slipped into his drink. It was also revealed that the spy agency used prisoners and patrons of brothels set up and run by the agency to test the drug's effects.

The graceful arches of wrought iron and glass covered the train concourse of the old Pennsylvania Station. This magnificent station, the predecessor to the current Penn Station, stood at Seventh Avenue between West 31st and 33rd Streets for only fifty-one years. *(FPG)*

777* Seventh Avenue

Taft Hotel—Jimmie C. Rodgers, the "Father of Country Music," died at this hotel on May 26, 1933, while in town for a recording session. Rodgers was the first "hillbilly singer" to become a nationwide star as a result of the phenomenal growth of the radio audience in the 1920s.

The Taft was also the site of the death of another entertainer on September 2, 1955. The actor Philip Loeb was found here, dead from an overdose of sleeping pills. Loeb, a victim of McCarthy-era blacklisting, was broke and despondent after losing his role on the popular *The Goldbergs* television show three years earlier. His career was finished after his name appeared in "Red Channels," a tattle sheet used to rout out possible Communists in the entertainment industry. The building is now a cooperative apartment house.

787 Seventh Avenue

Equitable Center*—The thirty-fifth floor of this high-rise was the scene of a major battle of man vs. machine. Garry Kasparov, the world chess champion, played a match with IBM's RS/6000 SP supercomputer, alias Deep Blue. On May 11, 1997, at 4:00 P.M., Deep Blue won the sixth and final game to win the match, 3 1/2 to 2 1/2. Advancing technology had finally made the victory inevitable. Deep Blue, with a total of 512 microprocessors working simultaneously, was able to consider 200 million moves per second. Kasparov was only human.

790 Seventh Avenue

Sheraton Center Hotel*—In the main ballroom, a little after midnight on November 8, 1989, David Dinkins gave his victory speech that marked the election of the first African American as mayor of the nation's largest city. Dinkins had defeated his Republican opponent Rudolph Giuliani, a former federal prosecutor in Manhattan, in the general election. He had defeated twelve-year Mayor Edward Koch in the Democratic primary in September.

870 Seventh Avenue

Park Central Hotel*—This hotel, now called the Omni Park Central, has been the scene of two mob shoot-outs, almost thirty years apart, both never solved. Arnold Rothstein was shot in Room 349 on November 4, 1928. Rothstein was a gambler who was rumored to be involved with the Black Sox Scandal of 1919. Albert Anastasia was murdered in the barbershop of this hotel—then named the Park Sheraton—on October 25, 1957. Anastasia had been a hit man for the mob.

EIGHTH AVENUE

Eighth Avenue and West 23rd Street, Northwest Corner

Grand Opera House—On January 9, 1868, the opera *Il Trovatore* was the opening performance at this theater, originally called Pike's Opera House. New owners Jay Gould and Jim Fisk, the infamous Stock Market manipulators, changed the name and used the upper floors for their offices the following year. Fisk's theatrical funeral was held in the auditorium after he was shot and killed by a jealous rival in January of 1872. In 1904 this same building housed a dancing school attended by five-year-old Fred Austerlitz, later known as Fred Astaire. The building burned in 1960.

Eighth Avenue between West 23rd and West 24th Streets

In spite of threats of violence, the annual Orange Societies Parade marched on Eighth Avenue on July 12, 1871. The parade celebrated the anniversary of the 1690 Battle of Boyne, when the Irish Protestants triumphed over the Irish Catholics.

EAs depicted shortly after opening in 1868, the lavish Pike's Opera House once stood on the corner of Eighth Avenue and West 23rd Street. After ninety-two years, it was one of the longest continuing theaters in New York theater history. Built to perform operas, it was also a stage, vaudeville, and motion-picture theater. *(Harper's Weekly, January 25, 1868)*

Based on an eyewitness account, this newspaper engraving recorded the gunfire during the Orange Societies Parade on Eighth Avenue between West 23rd and West 24th Streets. On July 12, 1871, the ensuing riot between Catholic and Protestant Irish immigrants and the police resulted in forty-seven deaths and many injuries. *(Harper's Weekly, July 29, 1871)*

Understandably, this parade was unpopular with the city's large population of Irish Catholic immigrants. More than 800 policemen and 2,200 state militiamen were assigned to protect the marchers. As the procession passed West 24th Street, snipers from tenement windows fired into the crowd. Regiments within the parade, the police, and the militia returned the fire. When the shooting stopped, there were forty-seven casualties. The *Irish World* newspaper called the debacle the "Slaughter on Eighth Avenue."

481* Eighth Avenue

Hotel New Yorker—The master inventor Nikola Tesla was found dead in his room in this hotel on January 7, 1943. Tesla, the holder of seven hundred patents, invented the first practical application of alternating electrical current. The eighty-six-year-old inventor died an impoverished eccentric, a hermit who spent the last years of his life feeding the pigeons on the steps of the New York Public Library and at St. Patrick's Cathedral.

782 Eighth Avenue

New York City society was shocked by the murder of Civil War hero Maj. Gen. Franz Sigel's granddaughter. The body of twenty-two-year-old Miss Elsie Sigel was found in a trunk in a furnished room above Sun Leung's chop-suey restaurant on June 18, 1909. She had been murdered by her Chinese lover, Leon Ling.

The two had met while Miss Sigel was active in missionary work in Chinatown. The case and the ensuing publicity inflamed "Yellow Peril" bigotry. Mr. Ling disappeared and was never brought to trial, but the police, under public pressure, did crack down on the violent "tongs," the Chinatown gangs.

Eighth Avenue between West 49th and West 50th Streets

Madison Square Garden—This was the site of the second and grittier Madison Square Garden, from 1925 to 1966, home to many smoky boxing matches and New York Rangers hockey games. On May 19, 1962, President John F. Kennedy's Forty-fifth Birthday Party Democratic Fund-raiser was held here. More than twenty thousand guests paid $1,000 a ticket to celebrate and see entertainers Harry Belafonte, Jimmy Durante, and Ella Fitzgerald. The unexpected highlight of the evening was Marilyn Monroe's breathy version of "Happy Birthday" to the president.

Shortly after her capture at the Howard Johnson Motor Lodge, Angela Davis is surrounded by FBI agents on October 13, 1970. Davis was arraigned on a California murder warrant. *(Daily News L. P. Photo)*

829 Eighth Avenue

Here were the offices for the *New York Morning Telegraph* newspaper. The one-time sheriff of Dodge City, William "Bat" Masterson, died at his desk here of a heart attack on October 26, 1921. The lawman-turned-sportswriter had worked for this paper for more than ten years.

851 Eighth Avenue

Howard Johnson Motor Lodge*—The FBI arrested the fugitive Angela Davis outside her room on the seventh floor of this hotel on October 13, 1970. She had been hiding for more than two months. She was wanted on kidnapping and murder charges.

987 Eighth Avenue

Reisenweber's Restaurant—The restaurant and dance club that long ago stood at the southwest corner of West 58th Street has earned an illustrious footnote in the history of jazz. Jazz, America's uniquely native music form, developed and natured by Southern African Americans during the latter half of the nineteenth century, was new to Northern white audiences until "The Original Dixieland Jass Band" debuted here on January 26, 1917. This unlikely all-white band, named with an early spelling of the word jazz, created a musical frenzy. Within a matter of days, on January 24, Columbia had the group record "Darktown Strutter's Ball" and "Indiana," the first phonograph recording of a jazz band. The ODJB, as they were later called, also made a record for Columbia's rival, the Victor company, in February. That recording of "Livery Stable Blues," led by cornet player Nick LaRocca, had the distinction of beating out Columbia's record and earned the claim of the first jazz-band record to be released.

EAST 15TH STREET

109* East 15th Street
Century Club—Auguste Bartholdi spoke here to raise money for the pedestal of his *Statue of Liberty* on January 2, 1877. The statue was a gift to the United States from the people of France, but the base was to be supplied by the Americans.

234 East 15th Street
The sixty-eight-year-old artist William Merritt Chase died here at his home on October 25, 1916.

240* East 15th Street
This was once the home of artist Reginald Marsh.

WEST 15TH STREET

27* West 15th Street
This was home for novelist Thomas Wolfe in 1928–29.

123* West 15th Street
Martha Held, who rented this brownstone in 1912, was a popular German opera singer. The house was also a hotbed of German sabotage in the years before World War I. German sea captains, spies, and even the German ambassador to the United States, Count Johann von Bernstorff, visited here to exchange information and plot against U.S. involvement in World War I. Plans were hatched here to blow up

the Black Tom Island munitions plant, the greatest act of foreign sabotage ever performed on American soil up to that time.

308 West 15th Street
Around 1895 two rooms at this residence were home to the painter Albert Pinkham. Ryder. The reclusive and eccentric symbolist artist lived here in squalor for fifteen years.

EAST 16TH STREET

East 16th Street and Irving Place, Northwest Corner
Westminster Hotel—In 1876 a group of dog lovers met to form the Westminster Kennel Club at the hotel that once stood on this corner. Since that first dog show in May of 1877 at Gilmore's Gardens, the club has had more than a hundred annual shows. The Westminster Show, named in honor of the hotel, is second only to the Kentucky Derby as the oldest continuous sporting event in America.

128* East 16th Street
The artist Winslow Homer lived in this house in 1859.

East 16th Street East of Avenue C
Willard Parker Hospital for Contagious Diseases—Typhoid Mary, born Mary Mallon, the famous chronic typhoid carrier, was forcibly taken here by police for tests on March 19, 1907. Mary, once called "the most dangerous woman in America," was eventually isolated by the Health Department for causing at least fifty-three cases of typhoid and three deaths. Dr. George Soper, the epidemiologist responsible for tracing the illness to Mary, later identified her as the most likely cause of more than 1,400 cases in Ithaca, New York, four years earlier. While working as a cook she had inadvertently infected her employers and their families. She was kept in almost complete isolation for the next thirty years until her death on November 11, 1938. She died in a little cottage the city provided for her on North Brother Island near Rikers Island.

WEST 16TH STREET

17* West 16th Street
From 1930 to 1973 this landmarked Greek Revival–style townhouse, with the unusual curved front, was the famed Margaret Sanger Clinic for family planning.

The house sits on land that was part of the seventeenth-century farm owned by Simon Congo, a free African American.

24* West 16th Street

The poet and editor William Cullen Bryant died here at his home on June 12, 1878. He had lived here since 1867. Margaret Anderson, the editor of the *Little Review,* lived in this same house in 1917.

41* West 16th Street

The ground-floor, one-bedroom apartment in this building was home to song-writer Joni Mitchell in the mid-1960s. It was here that she wrote her ode to the neighborhood, "Chelsea Morning." The country's first baby-boomer president Bill Clinton, a Joni Mitchell fan, was inspired by the song to name his only daughter Chelsea.

EAST 17TH STREET

East 17th Street and Park Avenue South, Northwest Corner

Everett House Hotel—This hotel was popular with entertainers employed in the Union Square theater district. But on the election night of November 7, 1876, it was filled with Democratic politicians here to celebrate the election as president of Samuel Tilden, New York governor and Gramercy Park neighbor. It was not to be. In an election widely regarded as having been stolen, Tilden won about 250,000 more votes than his Republican rival, Rutherford B. Hayes, but he eventually lost in the electoral college. A commission with a majority of Republican members declared Hayes the winner.

117* East 17th Street

This was once the residence of Katherine Anne Porter. She worked on her only novel, *Ship of Fools,* while living here in 1953.

122* East 17th Street

Erroneously called the "Washington Irving House," this corner house was home to Elsie de Wolfe from 1894 until 1911. This one-time actress, with help from Stanford White and her society friends, became America's first modern interior decorator. Famous for her simple white interiors, she offered a radical design

alternative to the busy Victorian clutter of the period. De Wolf lived and worked here, with her long-time companion Bessie Marbury, one of America's first literary agents. Marbury's most famous client, Oscar Wilde, lived in the house next door during an American tour. The lesbian couple were notorious for their grand parties where society and the arts met.

241* East 17th Street

Author William Dean Howells lived in this brownstone in 1891. He also lived at 330 East 17th Street, which is now the site of Beth Israel Hospital.

327 East 17th Street

A four-story townhouse that once stood here was home to Antonín Dvořák from 1892 until 1895. The conductor had come to America to be the director of the National Conservatory of Music. While at this address he wrote his *New World Symphony*. After an extended battle to save the house, including an appeal from Vaclav Havel, then the president of Czechoslovakia, Beth Israel Medical Center razed the building for the Robert Mapplethorpe Residence, an AIDS residence built with the help of the photographer's foundation.

WEST 17TH STREET

194 West 17th Street
Lola Montez, a performer who was the one-time mistress of Ludwig I of Bavaria, spent the last few months of her life in a barely furnished room at this address. She had suffered a stroke and died here on January 17, 1861. The once-great beauty was just forty-two years old.

EAST 18TH STREET

78 East 18th Street
Edwin P. Christy, the founder of the Christy Minstrels, the popular forerunner of early minstrel shows, died here at his home on May 21, 1862. He died as a result of injuries he received from a suicidal jump from a second-story window into the backyard earlier in the month.

136 East 18th Street
One of the city's greatest treasures, Central Park, was conceived and planned in the parlor of a townhouse that once stood at this address. It was the home of Calvert Vaux, the landscape designer who with his friend and partner Frederick Law Olmsted mapped out their design for the park during the fall and winter of 1857. The team's winning "Greensward Plan" almost missed the April 1, 1858, deadline and was the last entrant submitted to the judges.

129 East 18th Street
Pete's Tavern*—This corner bar was a favorite hangout of the writer O. Henry. A plaque above the front booth identifies the spot where he spent a great deal of time drinking while writing some of his short stories. Pete's Tavern bills itself as the oldest continuously operating bar in New York City. Posing as a florist shop, it was a speakeasy during Prohibition. Thirsty customers would enter through a refrigerator in the back of the shop.

142 East 18th Street
Stuyvesant Apartments—The five-story building by the architect Richard Morris Hunt that once stood at this address was considered the first true apartment house in the United States. Called "French flats" at the time it was built in 1869, the

Stuyvesant helped make apartment living acceptable to middle-class Americans, particularly widows and young couples. Up to this time, multiple-family housing was considered shocking by polite society because it offered no more privacy or propriety than the tenements built for the poor.

EAST 19TH STREET

28 East 19th Street
The actor Edwin Booth lived at this address from 1862 until 1865. His brother John Wilkes Booth, the assassin of Abraham Lincoln, often stayed here while visiting New York.

35* East 19th Street
This altered townhouse was the home of journalist Horace Greeley from 1850 to 1853. He was the editor and publisher of *The New York Tribune* while at this address.

132* East 19th Street
This address has been the home of many of America's greatest actresses. Mrs. Patrick Campbell, Theda Bara, Helen Hayes, Ethel Barrymore, and the Gish sisters, Dorothy and Lillian, all lived here in this seven-story studio building.

139* East 19th Street
Frederick Sterner, an English born-architect, bought this plain brick house and transformed it and eventually the rest of the block into a charming enclave of Mediterranean-style homes. Between Irving Place and Third Avenue, 19th Street is the landmarked "block beautiful" because of Sterner's efforts early in the twentieth century. After decorating his house with stucco, tiles, and ironwork, he bought other houses and did the same. A sanctuary for picturesque architecture, the block has also attracted writers and actors.

146* East 19th Street
The artist George Bellows bought this house in 1910 and lived here until his death in 1925. Bellows, who learned carpentry and bricklaying from his father, raised the roof of this house eight feet and made improvements to his studio here. Bellows and his wife, Emma, often entertained friends, playwright Eugene O'Neill, radical Emma Goldman, and writer John Reed, here.

151* East 19th Street

Carl Van Vechten, music critic for the *New York Times* turned novelist, lived in the top-floor apartment of this building, beginning in 1914. A leader in the Harlem Renaissance movement, he was also a legendary "Jazz Age" party-giver. Some of his guests included music greats George Gershwin and Bessie Smith.

227* East 19th Street

Columbus Hospital—Artist Andy Warhol was taken to this hospital, now with a new addition and new name Cabrini, after being shot at his Union Square "factory" on June 3, 1968. He was in surgery for more than five hours and spent his recovery here.

EAST 20TH STREET

28* East 20th Street

Theodore Roosevelt, the only New York City native to be elected president, was born at this address on October 27, 1858. He lived here until age fifteen. The original Gothic Revival four-story townhouse was demolished in 1916. Six years later the building was replicated by Theodate Pope Riddle, the first woman architect in the United States. Theodore's sisters and widow furnished the rooms to recall his boyhood home.

52 East 20th Street

This address was the home of Alice and Phoebe Cary. These sisters, both poets, held Sunday-evening receptions for literary figures of the 1850s here.

WEST 20TH STREET

20/22 West 20th Street

This was the home of Martin Bradley, a wealthy businessman, and his society-leader wife, reputed to be the most lavish party-giver in modern times. After their much criticized ball at the Waldorf Hotel

In 1922, three years after Theodore Roosevelt's death, his birthplace was reconstructed on its original site at 28 East 20th Street. As a child, the future president exercised in a top-floor gym to strengthen his lungs and overcome his asthma. *(Author's collection)*

on February 10, 1897, the city reassessed the value of this home and doubled the taxes. The embarrassed family moved to Europe.

333* West 20th Street

On November 5, 1938, the painter Thomas W. Dewing died here at his home at the age of eighty-seven. His paintings of solitary women lost in thought were popular in the early years of this century.

West 20th Street at the Hudson River

Chelsea Piers*—Now a huge sports and entertainment complex, these piers were originally designed to dock the White Star Line's transatlantic ocean liners. The *Titanic,* the world's most famous ship, never arrived as scheduled on April 17, 1912, at Pier 59. Instead, desperate crowds gathered, hoping for any news of their friends and family aboard the wrecked ship.

EAST 21ST STREET

24 East 21st Street

Samuel B. Ruggles, the developer and creator of Gramercy Park across the street, lived at this address.

41 East 21st Street

In 1901 this address was a movie studio for Thomas Edison's early film company. The interior scenes for the 1903 classic *The Great Train Robbery* were filmed in this skylighted brownstone, the country's first indoor motion-picture studio. This twelve-minute action Western was the fledgling movie industry's first hit; it remained the most famous and profitable film until *Birth of a Nation* in 1915. Edwin Stanton Porter, the director of *The Great Train Robbery* and many other pioneer films, recruited his movie stars at nearby Union Square, which was a popular hangout for unemployed stage actors. New York City was the center of the American film industry until the early studio moved to the West Coast around the time of World War I.

WEST 21ST STREET

34 West 21st Street

This address was once home to Chester A. Arthur. The future president of the United States lived here from 1859 to 1861.

EAST 22ND STREET

155* East 22nd Street

The artist John Sloan moved into an apartment at this address in June of 1911 and lived here until the end of 1912.

WEST 22ND STREET

5 West 22nd Street

This address was the last home of Samuel F. B. Morse, painter and inventor of the telegraph. As he lay dying, his doctor tapped him on the chest. "This is how we doctors telegraph," he said. "Very good," said Morse. These were the inventor's last words. He died here on April 2, 1872.

436* West 22nd Street

America's great Shakespearean actor Edwin Forrest once lived at this still-standing house. The actor's feud with British actor Charles Macready lead to the tragic Astor Place Riot on May 10, 1849.

EAST 23RD STREET

East 23rd Street and Broadway, Southeast Corner

Number 2 West 23rd Street was the studio of sculptor Jacques Lipchitz from 1942 until a fire on January 5, 1952, destroyed the studio. Only one or two bronzes survived the blaze that destroyed years of work, models, sketches, and drawings. At 6 East 23rd Street an even more devastating fire engulfed the American Art Galleries Building on October 17, 1966. Twelve fire fighters died after a floor collapsed. This fire was the worst disaster in the history of the fire department.

East 23rd Street and Park Avenue South

After coming ashore during the Battle of Kips Bay during the Revolutionary War, the advancing British forces chased the retreating revolutionaries inland toward this spot. It was roughly at the site of this present-day intersection that one detachment of Hessians captured three hundred soldiers.

145 East 23rd Street

Kenmore Hall Hotel*—This hotel, a haven for drug dealers and prostitutes, was seized by federal agents and New York City police in a morning raid on June 8, 1994. The takeover by authorities represented the largest seizure ever made by the government of a building being used to sell narcotics. Later, it was sold to a nonprofit organization and refurbished as low-income housing. In 1926 the writer Nathanael West worked here as a night manager, often supplying free rooms to his friends Dashiell Hammett, Maxwell Bodenheim, and his brother-in-law S. J. Perelman. Before the hotel was built, this was the site of a building where another author, Stephen Crane, lived in 1893. It was here that he wrote his novel *The Red Badge of Courage.*

WEST 23RD STREET

14* West 23rd Street
Edith Newbold Jones, the future novelist Edith Wharton, was born here in her parents' brownstone on January 24, 1862. The present structure has been greatly altered.

165* West 23rd Street
The writer Stephen Crane once lived on the top floor of this brownstone in 1895–96. The top floor was also the first New York City home of John Sloan, from September of 1904 until 1911. The painter used his view as subject matter for many of his city paintings.

222 West 23rd Street
Chelsea Hotel*—From its opening in 1884 as a pioneering co-operative apartment house to its present status as a hotel for the aspiring avant-garde, this imposing edifice has always been popular with actors, authors, artists, and musicians. A favorite with Sarah Bernhardt, the Victorian Gothic-style hotel has also been home to Thomas Wolfe, Dylan Thomas, Arthur Miller, the Jefferson Airplane, Bob Dylan, and others. It was the setting for Andy Warhol's underground movie *Chelsea Girls* in 1966. On October 12, 1978, it was also the setting for the murder of Nancy Spungen. The twenty-year-old was stabbed once in the stomach by her British musician boyfriend Sid Vicious.

362* West 23rd Street
In September of 1886 the actress Lillie Langtry was given the house at this address. The generous admirer was her American lover, Fred Gebhard. The couple grew apart, and she eventually sold the property in 1894.

West 23rd Street between Ninth and Tenth Avenues

Chelsea Mansion—Just south of present-day West 23rd Street was once the site of the ancestral home and birthplace, on July 15, 1781, of Clement Clark Moore. Moore, a professor of Greek and Oriental literature at the nearby General Theological Seminary and author of the nineteenth-century's primary Hebrew dictionary, is now known chiefly as the poet of "A Visit from St. Nicholas," later called "The Night Before Christmas," recited here for the first time during the holidays in 1822. The cherished poem created for his six children initiated Santa's nocturnal visit on December 24—not December 5, the eve of St. Nicholas's Day, as had been the tradition. It also helped improve Santa's image from that of a stern saint into a jolly old soul. The estate was subdivided and the mansion was demolished in 1854. Professor Moore moved to a house, also now gone, on the southwest corner of Ninth Avenue and West 23rd Street, which he shared with his daughter.

450* West 23rd Street

A downtrodden Edwin Arlington Robinson lived in this brownstone from 1901 until 1905. The poet described his top-floor furnished room as "my old cell." He was living here when *Captain Craig* was published.

EAST 24TH STREET

155 East 24th Street

RCA Victor Studios—The offices for the record division moved to this address in 1929. Musical performers as varied as John McCormack, Marian Anderson, Harry Belafonte, and Perry Como have used recording studios here. Elvis Presley recorded some of his biggest hits, including "Don't Be Cruel" and "Hound Dog," here on July 2, 1956. The building was replaced by Baruch College's academic complex in 1998.

WEST 24TH STREET

22* West 24th Street

Still standing, this building housed Stanford White's favorite hideaway for his legendary trysts, complete with a room entirely covered with mirrors and another with a red-velvet swing. It was here that the architect brought the sixteen-year-old Evelyn Nesbit in 1901 for the first time. This affair with the beautiful showgirl would cost White his life. Five years later he was shot by Nesbit's crazed husband, Harry K.

Thaw. In the trial, it came out that White would suggest to his guests "to see his drawings and etchings," kept here. This mock-seductive invitation to "come up and see my etching?" became a popular line with aspiring playboys for decades after this revelation.

47 West 24th Street

Martz Hotel—This hotel, now gone, was the first New York home of William Sydney Porter in 1902. He had just been released from an Ohio prison, serving time for bank fraud, which accounts for his taking the pseudonym O. Henry. It was here in his beloved adopted home, the New York City he called "Baghdad on the Subway," that he began his tremendously successful career as a short-story writer.

WEST 25TH STREET

1 West 25th Street

New York Club—On the night of March 12, 1888, an exhausted Roscoe Conkling collapsed in the lobby of this club after an arduous trek from his Wall Street office during the Blizzard of 1888, the worst snowstorm in New York's history. The former U.S. representative and senator and aspirant to the White House reached this address after a three-hour ordeal, which included being trapped for twenty minutes in a snow drift in Union Square. He died several weeks later on April 18 as a result of exposure. He became the most famous victim of the blizzard that took an estimated four hundred lives in the Northeast. A statue of Conkling was to be placed in Union Square near the spot where he struggled in the snow but was instead placed in the southeast corner of Madison Square Park.

EAST 26TH STREET

104 East 26th Street

The Armory built in 1906 replaced a yellow brick house that was once the home of Herman Melville. Long forgotten and misunderstood by the readers of his day,

Evelyn Nesbit posed for this portrait in 1905. Nesbit's jealous husband, Harry K. Thaw, shot and killed Stanford White on June 25, 1906. Thaw was obsessed with killing White after learning of his wife's earlier love affair with the architect. *(Collection of the New-York Historical Society)*

Melville's last popular novel was *Typee,* written in 1846. He lived and wrote at this address for almost thirty years. He finished his manuscript of *Billy Budd* three months before dying just after midnight on September 28, 1891. His wife, Elizabeth, considering the novel unfinished, packed it away. It wasn't discovered and published until 1924.

WEST 26TH STREET

37–41 West 26th Street
Miller's Hotel—A physically and mentally deteriorating Mary Todd Lincoln checked into this spa/hotel in October of 1882. The former first lady hoped to relieve her back problems. The hotel offered Turkish, electric, and Roman baths to relieve aches and pains. Louisa May Alcott also visited here, earlier in the fall of 1875; then the name of the hotel was the Bath Hotel.

WEST 27TH STREET

28 West 27th Street
This address was the home of Nathaniel Currier, the famous lithographer. He died here on November 20, 1888. His funeral was held here three days later.

EAST 28TH STREET

4 East 28th Street
Hotel Latham*—Ninety-nine-year-old photographer William Henry Jackson was living here when he fell and injured himself on June 26, 1942. His photographs, shown to members of Congress in 1872, were vital in the creation of Yellowstone, the country's first national park. The "grand old man of the national parks" died four days later at Midtown Hospital and was buried in the National Cemetery in Arlington, Virginia.

149 East 28th Street
Church of St. Stephen Roman Catholic*—The funeral Mass of Louis Moreau Gottschalk was held at this church on October 3, 1870. An overflowing crowd of

mourners came here to pay respects to the concert pianist, who had died the previous year on December 18, 1869, while on tour in Rio de Janeiro, Brazil. Gottschalk was the first American composer to achieve international recognition. Later that afternoon his body made the final journey to Brooklyn's Greenwood Cemetery.

WEST 28TH STREET

West 28th Street between Fifth Avenue and Broadway

This block of West 28th Street is known as the legendary Tin Pan Alley, the turn of the century's center of the sheet-music business. America's great composers, like Jerome Kern, George Gershwin, and Irving Berlin, all began their illustrious careers by creating popular songs on this block. Tin Pan Alley reached the peak of its influence around 1917; during that year more than two billion copies of sheet music were sold. Soon after, the development of radio and the movies radically changed how songs were produced, and New York's share of the music business moved uptown to Broadway at 46th Street.

EAST 29TH STREET

1 East 29th Street

Church of the Transfiguration*—In 1870, while searching for a church to perform the funeral services for the famous actor George Holland, his friend and fellow actor Joseph Jefferson was turned away by a pastor from a tony congregation who suggested they try "the little church around the corner where the matter might be arranged." So nicknamed, the church became a favorite of New York thespians. In addition to Holland's funeral, the church was the site of services for the actors Edwin Booth, James and Lester Wallack, and Richard Mansfield. The writer O. Henry's funeral was also held here. The Episcopal Actors Guild of America had its headquarters in the church building.

29 East 29th Street

Martha Washington Hotel*—When opened on March 2, 1903, this was the first hotel in the United States exclusively for women. The hotel is still open and is still only for women guests.

EAST 30TH STREET

323 East 30th Street

The home of sculptor Louise Nevelson was at this site from 1943 until 1959. In the garden she created an assemblage of painted wood scraps and found objects, which she called "the farm." She sold the four-story townhouse to the developers of the current buildings, the Kips Bay Plaza apartment complex.

WEST 30TH STREET

137 West 30th Street

29th Precinct Police Station—On December 14, 1882, a humiliated Oscar Wilde rushed into this police station, asking to see the captain on duty. He explained he had just been swindled out of $1,000. The English author on an American lecture tour had been approached on Broadway by a young man who suggested lunch and a game of dice. Before he realized it, he was deeply in debt to the other players. Later, Wilde was unable to locate the townhouse where the gambling took place, but he did manage to identify, with the help of mug shots, one of the men involved. He was a notorious con artist known as "Hungary Joe" Sellick.

WEST 32ND STREET

38 West 32nd Street

This address was once home to Commo. Matthew C. Perry, the naval officer who opened Japan to Western trade. He moved into the house that once stood here in 1855 and died here three years later on March 4, 1858, at age sixty-three.

WEST 33RD STREET

35 West 33rd Street

Major's Cabin Grill—While dining in this restaurant, New York lawyer Frank X. McNamara realized he was short of cash and unable to pay his bill. His embarrassment led to his creation of a new enterprise, the Diner's Club. His new company, allowing members to pay for meals on credit, gave birth to the modern credit card.

A few months after the founding in February of 1950, McNamara returned here for a congratulatory meal and executed the company's first transaction.

West 33rd Street to West 34th Street and from Eighth to Ninth Avenues

New York Institution for the Blind—A seventeen-year-old Grover Cleveland accepted a position as assistant teacher at this school in the fall of 1853. The future president taught the younger students reading, writing, arithmetic, and geography here for one year.

EAST 34TH STREET

East 34th Street between First and Second Avenues

This site was once the original shoreline of the East River in the eighteenth century, and on Sunday morning, September 15, 1776, it was the site of the Battle of Kips Bay. Here, in a ditch above that rocky beach, a contingent of revolutionary troops waited for the British troops to begin their attack. Offshore in the East River there were five British ships and about eighty flatboats loaded with more than four thousand Redcoats. At about 11:00, the ship's guns opened fire on the beach. After two hours of bombardment, the British landed and overpowered the remaining defenders. Generals George Washington and Israel Putnam tried to rally their troops, but the patriots were forced to flee before the oncoming British.

WEST 34TH STREET

1 West 34th Street

After tearing down the showplace of the "Sarsaparilla King," Dr. J. C. Townsend, department-store magnate Alexander T. Stewart built his fabled palace on this corner site for his wife, Cornelia. Once it was finished in 1867, he filled it with paintings—a Titian, a Rembrandt, and a Gilbert Stuart portrait of George Washington—and sculpture—*The Blind Girl of Pompeii* and *The Greek Slave*. But their marble museum wasn't a happy home. Ostracized by Knickerbocker society as common tradespeople, the Stewart couple, who never had children, lived a lonely life in the shadow of their disapproving and aristocratic neighbor across the street, Mrs. William Astor. After Stewart died here on April 10, 1876, he left the

This was the home of Alexander T. Stewart on the corner of West 34th Street and Fifth Avenue. The *American Architect* reported that the $2 million five-story marble mansion "has caused more surmise and gossip than any other house ever erected in America." *(Harper's Weekly, August 14, 1869)*

bulk of his $40 million estate to Cornelia. He also bequeathed to his friend and assistant Judge Henry Hilton $1 million. *Harper's Weekly* reported it was "the largest sum ever given by one man to another, not a relative, either in the United States or in Europe."

147 West 34th Street

Koster and Bial's Music Hall—The first official public showing of a projected moving picture for a paying audience took place at this address on April 23, 1896. It was here as part of a vaudeville show that Thomas Edison's Vitascope was demonstrated to an enthusiastic crowd. The audience was treated to several short filmstrips, including two dancers performing the "umbrella" dance and a boxing match. One of the films, *The Beach at Dover,* appeared so real to these early film-goers that several jumped up from their seats, afraid they were about to be drenched. This landmark in movie history was replaced by the present R. H. Macy's Department Store in 1902.

311 West 34th Street

Manhattan Center*—On April 23, 1941, aviation hero Charles A. Lindbergh gave his first New York City speech at an America First Committee rally, a short-lived isolationist group hoping to keep the United States out of World War II. Lindbergh, already perceived as friendly to the Germans, suggested among other things that England had already lost the war against Hitler. Two days later, President Franklin D. Roosevelt, asked his views on Lindbergh's speech, compared the aviator to those "sunshine patriots" at Valley Forge who wanted General Washington to surrender. Lindbergh took offense at Roosevelt's remarks and resigned his commission in the reserves. By the end of the year, it was something of a moot point. The American pacifist movement died after the Japanese bombing of Pearl Harbor.

An early poster advertising Thomas Edison's motion-picture invention the Vitascope. The first paying audience to see these moving pictures was at Koster and Bial's Music Hall on West 34th Street on April 23, 1896. *(FPG)*

EDISON'S GREATEST MARVEL

THE VITASCOPE

"Wonderful is The Vitascope. Pictures life size and full of color. Makes a thrilling show." NEW YORK HERALD, April 24, '96.

Charles A. Lindbergh, speaking to an audience of ten thousand attending an America First Committee rally at the Manhattan Center on West 34th Street on April 23, 1941. An additional twenty thousand people stood outside the hall and heard his isolationist speech on loudspeakers. *(Daily News L. P. Photo)*

WEST 35TH STREET

63–67 West 35th Street

Garrick Theater—As with most opening nights in the theater, the opening of the play *Mrs. Warren's Profession* on October 30, 1905, was full of anticipation. But this night in particular, since Anthony Comstock, the president of the New York Society for the Suppression of Vice, had threatened to stop the show. The comedy by George Bernard Shaw was about life in a brothel. Comstock, the ever-vigilant crusader, did manage to have the production closed for one performance, which yielded priceless publicity for the play. The English language was enhanced when Shaw invented the term "Comstockery" to describe misguided and prudish censorship.

EAST 36TH STREET

125* East 36th Street

After returning from their European honeymoon, Franklin and Eleanor Roosevelt moved into the house still at this address. The couple lived in this rented house from 1905 to 1908. Their first child, Anna Eleanor, was born here on May 3, 1906.

WEST 36TH STREET

16 West 36th Street
No longer here, the home of social arbiter Ward McAllister was once at this address. Dubbed by contemporary wits as "Make-A-Lister," Mrs. William Astor's master party planner was famous for his list of New York society's "400." He made the ultimate faux pas by writing an unflattering book, *Society As I Have Found It,* in 1890 and found himself ostracized from his former employers.

WEST 37TH STREET

11 West 37th Street
Nine-year-old Eleanor Roosevelt moved into this house of her grandparents in 1893 after her mother, Anna, died. The future first lady lived here until shortly before her marriage to the future president Franklin D. Roosevelt in 1905.

15 West 37th Street
This address was once the home of investigative reporter Nellie Bly. She moved here into the brownstone home of her new husband, industrialist Robert Livingston Seaman, in April of 1895. Already famous at twenty-eight years old, Nellie had married a seventy-two-year-old millionaire bachelor.

226 West 37th Street
Long Island–born Catherine Devine was found strangled at this address on January 5, 1908. Working as a prostitute, the once-famous beauty was the belly dancer "Little Egypt," who provoked a police raid on Herbert Barnum Seeley's bachelor's party at Sherry's. She named herself "Little Egypt," as did many erotic dancers, after the mythical dancer from the World's Columbian Exposition in Chicago in 1893.

EAST 38TH STREET

166 East 38th Street
A brownstone that once stood at this address was the home from 1901 until 1912 of Gutzon Borglum, the sculptor of Mount Rushmore. A remodeled stable in the back served as an artist studio.

EAST 40TH STREET

109 East 40th Street

Ernest Flagg, the architect, lived at this address for more than forty years. Flagg, who was an early automobile enthusiast, designed his house in 1906 to accommodate this recent invention. This innovative dwelling had a garage in the basement with an elevator to lift a car to street level. Flagg died here on April 10, 1947, at the age of ninety. The house and next-door office at 111 were demolished in 1979.

WEST 41ST STREET

315 West 41st Street

On April 9, 1874, the police arrived at this Hell's Kitchen tenement and removed a battered nine-year-old girl. "Little Mary Ellen," as she became known in the press, was a Civil War orphan who had been repeatedly beaten and burned by her foster mother, Mary Connolly. Henry Bergh, the recent founder of the American Society for the Prevention of Cruelty to Animals, was instrumental in protecting Mary Ellen from her guardian. The child's unprecedented rescue, along with the subsequent child-abuse trial, marked the beginning of child-protection laws in America.

EAST 42ND STREET

19 East 42nd Street

Hotel Manhattan—Sigmund Freud stayed in the hotel that once stood at this address while on his first and only trip to the United States in late August of 1909. The "Father of Psychoanalysis" had left Vienna to give a series of lectures at Clark University in Worcester, Massachusetts. While in New York, he went sight-seeing to Central Park, the Metropolitan Museum of Art, and Coney Island. One highlight of his trip to the city was his first visit to a motion-picture show.

Seven years later, in May of 1916, another guest, Senator Warren G. Harding of Ohio, began a love affair with Nan Britton at this same hotel. Their secret affair continued even after he was elected president in 1920. Their romance became public knowledge in 1927 after she wrote her book, *The President's Daughter*, about their child, Elizabeth Ann.

East 42nd Street between Park and Lexington Avenues

An eighty-seven-year-old twenty-inch water main a few feet below the pavement of 42nd Street ruptured and gushed million of gallons of water on October 17, 1991. The early-morning deluge created chaos and paralyzed one of the most congested traffic spots in the world. Below ground, the area's three subway tunnels filled with water and were closed to thousands of rush-hour commuters. At street level, automobiles were diverted around the buckled artery and nearby streets were closed. In the neighborhood's high-rises, offices and stores were forced to close because they lacked water. The disaster served as a nagging reminder of the city's vulnerability to its aging and neglected infrastructure.

125* East 42nd Street

Commodore Hotel—In 1980 this recently renovated hotel, with a new glitzy face-lift of reflective glass and a new name, the Grand Hyatt Hotel, became a symbol of the city's renewal after the fiscal crises of the 1970s.

Years earlier, it had been the site of a nervous meeting between Whittaker Chambers and Alger Hiss, the key players in a spy case that propelled Richard Nixon into the national limelight and eventually to the presidency. Chambers testified before the House Committee on Un-American Activities that he knew Hiss, a former State Department official, was a communist. On August 17, 1948, in room 1400 of this hotel, freshman Congressman Nixon and the committee members watched Hiss confront Chambers. Hiss, who had earlier denied knowing Chambers, now admitted his accuser was a man he had known nine years earlier as "George Crosley." Hiss denied spying and claimed he was framed. But a jury believed Chambers, and Hiss was sent to prison for perjury, indirectly labeled as a spy for the Soviets.

WEST 42ND STREET

33* West 42nd Street

Aeolian Hall—George Gershwin introduced his *Rhapsody in Blue* in the third-floor concert hall of this building on February 12, 1924. Paul Whiteman's orchestra, with Gershwin as the piano soloist, performed the symphonic jazz piece. The building was the long-time home of the Graduate Center of the City University of New York before it moved to the old B. Altman Department Store building on Fifth Avenue. It is now the College of Optometry of the State University of New York.

At 350 feet, the Latting Observatory at West 42nd Street and Sixth Avenue towered over midtown in 1853. It was the city's first skyscraper. The wooden tourist attraction and the Crystal Palace across West 42nd Street were both destroyed in separate spectacular fires. *(Author's collection)*

West 42nd Street between Fifth and Sixth Avenues, North Side

Latting Observatory—Built as an added attraction for the crowds attending the Exhibition of 1853 across 42nd Street, this 350-foot wooden observation tower opened on June 30, 1853. The novelty of riding one of the first steam elevators in the country was rewarded with a visit to an ice cream parlor at the very top. It was destroyed by fire on August 30, 1856.

214 West 42nd Street

New Amsterdam Theater*—This 1903 art-nouveau gem was the home of the famous Ziegfeld Follies. Beginning in 1913, Florenz Ziegfeld used this theater as his showcase for America's premier vaudeville talent. The stars of his elaborate musical revues were Fanny Brice, W. C. Fields, Marilyn Miller, Eddie Cantor, and Will Rogers. His composers included Irving Berlin, Victor Herbert, and Jerome Kern. In 1997 the Walt Disney Company's $34 million restoration and reopening of this theater spurred the rebirth of West 42nd Street.

234 West 42nd Street

Liberty Theater*—This movie theater is a landmark in the history of motion pictures. It was here that D. W. Griffith's epic film *Birth of a Nation* had its East Coast premier, March 3, 1915. The film was shown to capacity audiences, despite an admission price of $2. Still controversial after eighty years, Griffith's racial stereotyping and historical distortions of the Civil War and its aftermath nonetheless produced a masterpiece of filmmaking. *Birth of a Nation* provoked protests and riots at some showings yet is often credited with inspiring African Americans to organize for their civil rights.

EAST 43RD STREET

43* East 43rd Street

Hotel Biltmore—The fifth floor of this one-time hotel was the frantic headquarters in the fall of

The entrance to the New Amsterdam Theater is at 214 West 42nd Street. A small rooftop cabaret, created in 1915 to showcase new talent, was where Eddie Cantor, Norma Terris, and Will Rogers began their careers. *(Collection of the New-York Historical Society)*

1915 for Henry Ford's ill-fated peace mission to end World War I. The industrialist, who hoped to have the boys "out of the trenches by Christmas," bankrolled an international delegation to travel to Europe aboard his "Peace Ship" and stop the war. Ford, along with 120 other pacifists, set sail on December 4, 1915, and arrived in Stockholm three weeks later. The idealistic and quixotic venture failed almost immediately, and Ford returned to the United States, ill within a week.

The lobby of this hotel was a favorite meeting place for the coed set. "Meet me under the clock" became college campus buzzwords. This was where F. Scott Fitzgerald, also a favorite on campus, and his new wife, Zelda, spent part of their honeymoon, in room 2109 in April of 1920. The clock is still here, but now it watches over a stark atrium created when the entire structure was remodeled into a glass-clad office building in the early 1980s.

141* East 43rd Street

Saint Agnes Roman Catholic Church—The current Italian Renaissance–style church replaced a Gothic-style structure that was destroyed by fire in 1992. That earlier church was the site of the funeral for "Diamond Jim" Brady on April 16, 1917. The "King of the Great White Way" was a beloved character and spendthrift, who died in Atlantic City in his $1,000-per-week hotel room.

WEST 43RD STREET

108 West 43rd Street

Hotel Diplomat—On August 28, 1973, political activist Abbie Hoffman was arrested in a hotel room for selling two and a half pounds of cocaine to undercover drug agents. He spent the next six weeks in prison before being released on bail. While awaiting trial and a likely mandatory life sentence, he vanished. He spent the next six years in hiding, including stretches in Mexico and Canada. He also had plastic surgery to avoid being identified. The fugitive surrendered on September 4, 1980, pleaded guilty to a lesser charge, and served one year in prison before being released on parole.

229 West 43rd Street

The New York Times*—On June 13, 1971, the newspaper ran the first installment of the Pentagon Papers, a secret study of policy decisions that drew the United States into the Vietnam War. Two days later the Nixon administration obtained a court order halting the publication on the grounds of national security. The U.S. Supreme Court on June 30 upheld the right of *The New York Times* and the *Washington Post* to print the articles. The next year, the Pulitzer Prize in Journalism was awarded to *The New York Times* and Jack Anderson.

255 West 43rd Street, Northeast Corner of Eighth Avenue

Times Square Hotel*—Here on June 13, 1962, Lee Harvey Oswald, the assassin of President John F. Kennedy, his Russian wife, Marina, and new baby spent their first night back in the United States after leaving the Soviet Union. It was here Marina learned her first words of English, "hot" and "cold," from the bathroom faucets. They stayed only that one night; the next day Oswald's brother wired him money to return to Texas. Built in 1922, the hotel has housed tourists, transients, the elderly, and welfare tenants. It was recently renovated as one of the city's largest S.R.O.s, single-room-occupancy hotels.

EAST 44TH STREET

5 East 44th Street

Canfield's Gambling House—This illegal but well-known gambling casino was popular with New York society's "400" and millionaires such as John "Bet-a-Million" Gates. Richard Canfield, an art lover and bibliophile, operated this establishment, along with clubs in Saratoga and Newport, the two resorts popular with New York society in the Gilded Age. In a gentleman's club atmosphere, patrons wagered thousands of dollars on baccarat, roulette, and faro, a card game. During one rare raid, the police discovered $300,000 in IOUs from playboy Reginald Vanderbilt.

225 East 44th Street

Costello's—This bar was a favorite watering hole of James Thurber. The humorist and cartoonist decorated the walls with two sets of murals. After the first set, drawn in late 1934, were mistakenly painted over, he made new ones.

WEST 44TH STREET

59 West 44th Street

Algonquin Hotel*—Famous for the Round Table wits of the 1920s, the hotel was initially made well-known by Alexander Woollcott. In 1919 he was working as a newspaper reporter on assignment to write a piece on the hotel, and he fell in love with the apple pie served there. He kept coming back, each time bringing along friends such as Harold Ross, Heywood Brown, and Franklin Pierce Adams. The number of luncheon partners grew to include Robert Benchley, Dorothy Parker, and Robert Sherwood. The Algonquin has also been home over the years to John Barrymore, Douglas Fairbanks, James Thurber, and Alan Jay Lerner.

145 West 44th Street

Hudson Theater*—Now part of the Hotel Macklowe, this theater was the home of *The Steve Allen Show.* Premiering on July 27, 1953, the pioneering late-night television talk show was broadcast only locally on NBC. It proved very popular, and beginning on September 27, 1954, with guests Wally Cox and Willie Mays, it was broadcast nationally. Retitled *The Tonight Show,* the program became the longest-running talk show in history and the yardstick used to measure all future talk shows.

216 West 44th Street

44th Street Theater—The American Theatre Wing Stage Door Canteen was in the basement of this theater during World War II. The canteen opened on March 1, 1942, and operated until the end of the war. The combination soup kitchen/nightclub was host to more than two thousand servicemen on busy nights.

EAST 45TH STREET

45 East 45th Street

Roosevelt Hotel*—Guy Lombardo and his Royal Canadians orchestra made their New York debut in this hotel's Roosevelt Grill. Beginning on December 31, 1929, Lombardo played "the sweetest music this side of heaven" here for the next thirty-four New Year's Eves before moving to the Waldorf-Astoria Hotel in 1963.

East 45th Street East of First Avenue

Near the East River, there once stood a small stone house used by the British as an armory. In the spring of 1775 it was the target of a daring midnight raid by Marinus Willett and a band of "Liberty Boys." The patriots had sailed down from Greenwich, Connecticut, ambushed the guards, and made off with arms and ammunition for the new Continental Army. Willett later served as mayor of New York City in 1807. This site is now part of the seventeen-acre United Nations complex.

WEST 45TH STREET

128 West 45th Street

Peppermint Lounge—Officially recorded as the birthplace of the Twist in the summer of 1961, in reality, it was the nightclub where mainstream culture was introduced to the swiveling fad. Chubby Checker had popularized the dance on *American Bandstand* a year earlier, and most teenagers were already tired of it

The media-created dance craze, the Twist, started at the Peppermint Lounge in 1961. These couples are twisting at the club once located at 128 West 45th Street. *(Daily News L. P. Photo)*

when it became an overnight sensation here. "Jet-setters," celebrities, the Duke and Duchess of Windsor, and the accompanying press flocked to this club to dance the Twist.

332 West 45th Street

Billy Haa's Restaurant—New York State Supreme Court Judge and legendary missing person Joseph F. Crater waved goodbye to his dinner companions outside the chophouse and got into a cab at 9:15 P.M. on August 6, 1930. The six-foot dapper judge was never seen again. The search continued well beyond Crater's being declared legally dead in 1937. Investigators were digging up backyards in Yonkers as late as 1964, based on visions of a clairvoyant.

EAST 46TH STREET

East 46th Street between Lexington and Third Avenues
In one of the first acts of violence by the mob during the Draft Riots, Metropolitan Police Superintendent John A. Kennedy was beaten unconscious on this block early on the morning of July 13, 1863. He would have been killed but for a good samaritan who convinced the mob that the superintendent was dead and took him to police headquarters.

210 East 46th Street
Sparks Steakhouse*—Mob boss "Big Paul" Castellano and his bodyguard Thomas Bilotti were gunned down outside this restaurant on December 16, 1985. The killings, long denied by rival mobster John Gotti, resulted in his becoming head of the powerful Gambino crime family. It wasn't until Gotti's fourth racketeering trial that Salvatore "Sammy the Bull" Gravano, a former underboss turned government witness, testified that Gotti had indeed authorized the murders. Gravano also testified that he and his boss waited together down the block from the murder scene in their Lincoln sedan at the northwest corner of Third Avenue and 46th Street to direct the assassination. It was Gravano's courtroom confessions that finally convinced a jury to convict Gotti of murder and racketeering on April 2, 1992.

EAST 47TH STREET

231 East 47th Street
Now Dag Hammarskjöld Plaza, this address was the site of Andy Warhol's first "factory," his studio in 1963. The silver-painted and aluminum-foil-covered walls were the sets of his early films *Kiss, Haircut,* and *Eat.* The "50 Most Beautiful People" party was held in this loft in the spring of 1965. Judy Garland, Tennessee Williams, Allen Ginsberg, and other celebrities attended the party, which lasted until five o'clock the following afternoon.

WEST 47TH STREET

41 West 47th Street
Gotham Book Mart*—Marked with the sign "Wise Men Fish Here," this bookstore has been the spiritual heart of literary New York since its opening in 1920. This address is its third home. In addition to famous literary customers, the shop has employed Allan Ginsberg, Everett LeRoi Jones, and even Tennessee Williams as sales clerks.

412* West 47th Street
Editor Harold Ross and his wife, Jane Grant, bought this townhouse in 1922. His friend Alexander Woollcott moved in shortly after, and the house became a meeting place for the writers of the 1920s. It was here that Ross founded *The New Yorker* in 1925.

EAST 48TH STREET

237* East 48th Street
Journalist Dorothy Thompson lived at this address from 1941 until 1957.

WEST 48TH STREET

157 West 48th Street
48th Street Theater—The theater that was once at this address was the scene on April 18, 1926, of the first major dance concert of Martha Graham. This concert helped establish her as the leading exponent of modern dance in America.

West 48th Street at the Hudson River
Early in 1942, while berthed at Pier 88, the French ocean liner S.S. *Normandie* was being transformed into a troop ship for the Allied war effort. On February 9 she caught fire. The blaze was confined to the upper decks and was pretty much under control in a few hours, but all the water pumped into the ship from fireboats and the engines on the pier caused the ship to list to port. Eventually, the luxury liner rolled over into the icy Hudson. The lifeless hulk spent the remainder of the war in New York and was then sold for scrap. Possible explanations for the destruction ranged from Nazi sabotage to mob blackmail to just plain carelessness.

Smoke billows from the French liner S.S. *Normandie* as fire fighters pour water on the doomed ship on February 9, 1942. While in her Hudson River pier at West 48th Street, being refitted as a World War II troop carrier, she caught fire. *(FPG)*

WEST 49TH STREET

239 West 49th Street

St. Malachy's Roman Catholic Church*—This neo-Gothic church and its separate "The Actors' Chapel" has been a spiritual sanctuary for the Broadway community since 1903. The funeral Mass for silent-screen star Rudolph Valentino was held here on August 30, 1926. Mary Pickford, Gloria Swanson, and Pola Negri attended the service. Fred Allen was married here, as were Jimmy Durante and Joan Crawford.

EAST 50TH STREET

100 East 50th Street

Waldorf Towers*—This twin-towered annex to the famed hotel is reserved for residential suites. The list of residents reads like a Who's Who in America: Adlai Stevenson, Gen. Douglas MacArthur, and Cole Porter. Former president Herbert

Hoover lived here for almost thirty years. He died in suite 31A on October 20, 1964, from a massive internal hemorrhage. European royalty, the Duke and Duchess of Windsor and Prince Rainier and Princess Grace of Monaco, used the hotel as their home while in New York.

WEST 50TH STREET

West 50th Street near Seventh Avenue, North Side

Roxy Theater—Built by theater entrepreneur S. L. Rothapfel and christened with his nickname, this 5,920-seat movie "palace" was one of the most elaborate of the Roaring Twenties. The opening on March 11, 1927, was the gala premier of *The Love of Sunya.* The distinguished guests included his honor the mayor, Jimmy Walker; the governor of New Jersey; and four U.S. senators. Charlie Chaplin, Harold Lloyd, and star of the show Gloria Swanson represented Hollywood. Swanson was also on hand to bid a final farewell on March 9, 1960, when the theater was demolished.

345 West 50th Street

New York Polyclinic Hospital—The writer O. Henry died at this hospital on June 5, 1910. Silent-screen idol Rudolph Valentino also died here of peritonitis on August 23, 1926.

West 50th Street at the Hudson River

The *Queen Mary* docked here at Pier 90 on June 20, 1945. The former luxury liner, still doing war duty as a deep-gray-painted troop carrier, brought home the first shipload of American troops from Europe after VE Day. The waterfronts of Staten Island, Brooklyn, and Manhattan along the Hudson River were lined with well-wishers. New York Harbor was filled with a flotilla of boats. The dock was crowded with wives and sweethearts. Many of those 14,526 servicemen and -women

Former president Herbert Hoover arrives at his new home at the Waldorf Towers, the annex to the Park Avenue Hotel, on March 4, 1933. Hoover left Washington, D.C., immediately after the inauguration of his successor, President Franklin D. Roosevelt. *(FPG)*

Shown in this 1930 photograph, the Roxy Theater, known as "the cathedral of the motion picture," was equipped with six box offices, smoking and hospital rooms, and its own symphony orchestra and ballet company. The lobby and marquee extended into the first floor of the Taft Hotel on Seventh Avenue. *(FPG)*

aboard, though, were only on a short furlough and soon left to fight the war in the Pacific. The *Queen Mary* would later help reunite English war brides with their American husbands. The ship is now permanently docked in Long Beach, California, as a floating hotel.

EAST 51ST STREET

22 East 51st Street
The four-story brownstone that once stood at this address was the home of railroad magnate Edward Henry Harriman. It was here on November 15, 1891, that his son William Averell was born. W. Averell was governor of New York and adviser to several presidents.

East 51st Street and First Avenue, Northwest Corner
Mount Pleasant—James Beekman's mansion was at this location from 1763 until 1874. This house, with the first greenhouse in America, served as the headquarters

of General Howe of the British Army during the Revolutionary War. It was here that patriot Nathan Hale was condemned to death as a spy on September 21, 1776.

WEST 51ST STREET

51 West 51st Street
Toots Shor's Restaurant—Opened in 1940 by former B.V.D. underwear sales and speakeasy bouncer Toots Shor, this was the site of his first restaurant. Shor, a brassy host, lorded over the assembled "crumb bums"—sport figures, sports writers, and celebrities—who gathered here. In 1958 he sold his lease for $1.5 million. His lot, the last holdout, became the Sperry-Rand Building, and Toots moved on to several other locations.

West 51st Street West of Broadway, North Side
A vicious mob attack on journalist Victor Riesel took place here in the shadows near the Mark Hellinger Theater at about 3:00 A.M. on the night of April 5, 1956.

On June 20, 1945, the *Queen Mary* sails up the Hudson River to Pier 90 at West 50th Street, her decks crammed with the first returning troops from Europe after VE Day. *(National Archives)*

After leaving Lindy's restaurant, Riesel confronted a small-time hood who threw acid in his face, permanently blinding him. Riesel, an outspoken critic of corruption, had spoken earlier on mob racketeering in labor unions. The mob had the attacker, Abraham Telvi, killed two weeks later. Despite his blindness, Riesel continued his crusade in his newspaper column.

332* West 51st Street

Just steps from his apartment at this address, Alvin "Shipwreck" Kelly collapsed and died of a heart attack on October 11, 1952. The flagpole sitter's stunts epitomized the "era of wonderful nonsense" of the 1920s. He once spent forty-nine days atop a flagpole in Atlantic City. He was holding a scrapbook of his exploits when he died.

EAST 52ND STREET

435 East 52nd Street

River House—Edwin Howard Armstrong, the inventor of FM radio, plunged to his death from his thirteenth-story apartment on the night of January 31, 1954. He was despondent over his relationship with his wife and protracted legal battles concerning his radio-related patents. Other tenants in this building were Henry and Clare Booth Luce, who lived here from 1936 until 1960.

450 East 52nd Street

The Campanile—When screen actress Greta Garbo wanted to be alone, she came here, her home of more than forty years. In addition to the famous recluse, this apartment building was also home to Noel Coward and Alexander Woollcott.

WEST 52ND STREET

West 52nd Street between Fifth and Sixth Avenues

Nicknamed "Swing Street," this block was once lined with rundown brownstones that housed small jazz clubs. Dizzy Gillespie, Charlie Parker, Miles Davis, Sarah Vaughan, Count Basie, Buddy Rich, and many more great musicians played here during the block's heyday in the thirties and forties. The first club to open was the Onyx, later called the "Cradle of Swing." Other clubs included the Famous Door (first at 35 West 52nd Street), the Three Deuces (75 West 52nd Street), and the Downbeat (66 West 52nd Street).

416 West 52nd Street

Gene Tunney, the champion heavyweight fighter, was born at this address on May 25, 1898. He lived here until about the age of three months, then his family moved to Greenwich Village.

EAST 53RD STREET

3 East 53rd Street

Stork Club—It was at this locale on the evening of October 16, 1951, in one of the city's choicest night spots, that America was again painfully reminded of the country's racial bigotry. The American-born black dancer and French sensation Josephine Baker was badly treated and refused service here during her U.S. tour. The sordid affair escalated the next day when Baker denounced the club and another diner, the powerful columnist Walter Winchell, for not coming to her aid. Winchell's initial embarrassment soon turned to wrath, and he used his gossip column to smear Baker. Baker lost club engagements, and she returned to France, embittered by her homeland's intolerance. Today, this site is the serene Samuel Paley Park.

Protesters outside the Stork Club on East 53rd Street demonstrate against the nightclub's racial discrimination against singer Josephine Baker in October of 1951. *(FPG)*

WEST 53RD STREET

11 West 53rd Street

*Museum of Modern Art**—In the garden of the museum on March 17, 1960, a sculpture designed to destroy itself, called *Homage to New York,* did destroy itself in just twenty-three minutes. Created by Swiss motion artist Jean Tinguely, the work incorporated gunpowder, smoke bombs, and fireworks. The artist wanted to destroy art "before it's too late—i.e. before the vital spirit drowned in the rising tide of mass appreciation, publicity, and over exposure in reproductions." The next day he took the remains to the dump.

410* West 53rd Street

Five sunbathers on the roof of this apartment house had their 1993 Fourth of July lazy sojourn interrupted when a 160-foot blimp named *The Bigfoot* crash-landed on their tar beach. The bathers watched in disbelief as the large white ship slowly circled downward as it lost helium. The $4 million blimp was on its maiden voyage across the country to advertise Pizza Hut's new twenty-one-slice pizza. The pilot and copilot were treated for minor injuries at nearby St. Luke's-Roosevelt Hospital. None of the rooftop witnesses was hurt. One year later a report by the National Transportation Safety Board suggested that the accident, caused by a thirty-eight-foot gash, may have been averted by rip-resistant fabric.

EAST 54TH STREET

24 East 54th Street

A modern two-story building that once stood at this address was the first home of the Solomon R. Guggenheim Museum of Non-Objective Art in 1939. The museum moved to its current site in 1947, to a building that was later demolished for the celebrated structure designed by Frank Lloyd Wright.

60 East 54th Street

*Hotel Elysee**—One of America's preeminent playwrights, Tennessee Williams, died in his suite at this hotel on February 24, 1983. Long addicted to drugs and alcohol, Williams didn't die of an overdose but was asphyxiated by a medical bottle cap lodged in his throat.

WEST 54TH STREET

4 West 54th Street

This site was the New York City home of John D. Rockefeller, founder of the family oil empire. Built in 1865, it was one of the first townhouses in this newly fashionable section of upper Fifth Avenue. In 1884 Rockefeller, forever frugal, bought the modest four-story brownstone rather than building a European-inspired mansion like other robber barons of his age. He and his wife, Laura, made very few decorating changes and split their time after he retired in the 1890s between this house and the family's Pocantico Hills estate. After Rockefeller died in 1937, the house was torn down to make room for the Sculpture Garden of the Museum of Modern Art, a leading recipient of the family's charity.

13* West 54th Street

This brownstone was the childhood home of Nelson Rockefeller, New York governor and U.S. vice president, across the street from his grandfather John D. Rockefeller's house. It was here that Nelson had his fatal heart attack on the night of January 26, 1979.

254* West 54th Street

Studio 54—Built originally as the Gallo Theater in 1927, this cavernous space became the high temple of the disco culture of the late 1970s. Patrons like Truman Capote, Bianca Jagger, Andy Warhol, and the designer Halston mingled with other celebrities and politicos long into the night under the spell of drugs, flashing lights, and blaring music. The club closed in 1980 after its owners, Steve Rubell and Ian Schranger, were convicted of tax evasion.

EAST 55TH STREET

10 East 55th Street

This site was the home of Joseph Pulitzer from 1887 until a fire on January 9, 1900. The house-

One of America's richest men, John D. Rockefeller, lived in a house that once stood at 4 West 54th Street for fifty-three years. Several rooms from this house have been recreated at the Museum of the City of New York. *(FPG)*

keeper and a governess were trapped and died, but seventeen other servants and the family escaped. The blaze destroyed the journalist's valuable art collection. The St. Regis Hotel, a favorite with author Ernest Hemingway and painter Salvador Dalí, is now at this corner.

EAST 56TH STREET

65 East 56th Street

Coq Rouge—The restaurant Coq Rouge—once at this address—was the site of surrealist artist Salvador Dalí's farewell party, billed as the "Dream Betrayal Ball," on February 18, 1935. Guests, some of whom wore bird cages and headdresses, were instructed to come dressed as their dreams. Upon entering, they were given sausages to represent their "link in the endless chain."

330* East 56th Street

Sutton Club—In the fall of 1930 the writer Nathanael West worked as a night manager at this hotel, just as he had a few years earlier at another family property, the Kenmore Hall Hotel on East 23rd Street. Again he supplied cheap or free rooms to fellow writers. But it was here that his experience with the hotel guests, many defeated and embittered by the Great Depression, gave him inspiration for characters in his famous novel *Miss Lonelyhearts.*

353 East 56th Street

Forced to flee his native Holland for England in 1939, artist Piet Mondrian fled again after the Nazis started bombing London. He moved to this address, his first New York apartment and studio. It was here that he completed his last painting, *Broadway Boogie Woogie,* a lively variation on his grid patterns, as an homage to his adopted city's street patterns.

411* East 56th Street

Composer Jerome Kern was born at this address on January 27, 1885.

WEST 57TH STREET

2 West 57th Street

On August 29, 1896, President Grover Cleveland and members of his cabinet met with Li Hung, the Chinese viceroy, at this address. Li Hung was the first representative of the Chinese government to visit the United States. This was the home of W. C. Whitney, an ex-secretary of the navy.

4–6 West 57th Street

A teenaged Theodore Roosevelt moved here with his family in 1873. He later returned here, in 1880, with his new bride, Alice Lee, to live in an apartment made for them on the third floor. But this address would bring on horrible memories for the future president. It was in this house that both his wife and mother would die on the same day, February 14, 1884. Alice, who had just delivered the couple's first child, died of Bright's disease, and his mother, Mittie, died of typhus fever. The Crown Building now occupies the site.

Theodore Roosevelt wrote his book *The Naval War of 1812* in the library of his home that stood at 6 West 57th Street. His wife, Alice, and mother, "Mittie," both died here on the same day, St. Valentine's Day, 1884. *(Theodore Roosevelt Collection, Harvard College Library)*

Crown Building*—The current office building (730 Fifth Avenue), originally named the Heckscher, on this site was the first home of the Museum of Modern Art from 1929 until 1932. The building was involved in years of legal battles and international intrigue when it was discovered that Ferdinand Marcos, the Philippine president, had secretly bought it in 1981. After the dictator was deposed, the Philippine government hoped to claim the profits from the sale of the building. In a compromise, the courts decided that the proceeds would be split between all the competing parties.

30* West 57th Street

Art of This Century Gallery—Heiress and high priestess of modern art Peggy Guggenheim and her new husband, the artist Max Ernst, opened her gallery on October 21, 1942, in this building. It quickly became a showcase for abstract expressionism and surrealism. Artists Jackson Pollock, Robert Motherwell, Hans Hofmann, Adolph Gottlieb, and Mark Rothko were all promoted and exhibited here. Guggenheim was quoted as hoping the gallery "serves its purpose only if it succeeds in serving the future instead of recording the past." The gallery stayed open until 1947, when Guggenheim moved permanently to Venice.

60 West 57th Street

Hemisphere House*—Novelist Jerzy Kosinski had an apartment here. Sometime after midnight on May 3, 1991, the author committed suicide with a combination of alcohol, barbiturates, and a plastic bag, the same method detailed in his most recent novel, *The Hermit of 69th Street.*

101 West 57th Street

Buckingham Hotel*—Ignace Paderewski, pianist and statesman, died of pneumonia in this hotel on June 29, 1941. Paderewski, who had been the prime minister of Poland after World War I, was working in America for the Polish cause since the German occupation of Poland in 1939. He was buried in Arlington Cemetery in Washington, D.C., and finally returned to his native Poland in 1992 after the fall of the Communist government. Broadway chronicler Damon Runyon lived at this hotel for several years before his death in 1946. As requested in the writer's will, his friend Capt. Eddie Rickenbacker, the World War I flying ace and head of Eastern Airlines, scattered Runyon's ashes over Manhattan from a small plane on December 18, 1946.

120* West 57th Street

Hotel St. Hubert—A leading figure in the evolution of American literature, William Dean Howells, lived here in this building—then a hotel—from 1910 until his death on May 11, 1920. The eighty-four-year-old author had caught a cold three weeks earlier and died in his sleep.

130* West 57th Street

This address was the long-time studio of painter Childe Hassam from 1908 until his death in 1935. Here, the artist created many of his cityscapes, including his famous flag-draped scenes of Fifth Avenue during World War I.

154 West 57th Street

Carnegie Hall*—Peter Ilyich Tchaikovsky, making his only trip to America, formally opened the hall directing his *Marche Solennelle* on May 5, 1891, while donor Andrew Carnegie sat in box number 33. For more than one hundred years great entertainers have performed here: Ignace Paderewski, Antonín Dvorák, and Vladimir Horowitz. Leonard Bernstein made a triumphal appearance on November 15, 1943, as a replacement for conductor Bruno Walter, who was ill. Not only a showcase for classical music, the auditorium has heard the sounds of Benny Goodman, Duke Ellington, and the Beatles. The hall has also served as a lecture platform for Mark Twain, Woodrow Wilson, Winston Churchill, and Martin Luther King Jr. Carnegie Hall has been more than just a spiritual home for artists; 140 studios in this building have served as physical homes. Charles Dana Gibson, John Philip Sousa, Isadora Duncan, Agnes de Mille, and Marlon Brando have lived here over the years.

205 West 57th Street

Osborne Apartments*—Leonard Bernstein wrote *West Side Story* while he lived in this building. On October 19, 1978, it was the site of murder and suicide. Oscar-winning actor Gig Young shot his new bride and then shot himself in their bedroom.

215 West 57th Street

Art Students' League*—Anthony Comstock, founder and special agent of the Society for the Suppression of Vice and U.S. postal inspector, raided this famous art school on August 2, 1906. This overzealous reformer confiscated the recent issue of the league's magazine, *The American Art Student.* The issue, which Comstock found "indecent," contained illustrations of nudes drawn by some of the students. A list of the faculty and students of this school reads like a Who's Who of American art: William Merritt Chase, Thomas Hart Benton, Thomas Eakins, Augustus Saint-Gaudens, Robert Henri, George Bellows, Edward Hopper, John Sloan, and Jackson Pollock.

318 West 57th Street

West Side, Young Men's Christian Association—Often a first stop for many of the city's newcomers, this "Y" was the home for artist George Bellows from Columbus, Ohio, in 1904. The gym and locker rooms were subjects of many of his prints.

340 West 57th Street

Parc Vendome*—James Montgomery Flagg, one of America's most famous illustrators, died here in his apartment on May 27, 1960. The eighty-two-year-old artist created the World War I recruiting poster of Uncle Sam with the caption "I Want You."

EAST 58TH STREET

38* East 58th Street

Newlyweds Georgia O'Keeffe and Alfred Stieglitz moved into a studio apartment in this building in 1924.

WEST 58TH STREET

202 West 58th Street

Elysee Theater—Long-time health-food guru and publisher Jerome Irving Rodale was at this theater for a taping of the *Dick Cavett Show* on June 7, 1971. After his interview, the seventy-two-year-old author quietly slumped over in his chair and died of a heart attack. ABC never ran the show, replacing it with a rerun.

EAST 59TH STREET

5* East 59th Street

Playboy Club—On February 5, 1963, a newly trained Playboy waitress, Marie Catherine Ochs, reported for work here at this fading bastion of male supremacy.

This particular "bunny" on her first day was actually Gloria Steinem, the twenty-eight-year-old budding feminist author who had infiltrated the club to write "A Bunny's Tale," her article that originally appeared in *Show* magazine. Ms. Steinem's tale helped foster her as a voice of the newly emerging women's movement. Deborah Harry was also a "bunny" here before becoming the lead singer of the band Blondie.

WEST 59TH STREET

447 West 59th Street
Sloane Hospital for Women—Former first lady Nancy Reagan was born at this hospital on July 6, 1921.

View up Broadway from 62nd Street. *(FPG)*

ABOVE 59TH STREET

ADAM CLAYTON POWELL JUNIOR BOULEVARD

2090* Adam Clayton Powell Junior Boulevard

Hotel Theresa—Once called the Waldorf of Harlem, this landmark in African American history didn't even begin admitting blacks as hotel guests until it was purchased by African American businessman Love B. Woods in 1937. From that time on, it was the premier social hub for African American celebrities and entertainers. Famous guests have included Joe Louis, Jimi Hendrix (room 406), and Malcolm X (suite 128). Premier Fidel Castro of Cuba, in a gesture of egalitarianism, insisted on staying in this hotel while attending meetings at the United Nations in September of 1960. It was here that he met with Nikita Khrushchev, Gamal Abdal Nasser, and Jawaharlal Nehru. Now called the Theresa Towers, it is an office building.

2305 Adam Clayton Powell Junior Boulevard

A second-floor office at this address was the site of Dr. Elizabeth "Bessie" Delany's first dental practice. She earned her degree in dentistry from Columbia University in 1923 and was the second African American woman licensed to practice in New York City. In 1994 she and her sister, Sadie, both over a hundred years old, were the authors and subjects of a best-selling book based on their long lives, *Having Our Say,* later turned into a play by the same title.

2309 Adam Clayton Powell Junior Boulevard

Comedian Bert Williams died here at his home on March 4, 1932.

2588 Adam Clayton Powell Junior Boulevard

Paul Laurence Dunbar Apartments—This six-building complex, named for the African American poet, was developed by John D. Rockefeller Jr. as the first large co-operative project in the country built for African Americans. The innovative complex is centered around a large interior garden

After it ended its policy of racial segregation in 1937, the focal point of African American social life in Harlem was the Hotel Theresa at 2090 Adam Clayton Powell Junior Boulevard. Secretary of Commerce in the Clinton Administration Ron Brown, whose father was the hotel manager, lived here as a child. *(FPG)*

court. One of the first tenants in 1928 was the editor W. E. B. Du Bois, who lived here until 1934. Other celebrated tenants were Paul Robeson, singer and actor; A. Philip Randolph, labor leader; Matthew A. Henson, North Pole explorer; and Bill "Bojangles" Robinson, dancer.

AMSTERDAM AVENUE

108 Amsterdam Avenue
This was the family home of nineteen-year-old Gertrude Ederle, who was the first woman to swim across the English Channel. On August 6, 1926, she completed her swim in a record-breaking time—fourteen hours and thirty-one minutes, two hours faster than the men's record. This favorite New York City daughter was honored with a ticker-tape parade on Broadway.

Over one hundred years in the making, St. John the Divine Cathedral, the world's largest Gothic cathedral, is still unfinished today. This photograph, taken during the 1920s, shows the cathedral on Amsterdam Avenue surrounded by the familiar scaffolding. *(FPG)*

854 Amsterdam Avenue

Artist Norman Rockwell was born at this address, a fifth-floor walk-up, on February 3, 1894. The *Saturday Evening Post* cover illustrator lived in the city until he was six, and then his family moved to Westchester County. He received his training at the Art Students League.

Amsterdam Avenue between West 110th and 112th Streets

*Cathedral of St. John the Divine**—The cornerstone was laid on December 27, 1892, the feast day of Saint John, on what is intended to become the largest Gothic cathedral in the world. It is the principal church of the Episcopal Diocese of New York. Nicknamed "St. John the Unfinished," this cathedral has endured more than a hundred years of starts and stops and several major design changes. Such major-league players as John Pierpoint Morgan, John D. Rockefeller, and Franklin D. Roosevelt have helped with the constant fund-raising needed to build the landmark.

Amsterdam Avenue and West 114th Street, Northeast Corner

*Saint Luke's Hospital**—In the initial days of the then-unrecognized and -unnamed AIDS epidemic, a patient with a strange new disease underwent a brain biopsy and was diagnosed with toxoplasmosis. This opportunistic infection later became commonly recognized as an early sign of AIDS. The young man who died here on January 15, 1981, is now considered one of the earliest deaths due to AIDS in the United States.

1150 Amsterdam Avenue

*Philosophy Hall, Columbia University**—In 1913, in a basement laboratory, Edwin Howard Armstrong, recent Columbia graduate, was demonstrating his new invention, the regenerative circuit, which greatly improved the reception of wireless messages. One of the witnesses to this demonstration was David Sarnoff, the future chairman of Radio Company of America, RCA. These two radio visionaries had another meeting in this same laboratory twenty years later in 1933, this time to witness another of Armstrong's inventions, frequency modulation, or FM.

BROADWAY

1883 Broadway

Colonial Theater—At this theater Charlie Chaplin made his American debut in a vaudeville skit called "The Wow-wows, or a Night in a London Secret Society" on

Taken about 1905, this is the view from Broadway and West 62nd Street, looking north. On the left is the Colonial Theater. The theater is now gone. Two other Upper West Side landmarks visible in the picture, the Ansonia and the miniature Statue of Liberty, are still standing today. *(FPG)*

October 3, 1910. Also introduced here at the Colonial in the play *Runnin' Wild* on October 29, 1923, was a dance craze, the Charleston. The snappy dance, created on the docks in Charleston, South Carolina, came to epitomize the abandon of the Roaring Twenties. The comedy team of George Burns and Gracie Allen also appeared on the Colonial's stage.

Broadway and West 63rd Street, Northwest Corner

Lincoln Arcade Building—This building was a popular site for artist's studios in the early part of this century. George Bellows, Thomas Hart Benton, Rockwell Kent, Milton Avery, and Marcel Duchamp all had space to work here. This was also home to Robert Henri's School of Art from 1909 to 1912. Some of Henri's students were Yasuo Kuniyoshi, Edward Hopper, and Stuart Davis. Another artist with space here was Pat Sullivan, the creator of "Felix the Cat," America's first successful animated cartoon character. The arcade was destroyed in a three-hour blaze on January 29, 1931.

1970 Broadway

Frank E. Campbell's Funeral Chapel—From August 24 to 30, 1926, this address was the scene of a near riot among the mourners waiting to view the body of the silent-screen idol Rudolph Valentino. Mounted police had to be called to control the frenzied crowd. More than one hundred people were injured, some after crashing through the funeral home's front window. Eventually, ninety thousand fans filed through the Gold Room to see Valentino, laid out in a silver-bronze coffin with a glass cover. An honor guard, supposedly sent by Italian dictator Benito Mussolini, supplied additional protection from inconsolable fans.

2107 Broadway
The Ansonia*—An old friend rising above Broadway, this landmarked apartment house has been home to many musical artists, such as Enrico Caruso, Arturo Toscanini, Ezio Pinza, Lily Pons, and Igor Stravinsky. In the basement, Plato's Retreat was at different times a straight and gay sex club. The club closed its doors in the mid 1980s due to changing sexual attitudes and the fear of AIDS.

2120–22* Broadway
Hotel Kimberly—Aspiring actress and model Lucille Ball stayed in room 712 in the late 1920s. The building has become a condominium and was renamed the Fitzgerald.

Candles and mountains of flowers surround Rudolph Valentino's coffin at Frank E. Campbell's Funeral Chapel at 1970 Broadway. The flowers reportedly cost more than $50,000. The blanket of red roses on the coffin was a gift from Pola Negri, who announced she and Hollywood's leading man were planning to wed. *(Daily News L. P. Photo)*

Broadway and West 75th Street, Northwest Corner

Somerindyke House—Hessians occupied the house that once stood just north of this intersection during the Revolutionary War. Later, in the 1790s, Louis Philippe, citizen king of France from 1830 to 1848, lived and taught school here for a short time while in exile during the Napoleonic regime.

Broadway and West 77th Street

"Wood Lawn"—This section of the city was still in the country when Mayor Fernando Wood had a home near this present-day intersection. It was here that he entertained ex-president Millard Fillmore and the Prince of Wales for lunch on October 12, 1860, during the prince's U.S. visit.

2745 Broadway

This address was once the home of Isidor Straus, a co-owner of R. H. Macy's Department Store. Both he and his wife, Ida, lost their lives on the *Titanic*. A monument to the disaster in a nearby park at West End and Broadway is dedicated to their memory.

Broadway and West 106th Street

Once the buckwheat field on the Jones farm, this present-day intersection was the site of the Battle of Harlem Heights on September 16, 1776, during the Revolutionary War. More of a scrimmage than a battle, the shooting began shortly after patriot Lt. Col. Thomas Knowlton engaged the British Light Infantry. By the time the fighting was finished, the action had moved north to Broadway near today's West 120th Street. In spite of the death of Knowlton, it was considered an American victory and a needed boost of the rebels' low morale.

2911 Broadway

West End Cafe*—Still a local hangout for Columbia University faculty and students, this restaurant was popular with the beat poets and writers Allen Ginsberg, William Burroughs, and Jack Kerouac in the late 1940s.

Broadway and West 114th to West 120th Streets

Bloomingdale Insane Asylum—Open in 1821, this was the first mental hospital in New York State. The hospital moved to White Plains, New York, in the 1890s.

   Columbia University Campus*—This hilltop location became the third and current home of Columbia University in 1897. Charles F. McKim, who was also the architect of many of the initial buildings, designed the uncompleted master plan of the campus. McKim's masterpiece is the monumental Low Memorial Library. The sculpture *Alma Mater* by Daniel Chester French on the surrounding terrace in front of the library became a focal point for the student protest movement of the late 1960s. A student sit-in at several university buildings led to the closing of the school on April 26, 1968. Four days later, one thousand riot police stormed the campus and began dragging away the student protesters in the five closed buildings. Many students were arrested and injured. They were opposed to the new gymnasium planned for Morningside Park and the university's affiliation with a consortium that did military research for the government.

2960 Broadway

Dodge Hall, Kathryn Bache Miller Theater, Columbia University*—On Sunday, September 22, 1991, previous winners along with the 1991 winners celebrated the seventy-fifth anniversary of the Pulitzer Prizes in this Columbia University auditorium. The journalism prizes, founded by publisher Joseph Pulitzer and administered by the university, are awarded "for the encouragement of public service, public morals, American literature, and the advancement of education."

3030 Broadway

Pupin Physics Hall, Columbia University*—Enrico Fermi and John R. Dunning started the final experiment with the cyclotron to split a uranium atom in a basement laboratory of this building on January 25, 1939. The Atomic Age began with this research, which led to the development of atomic power and the bomb. Fermi had become a professor of physics here at Columbia University after he had fled Fascist Italy.

3032 Broadway

Horace Mann School, Columbia University*—In the auditorium of this building, Albert Einstein, lecturing on his theory of relativity, introduced "time" as the fourth dimension on April 15, 1921. Professor Einstein, speaking in German, explained one of the most revolutionary theories of twentieth-century science to a room packed with students and faculty.

Broadway and West 120th to West 122nd Streets

Today the Union Theological Seminary occupies this spot, but on September 16, 1776, it was a wheat field. It was here that the heaviest fighting of the Battle of

Harlem Heights during the Revolutionary War took place. A British force of about five thousand men faced off against about two thousand patriots. After the battle ended later that day, the American losses were about thirty soldiers killed, while the British had fourteen casualties.

3755* Broadway

American Geographical Society—Part of the Audubon Terrace complex, it was here, during the late summer of 1917 in the midst of World War I, that a group called the "Inquiry" met to discuss a possible permanent international association to preserve peace. Under secret orders from President Woodrow Wilson, Colonel House, his trusted adviser, Walter Lippmann, and others met to plan for the postwar age and to draft a constitution for the president's cherished League of Nations, forerunner to today's United Nations. The building now houses Boricua College.

Broadway and West 165th to West 168th Streets

Hilltop Park—Once solid rock, this site was carved out of the ramparts of Washington Heights to build this all-wood baseball stadium. One of the highest spots in Manhattan, the ballpark was the first home of the New York Yankees, then called the Highlanders. Their first game was on April 30, 1903, when the Highlanders beat Washington 6 to 2. After the Yankees played their last game here in 1912, the stadium was torn down two years later. The hilltop was then chosen as the site of a tabernacle where Billy Sunday, a baseball player turned evangelist, preached to the faithful. At his most successful revival here in 1917, he tallied up 98,264 conversions. Columbia Presbyterian Medical Center replaced the tabernacle in 1925.

3950 Broadway, Southeast Corner of West 165th Street

Audubon Ballroom*—Built in 1912 by Thomas Lamb, this was the site of the nation's first dance marathon, which began on March 30, 1923. Alma Cummings won the contest by dancing continuously for more than twenty-four hours. Popular jazz and big bands played here in the thirties, forties, and early fifties. It was here on February 21, 1965, that Malcolm X was assassinated. The charismatic African American leader was just about to address his audience when he was shot and killed on stage. The motive for the killing and identity of the assassins are still being questioned, but three men were convicted of the murder and given life sentences. A year earlier, Malcolm X had broken away from his mentor Elijah Muhammad and his Nation of Islam and formed his own group of followers. The ballroom was slated to be demolished for Columbia University's Biomedical Science and Technology Research Center, but community pressure ensured that the restored façade of the Audubon remained as a memorial.

5030 Broadway

New York Telephone Company Office—This building was the scene of a large explosion on October 3, 1962. At 12:07 P.M., the beginning of the lunch hour, a steam boiler weighing more than a ton blasted through a basement wall in the company's cafeteria. The boiler rocketed across the room, which was filled with employees. Twenty-three people were killed, and scores were injured.

CENTRAL PARK

Political leaders and reformers, including William Cullen Bryant, realized the need for a public park for the rapidly growing city in the 1840s. They were concerned about the influx of foreign immigrants forced to live in crowded urban neighborhoods. A "rural" park setting was envisioned as a release valve for these new social tensions. Their most idealistic goal was that of a park as a democratic meeting ground, where all classes of people could relax in a pastoral setting.

In 1856 land was acquired and the Central Park Commission created. A design contest for the park was established. Frederick Law Olmsted and Calvert Vaux won with their joint "Greensward" based on English landscape principles. Central Park became the first landscaped public park in the United States. Sixteen hundred residents of small settlements, including Seneca Village on what is now the west side of the park near the Great Lawn, were removed from the land. More than twenty thousand workers labored in the age of horsepower to transform the natural glacier-formed setting into a park. The bedrock was blasted away, mountains of dirt and rocks moved, streams were diverted, and lawns and meadows were formed to create the pastoral vistas. More than 270,000 trees and shrubs were planted. In the midst of this picturesque landscape, a formal area was created for promenading, a popular pastime for those early Victorian visitors. One of the Olmsted-Vaux team's most innovative ideas was to separate the crosstown traffic from the park in four sunken transverse roads, a vision created long before the automobile age.

Central Park has served as the city's backyard, witnessing the joys and tragedies of urban life for more than 140 years. It can be experienced collectively in any of the park's gathering points or virtually alone in the rural areas. One private moment took place on June 13, 1859, when Frederick Law Olmsted married Mary Olmsted, his brother's widow, in the park. It has been home to the homeless, the most visible during the Great Depression in so-called "Hoovervilles" on the Great Lawn. The park has been the site of rallies, concerts, protests, and a few well-publicized murders. Yet it is incredibly safe, still the tranquil retreat envisioned by its designers. The changing seasons in the park help keep the city in touch with nature. Each season brings its own fitting activity, whether ice-skating on the pond or sunbathing on the Great Lawn. Each fall is marked by the New York City Marathon, first run entirely in the park on September 13, 1970.

Central Park is remarkably resilient, given the increasing number of visitors over the years. What was considered a large crowd of twenty thousand attended the unveiling of Cleopatra's Needle in February of 1881. But that number seems small compared with the eight hundred thousand visitors during the *Statue of Liberty* centennial weekend, July 5, 1986, which is believed to be the largest crowd ever.

The newly planted Central Park is slightly barren in this engraving from 1861. The Arsenal, which was built ten years before the park, is still standing. It was the first home of the American Museum of Natural History in 1869. *(Author's collection)*

The park has fought off many encroachments over the years, including the construction of Grant's Tomb, an amusement park, numerous parking lots, and even an airport. One such encroachment, not fought off by the park nor the environment of the North American continent for that matter, was the introduction of nonnative species of the European starling. On March 6, 1890, Eugene Scheifflin released eighty of the birds here. His well-intentioned plan to introduce all the birds mentioned in the works of Shakespeare to America was an ecological disaster.

A national historic landmark since 1964, the park has been dramatically improved in the last twenty years. The private sector has taken on many projects, particularly the upkeep and restoration of Olmsted/Vaux's vision.

CENTRAL PARK NORTH

Central Park North between Fifth and Lenox Avenues, North Side
The First Polo Grounds—The publisher James Gordon Bennett Jr. once owned this block—and as far north as 112th Street—using the land to play polo, a game he and other New York sportsmen had recently introduced to America. Baseball games shared the field as early as 1880. The first National League game, here, on May 1, 1883, was between the Gothams, later renamed the New York Giants, and Boston. More than fifteen thousand fans, including former president Ulysses S. Grant—the largest crowd in New York baseball history up to that time—came out to root for the home team. Another footnote in the history of baseball took place here on October 23, 1884, the beginning of a three-game series for "the championship of the United States." The Providence Grays of the National League and the New York Metropolitans of the American Association met in the sport's first post-season championship games, a forerunner to the first World Series begun nineteen years later in 1903.

CENTRAL PARK WEST

50 Central Park West
*The Prasada**—The author Edna Ferber had an apartment with a view of the park in this building from 1923 until 1929. She wrote *Show Boat* while living here.

115 Central Park West

*Majestic Apartments**—A carpenter named Richard Bruno Hauptmann was hired to work on the construction of this building. Hauptmann was later tried and executed for the kidnapping and death of the baby son of Charles A. Lindbergh, the hero aviator. The prosecution used Hauptmann's altered time sheet for the day of the kidnapping, March 1, 1932, supposedly showing he was not at work, to help convict him during the sensational trial.

Twenty-five years later, on May 2, 1957, another footnote in the history of crime took place in this lobby. Gangster Frank Costello was returning to his seven-room penthouse when he was shot in the head by a mob hit man. Costello survived his wound and lived to the ripe old age of eighty.

Central Park West and West 74th Street

At age sixty-eight, real-estate broker Henry H. Bliss became the country's first automobile fatality at this intersection on September 13, 1899. He had just gotten off a southbound trolley when he was knocked down and run over by an electric cab driven by Arthur Smith. Bliss died later in a hospital.

Central Park West between West 77th and West 81st Streets

*American Museum of Natural History**—The Star of India—at 563 carats the world's largest star sapphire—was stolen from the Gem Hall at the museum on October 29, 1964. The priceless "Star," along with other gems, was reportedly uninsured. Within two days of the heist, Miami's Jack "Murph the Surf" Murphy and two accomplices were arrested and later sentenced to three years in prison. The gems were recovered in a bus depot locker in Miami.

211 Central Park West

Beresford Hotel—A hotel that once stood at this corner of 81st Street was the birthplace of Henry Morgenthau Jr. on May 11, 1891. He was secretary of the treasury from 1934 until 1945 during much of Franklin Roosevelt's administration, a period of tumultuous financial history that included the Great Depression and World War II.

*The Beresford**—The current apartment house named after an earlier hotel was home to the famed anthropologist Margaret Mead from 1966 to 1978. She worked across the street at the American Museum of Natural History.

CLAREMONT AVENUE

35 Claremont Avenue
Lionel Trilling, the literary critic, died here at his home on November 5, 1975.

COLUMBUS AVENUE

Columbus Avenue between West 65th and West 66th Streets, East Side
Sharkey's—A saloon that once stood on this site was run by an ex-boxer named "Sailor Tom." In the days when boxing was illegal in New York State, a loophole in the law permitted athletic clubs to stage fights. On nights there was a fight here the saloon became an athletic club. Sharkey's was immortalized in the paintings and prints of the artist George Bellows. Begun in 1907, his "boxing" paintings are full of energy and color and have now become icons in American art.

490 Columbus Avenue
Hellmann's Delicatessen—German immigrant Richard Hellmann, the owner of this delicatessen, introduced Hellmann's Blue Ribbon Mayonnaise in 1912. His dressing was so popular that within three years he gave up his store to devote his complete attention to his new mayonnaise plant in Astoria, Queens.

COLUMBUS CIRCLE

The reputed head of the Brooklyn Mafia, Joe Colombo Sr., was shot in the head at an Italian-American Civil Rights League rally here on June 28, 1971. Colombo, the organizer of the event, died after seven years in a coma. Jerome Johnson, the assailant, was killed at the scene. Johnson's reason for the attack was never known, but it was believed he was hired by a rival gang.

CONVENT AVENUE

287 Convent Avenue
*Hamilton Grange National Memorial**—The Grange was the country home of Alexander Hamilton, the author of much of *The Federalist* and the nation's first secretary of the Treasury. The only home Hamilton ever owned, the two-story Federal-style house, named after his ancestral home in Scotland, was built for him

Recorded in its original location near West 145th Street, the clapboard house is Alexander Hamilton's country home, the Grange. The stand of trees enclosed within the picket fence was George Washington's gift to Hamilton. *(Collection of the New-York Historical Society)*

in 1802 by architect John McComb. The thirty-five-acre estate had a grove of thirteen gum trees, representing the original colonies, given to Hamilton by George Washington. He was very happy here and once wrote of his beloved retreat, "I am always sure to find a sweet asylum from care and pain." Unfortunately, he spent only two years here before he died as a result of his duel with Aaron Burr. The house was originally located about two blocks north but was moved to this site in 1889 to escape demolition. It later served as a chapel and rectory for the adjoining St. Luke's Episcopal Church. There have been recent discussions about moving the house yet again to a less cramped and more suitable location.

EAST END AVENUE

120* East End Avenue

This current apartment house was the last home of ex-mayor Jimmy Walker from 1944 until 1946. He lived here with his son, along with his sister and her two sons.

EDGECOMB AVENUE

409–17 Edgecomb Avenue

*Colonial Parkway Apartments**—This thirteen-story apartment house was the heart of Harlem's exclusive Sugar Hill section, so named because life was "so sweet" for those celebrated African American residents who could afford to live here from the 1930s to the 1950s. Tenants who have lived here include W. E. B. Du Bois, Roy Wilkins, William Stanley Braithwaite, and Thurgood Marshall.

555 Edgecomb Avenue

*Roger Morris Apartments**—Another fashionable address for successful African Americans, this building was once home to Count Basie and Paul Robeson.

FORT WASHINGTON AVENUE

177 Fort Washington Avenue

*Milstein Hospital**—For more than a decade, Sunny Von Bulow has been a patient here in a ninth-floor room with a panoramic view of the Hudson River. The wealthy heiress has been the tranquil eye of a legal hurricane, since she slipped into an irreversible coma the night of December 21, 1980, in Newport, Rhode Island. Her husband, Claus, was tried twice and eventually acquitted of her attempted murder. The prosecution claimed he tried to kill her with a lethal injection of insulin, which induced her coma.

LENOX AVENUE

272* Lenox Avenue

The ground floor of this brownstone was the photography studio of James VanDerZee. For more than sixty years he documented the life of Harlem in his photographs.

506 Lenox Avenue

*Harlem Hospital**—James Baldwin, the novelist, was born at this hospital on August 2, 1924.

596 Lenox Avenue, between West 140th and West 141st Streets

Savoy Ballroom—Billed as "the world's most beautiful ballroom," the Savoy was also one of the largest. On busy nights it accommodated crowds of up to five thousand. The second-floor dance floor extended the length of the entire block. After opening on March 12, 1926, and for the next two decades, this spot became the place to dance. Many new dances originated and were popularized here, including the Black Bottom and the Lindy Hop. Drummer and bandleader Chick Webb, the "King of the Savoy," challenged other bands in the popular "battle of the bands." Benny Goodman's hit rendition of "Stompin' at the Savoy" in 1936 served as a tribute and advertisement for the club.

644 Lenox Avenue

Cotton Club—First opened and owned by former heavyweight boxing champion Jack Johnson in 1920 as the Club Deluxe, it was reopened for white customers only in 1923 as the Cotton Club. The "Old South" decor, complete with slaves' cabins and cotton plants, was the stage set for such entertainers as Duke Ellington, Cab Calloway, Bill "Bojangles" Robinson, Ethel Waters, and the Nicholas Brothers. The club was popular with the adventurous set looking for new thrills, including the city's "Night" Mayor Jimmy Walker. After the race riot on March 19, 1935, Whites stopped coming uptown, and the club moved to Times Square.

LEXINGTON AVENUE

1342* Lexington Avenue

Rising star artist Andy Warhol bought this four-story townhouse in 1959. He lived here with his mother until the late 1960s.

MADISON AVENUE

816 Madison Avenue

In 1886 Grover Cleveland was the first president to marry in the White House. Two years later he and his new bride, Frances, moved into a four-story townhouse that once stood at this address. The president had just lost his reelection bid to Benjamin Harrison. While Cleveland was in "retirement" in New York, his daughter, Ruth, was born on October 3, 1891. The "Baby Ruth," a popular candy bar, was named after her. The following year Cleveland made a comeback in a rematch with Harrison. He won the presidency and returned to Washington, D.C., with his new family.

MORNINGSIDE DRIVE

60 Morningside Drive

President's House, Columbia University*—Before he became the thirty-fourth president of the United States, Dwight D. Eisenhower was the president of Columbia University. He was reluctant to take the position but felt pressured by the university trustees, who were determined to have the World War II hero as president. Eisenhower was released from his Pentagon duties and moved to this house in June of 1948. It was an unhappy match from the start. The general and the professors were not very compatible. After just two years, Eisenhower gladly took on the job of advising the first Secretary of Defense James Forrestal, in his newly created cabinet post, and shortly thereafter Eisenhower was made the commander of the North Atlantic Treaty Organization (NATO). He took a leave of absence and then resigned in 1952.

May 4, 1948, was the first day of school for Gen. Dwight D. Eisenhower as he began his tenure as president of Columbia University. He is seen posing on the steps of the Low Memorial Library. Daniel Chester French's statue Alma Mater is in the background. *(FPG)*

PARK AVENUE

570* Park Avenue

Author Willa Cather moved to an apartment in this building in 1932. She died of a massive cerebral hemorrhage here on April 24, 1947.

730* Park Avenue

Eighty-two-year-old writer Edna Ferber died here at her home on April 16, 1968. She wrote *Giant* and *Ice Palace* while in this building. This address was also home to songwriter Richard Rodgers from 1945 until 1971.

733 Park Avenue, Northeast Corner of East 70th Street

Elihu Root, statesman and secretary of state, built the Georgian-style townhouse that once stood on this corner in 1905. The construction of this mansion was regarded as a turning point in the development of the Upper East Side as a wealthy residential enclave.

740* Park Avenue

This was the childhood home of Jacqueline Kennedy Onassis, from the age of three to nine. Her grandfather James T. Lee, who also lived here, was a very successful developer who had built this luxury apartment house in 1929. The year before, Jacqueline's mother, Janet Lee, had married John Vernou Bouvier III. Bouvier, a handsome free-spender, lived here because of his father-in-law's charity. The marriage ended in divorce the year they moved out—1938.

778* Park Avenue

Dag Hammarskjöld, the secretary general of the United Nations, lived in this building from 1954 until his death in 1961.

820* Park Avenue

This address was home to Herbert Henry Lehman, who was governor of New York from 1932 until 1942. He died in his apartment on December 5, 1963, the day he was to leave for Washington, D.C., to receive the Presidential Medal of Freedom from President Johnson. This was also the last home of another New York governor, Al Smith. He lived here from the late 1930s until his death in 1944.

890 Park Avenue

*St. Ignatius Loyola Church**—This Catholic church was the site of Jacqueline

Kennedy Onassis's funeral on the morning of May 23, 1994—the same neighborhood church where she was baptized as an infant and confirmed as a teenager. After the private service, the family accompanied the body aboard a chartered plane to Washington, D.C., where they were met by President William Clinton for the journey to Arlington National Cemetery. The former first lady was buried next to her husband, President John F. Kennedy, and two of their children, an unnamed daughter, stillborn in 1956, and an infant son, Patrick, who died in 1963.

895* Park Avenue

Ninety well-heeled guests attended a party here at the duplex apartment of composer Leonard Bernstein on January 14, 1970. The gathering was a fund-raiser for the Black Panthers. In addition to the $10,000 raised for the militant left-wing group, the party aroused the interest of the FBI and the media. Tom Wolfe satirized the party in an article for *New York* magazine and labeled it "radical chic."

1035* Park Avenue

George S. Kaufman, the playwright, lived in this apartment building from 1951 until his death, here, on June 2, 1961.

Park Avenue and East 93rd Street, Northwest Corner

This was the site of the summer home of Gen. Winfield Scott. Scott was a hero of the Mexican-American War and a presidential candidate in the election of 1852.

RIVERSIDE DRIVE

33* Riverside Drive

Still standing, this apartment house was home to composer George Gershwin from 1929 until 1933. He lived in the penthouse next door to his brother Ira. Another composer, Sergei Rachmaninoff, lived in this building from 1921 until 1942.

137 Riverside Drive

Clarendon Apartments—William Randolph Hearst lived in one of the city's largest apartments here from 1908 until 1926. Five years after moving in, he bought the entire building in order to expand his already huge apartment. Over the years his palatial home grew to include the top five floors of the twelve-story building. The thirty-room apartment contained the "English Room," the "Gothic Room," and a "Tapestry Gallery" that was two stories high and ran the entire length of the building.

160* Riverside Drive

Brooks Atkinson, the drama critic of *The New York Times,* lived at this address from 1928 until 1969.

435 Riverside Drive

Colosseum*—Harlan Fiske Stone lived in this apartment building while he was the dean of Columbia Law School from 1920 to 1925. He later became chief justice of the U.S. Supreme Court.

490 Riverside Drive

Riverside Church*—On April 4, 1967, the Reverend Dr. Martin Luther King Jr. spoke here in favor of merging the civil-rights and anti–Vietnam War movements. He warned that the war threatened the struggle for equal rights for African Americans. His speech, which encouraged draft evasion, called the U.S. government "the greatest purveyor of violence in the world today." Eleven days later Dr. King helped lead the largest antiwar demonstration to date—more than one hundred thousand people—from Central Park to U.N. headquarters.

Riverside Drive and West 122nd Street

Grant's Tomb*—The city's most popular tourist attraction at the turn of the century, the tomb is largely overlooked today. Built not only to house the remains of the eighteenth president and Civil War hero, it was conceived as a grand monument, in the age of monuments, to the growing self-assurance of America's standing in the modern world.

On August 8, 1885, the gathering of mourners along the funeral route from City Hall was the largest ever seen in the city. Twelve years later on "Grant Day," April 27, 1897—the seventy-fifth anniversary of his birth—the crowds were even larger for the formal dedication of the finished edifice. Millions of spectators, along with President William McKinley, Vice President Garret A. Hobart, and thirteen governors, watched sixty thousand marching troops and a parade of ships in the Hudson during the ceremonies. The pomp and significance of the event were compared by contemporary observers to the transfer of Napoleon's remains from St. Helena to Paris.

Grant's tomb was also a focal point in the fall of 1909 for the Hudson-Fulton Celebration, which saluted the anniversaries of Henry Hudson's discoveries in 1609 and Robert Fulton's successful development of the steamboat in 1809.

Many of these events were staged along the banks of the Hudson River. One of the highlights was Wilbur Wright's flight in an airplane over Grant's Tomb on October 4, 1909. The pioneer aviator took off from Governors Island, flew up the Hudson, circled the monument, and returned to Governors Island. The plane was outfitted with a red canoe in case of a water landing. This historic thirty-three-minute trip included the first airplane flight over the island of Manhattan.

765 Riverside Drive

This address marks the spot where the home of John James Audubon stood until 1930. In 1841 the painter and naturalist bought twenty-four acres and built a home he called "Minnie's Land," in honor of his wife. He died here on January 27, 1851. Nearby Trinity Cemetery was once part of the Audubon farm and is also where he is buried.

Twelve years after the death of Gen. Ulysses S. Grant, his body was moved into this tomb on Riverside Drive at West 122nd Street. The design was based on the ancient tomb in Halicarnassus of Mausolus, where the term mausoleum is derived. After her death in 1902, Julia, his wife, was laid to rest beside her husband. *(FPG)*

Dilapidated and neglected in 1921, this house that once stood at 765 Riverside Drive was the beloved home of John James Audubon. The naturalist spent the last ten years of his life here. Inventor Samuel F. B. Morse rented a room here in 1846 to conduct long-distance experiments with his telegraph. *(FPG)*

SAINT NICHOLAS AVENUE

Saint Nicholas Avenue and 145th Street

The single worst accident during the construction of the subway took place sixty feet below this intersection on October 24, 1903. This cut of the subway system, the second-longest two-track rock tunnel ever built in the United States and the deepest in the entire New York City system, was a complicated engineering feat. A crew of subway workers, having just heard the all-clear call from their foreman, returned to the recent blast site. A forty-four-foot boulder dropped from the roof of the tunnel, killing six men instantly and seriously injuring eight more. The foreman and nine of the workers, mainly immigrant Italian laborers, died.

935* Saint Nicholas Avenue

Musician Duke Ellington lived at this address for twenty-two years, 1939 to 1961, in apartment 4A.

SAINT NICHOLAS PLACE

10* Saint Nicholas Place

Built in 1888, this landmarked Romanesque Revival mansion was home for James Anthony Bailey, partner in the famous Barnum and Bailey Circus. The thirty-room limestone residence—one of the few surviving freestanding mansions in Manhattan—is now a funeral parlor.

WEST END AVENUE

128 West End Avenue

Consolidated Edison Company's Energy Control Center—At 5:15 P.M. on November 9, 1965, the first indication of serious trouble for the city's power supply appeared on the instruments here. Within minutes, the lights in the room flickered and the city slipped into darkness. This was the beginning of the nation's worst blackout. The power failure, which spread across nine states and three Canadian provinces, affected thirty million people. Power was not restored to the full city until thirteen hours later.

YORK AVENUE

1270 York Avenue

Rockefeller Institute for Medical Research—It was here in the early 1940s that biologist Oswald Avery and his colleagues discovered that the substance responsible for recording hereditary information in cells is DNA.

FIRST AVENUE

First Avenue between East 70th and East 75th Streets, East Side

Jones Woods—A beautiful wooded tract of land that swept down to the shore of the East River, Jones Woods was considered a likely candidate for the city's new park in 1851 but was rejected in favor of the current Central Park. On September 17, 1860, Stephen Douglas, the Illinois senator and Democratic candidate for the presidency, was the guest of honor at a campaign rally and barbecue here. Three thousand loyal supporters attended and listened to the senator and his running mate Hirschel V. Johnson offer their solutions to the crisis of slavery and possible secession of the Southern states. On election day, Douglas received almost two-to-one votes in the city, but Abraham Lincoln carried the state's thirty-five electoral votes and won the presidency.

1901 First Avenue

Metropolitan Hospital*—Legendary jazz great Billie Holiday ended her long-running battle with drug addiction and the police at this hospital. While here, she was placed under arrest for heroin possession after a nurse reported finding the drug in a silver-foil package in her room. She died here on July 17, 1959.

SECOND AVENUE

1994 Second Avenue

Henry Louis "Lou" Gehrig, the beloved Yankee baseball star, was born here at the home of his parents on June 19, 1903.

THIRD AVENUE

Third Avenue and East 66th Street, Northwest Corner

Sign of the Dove Tavern—The British captured Nathan Hale, the Connecticut school-teacher-turned-American-spy, at this tavern on September 21, 1776. Legend has it that he said his famous last words, "I only regret that I have but one life to lose for my country," and was hung nearby the next day.

FIFTH AVENUE

781 Fifth Avenue

Sherry Netherland Hotel*—Jesse Livermore, infamous stock-market operator, shot and killed himself outside the men's room of this hotel on November 28, 1940. Livermore, nicknamed the "Boy Plunger of Wall Street," was a speculator often singled out for contributing to the crash of 1929.

810* Fifth Avenue

After losing the governorship of California, Richard Nixon left his native state and moved to this apartment building in 1963. In spite of his "last press conference" vow that "you won't have Nixon to kick around anymore...," he began campaigning for Republican candidates and rebuilding his political career. From here he moved to the White House, when he won the presidential election of 1968.

820* Fifth Avenue

William S. Paley, entertainment entrepreneur and the founder of the Columbia Broadcasting System, moved to a twenty-room duplex apartment in this building in 1965. He died here on October 26, 1990.

Fifth Avenue and 67th Street

Winston Churchill, forgetting that Americans drive on the right-hand side of the street, stepped in front of an oncoming car at this intersection on December 11, 1931. He was dragged several feet and fractured two ribs. The future British prime minister was taken to Lenox Hill Hospital, where King George telephoned to ask about his condition.

920* Fifth Avenue

Composer Igor Stravinsky died in his newly purchased apartment in this building on April 6, 1971.

Fifth Avenue and East 70th Street, Northeast Corner

The world's costliest residence, when built, was on this corner. Built by millionaire Montana Senator William Andrews Clark, it stood only twenty-four years, from 1903 until it was torn down in 1927. This proud monument was celebrated in 1904 in a poem by Wallace Irwin.

Senator Copper of Tonapah Ditch
  Made a clean billion in minin' and sich
Hiked for Noo York, where his money he blew
  Buildin' a palace on Fift' Avenoo.
"How," sez the Senator, "can I look proudest?
  Build me a house that'll holler the loudest."

The Fifth Avenue mansion of Senator William Andrews Clark, "The Copper King" from Montana, was a French Empire-style towered concoction made of white granite. The 130-room palace was a testament to what money could buy at the beginning of the twentieth century. *(FPG)*

Fifth Avenue between East 80th and 84th Streets

Metropolitan Museum of Art*—The museum's most famous visitor was the Mona Lisa by Leonardo da Vinci, which went on exhibit beginning February 7, 1963. The lady with the enigmatic smile was displayed behind bullet-proof glass and given Secret Service protection. Sixteen thousand visitors waited in line to see her that first day.

993* Fifth Avenue

This was the last home of George M. Cohan, one of America's leading songwriters of the musical stage. He died in his bedroom on November 5, 1942.

995 Fifth Avenue

Stanhope Hotel*—Charlie "Bird" Parker, the jazz alto-saxophone musician, died here in the suite of his friend and jazz maven Baroness "Nica" de Koeningswarter, a heiress to the Rothschild fortune. Parker, a long-time abuser of drugs and alcohol, had refused to be taken to the hospital and died of a heart attack on March 12, 1955, at the age of thirty-four.

1040* Fifth Avenue

In 1964 Jacqueline Kennedy, the widow of President John F. Kennedy, moved to this apartment building, hoping to find some privacy for herself and her children, Caroline and John Jr. She lived here in her fourteenth-floor apartment until her death on the night of May 19, 1994. She died of cancer of the lymphatic system at the age of sixty-four.

1107* Fifth Avenue

This site was once the townhouse of society leader Marjorie Merriwether Post Hutton, heir to the Post cereal fortune. In 1924 she was persuaded by a builder to tear down her home and allow him to build her a fifty-four-room triplex residence atop the current apartment house. A separate entrance and elevator allowed for her privacy. She lived in her triplex here until 1941. Because her spacious home was unable to be rented out, it was eventually divided up into six different apartments.

1130* Fifth Avenue

International Center for Photography—Now ICP, this was once the home of Elbert Gary, a founder and long-time chairman of United States Steel Corporation. When he died here on August 15, 1927, his company was the largest industrial corporation in the world. It was widely speculated that the news of his death was delayed until after the close of the stock market for fear of the effect on the company's stock.

1489 Fifth Avenue

Dressmaker and entrepreneur Lena Bryant opened a shop at this address in 1904. While here, she created her well-known design for a modern stylish maternity dress. The success of this dress enabled her company, Lane (an early misspelling) Bryant, to grow into today's clothing retail giant.

2078* Fifth Avenue

The country's ultimate pack rats, Homer and Langley Collyer, lived in this brownstone for thirty-eight years. The brothers—Homer, a lawyer, and Langley, a concert pianist—moved here in 1909. On March 21, 1947, the police were summoned to this address to look for the reclusive brothers. What they found, after a day of burrowing through tons of refuse, was the emaciated body of Homer. It took another three weeks to find Langley's body. He, like his older sibling, apparently starved to death, trapped in his own burglar booby trap. The brothers had filled the house with more than 120 tons of junk, including five pianos and a Model-T Ford automobile. They also left an estate worth $300,000.

Recluse Langley Collyer, captured by a camera flash-bulb, sneaking into his own home at 2078 Fifth Avenue. Langley and his brother were found dead here in their booby-trapped townhouse in March of 1947. *(FPG)*

EAST 60TH STREET

14 East 60th Street

Hotel Fourteen—Still located at this address, this residential apartment house was the headquarters in June, 1945, for David Ben-Gurion and other emissaries from Palestine, so many in fact that it was nicknamed "Kibbutz 14." They were making plans for a future British withdrawal from Palestine and the establishment of a Jewish state. Ben-Gurion, the future first prime minister of Israel, was in New York to find American Jews willing to bankroll and support the fight for independence.

EAST 61ST STREET

6 East 61st Street
Hotel Pierre*—Built by famed chef Charles Pierre, this hotel opened for business one year after the stock market crash of 1929. Wealthy guests, seemingly unfazed by the Depression, dined on opening night, October 1, 1930, at a dinner prepared by another renowned epicurean, eighty-five-year-old Auguste Escoffier, who was hired to set up the hotel's kitchen.

Many guests were decidedly upset on January 2, 1972. That morning the largest hotel jewel robbery in history took place here. Five burglars wearing masks and tuxedos stole an estimated $10 million in cash and precious gems from the hotel's safe-deposit boxes. The two-hour heist was never solved, but $1 million worth of the jewels were eventually recovered.

151* East 61st Street
At 12:55 A.M. on June 3, 1919, a bomb rocked this address, the home of Judge Charles Cooper Nott Jr. The homemade bomb exploded prematurely, killing the man and the woman who were planting it on the front stoop. The judge was away in Connecticut, and no one in the house was injured. This bombing was one of many that evening in what was believed to be a nationwide plot to retaliate against the U.S. Justice Department's crackdown on perceived radicals and anarchists. Bombs went off in Boston, Cleveland, and Pittsburgh. An explosion also damaged the home of Attorney General A. Mitchell Palmer in Washington, D.C. Again, the bomber was killed by the blast and his target escaped injury.

217* East 61st Street
Still standing, this townhouse was a wedding present from President Theodore Roosevelt to his flamboyant daughter Alice in 1906. Alice married, in a White House ceremony, U.S. Congressman Nicholas Longworth, who later became speaker of the House. Critic Clifton Fadiman also lived in this house, as did the actor Montgomery Clift, who died of a fatal heart attack here on July 23, 1966.

Police inspect the damage to the home of Charles Cooper Nott Jr. at 151 East 61st Street on the morning of June 3, 1919. Bolshevik and anarchist leaflets were scattered by the bombers at several of their other targets. *(FPG)*

EAST 62ND STREET

211* East 62nd Street

Eleanor Roosevelt lived in a garden duplex apartment in this building between 1953 and 1959.

EAST 63RD STREET

16* East 63rd Street

Sixties flower child and drug addict Edie Sedgwick lived in an apartment at this address during her "fifteen minutes of fame." Daughter of wealthy parents, Edie was discovered by Andy Warhol and transformed into his companion, alter ego, and star of several of his movies.

120* East 63rd Street

At 5:32 P.M. on December 5, 1933, the state of Utah ratified Article 21 of the U.S. Constitution, officially repealing Prohibition and ending "The Noble Experiment." Three minutes later, on a sidewalk at this address, Herbert Chase had the distinction of being the first post-repeal person to be arrested for publicly drunken behavior. The twenty-six-year-old was arraigned in night court and given a suspended sentence.

140 East 63rd Street

Barbizon Hotel—This Gothic-style residential hotel is for women. Before she was a movie star and the princess of Monaco, Grace Kelly was an aspiring actress who lived here. The author Sylvia Plath also lived in this hotel in 1953. She wrote about her experience here in her novel *The Bell Jar*.

Herbert Chase, obviously feeling no pain, pleads his case at his arraignment for public drunkenness on December 5, 1933. New Yorkers, delighted with the end of Prohibition, had never really stopped drinking. There were more than ten thousand speakeasies, by one estimation, in the city in the decade before repeal. *(Daily News I. P. Photo)*

WEST 63RD STREET

22 West 63rd Street

Daley's 63rd Street Theater—After playing for more than forty-one weeks, the universally panned but provocative play *Sex* was just about to close when a lucky thing happened. On February 9, 1927, the police raided the theater and arrested the star and playwright Mae West and the rest of the cast. The bawdy West was told that if she canceled the show, the officials would drop the charges. But West chose to fight the charges. At her court date, April 19, 1927, she was found guilty of corrupting the morals of youth and sentenced to prison for ten days and fined $500. The publicity made West a celebrity.

243 West 63rd Street

Thelonious Monk, the acclaimed jazz musician, lived most of his life in a building that once stood at this address. Down the block, the intersection of West 63rd Street and West End Avenue is named Thelonious Sphere Monk Circle.

EAST 64TH STREET

29* East 64th Street

Mary Scott Dimmick Harrison, the widow of President Benjamin Harrison, died here in her apartment on January 5, 1948. Mrs. Harrison, the president's second wife, married him after his term expired and never lived in the White House. She was active in Republican politics well into her eighties.

30 East 64th Street

This address was once home to Seth Low. Low was mayor of the city from 1901 to 1903. He was also mayor of Brooklyn from 1882 to 1886, before the boroughs were consolidated, and president of Columbia University from 1890 to 1901.

WEST 64TH STREET

20 West 64th Street

One Lincoln Plaza*—Forty-three stories tall, this condominium apartment tower was the site of a five-alarm blaze on January 7, 1997. The fire started in the twenty-eighth-floor home of one of the building's most renowned residents, jazz great Lionel Hampton. A halogen lamp in Hampton's bedroom tipped over and set his bed on fire. The eighty-three-year-old musician was evacuated in his wheelchair unharmed, but his apartment was totally destroyed. Several residents were treated for smoke inhalation, but there were no fatalities.

EAST 65TH STREET

47–49* East 65th Street

These are two separate townhouses with a shared neo-Georgian front entrance. The one townhouse was a 1905 Christmas present from Sara Roosevelt to her only son, Franklin D. Roosevelt, and his new bride, Eleanor, and the other was a home for herself. The future president and his family lived in the one half, number 49, and Sara lived in the other at number 47. This living arrangement reflected the close relationship between Franklin and his mother, and it also explains the often strained relationship between Eleanor and her mother-in-law. Twice in his life he returned here to recuperate, each time from one of the most frightening diseases of the twentieth century. On September 19, 1918, Roosevelt, who was then the assistant secretary of the navy, had just landed on the troop ship USS *Leviathan*. He nearly died from the Spanish Influenza of 1918, one of the world's worst epidemics, which killed more than twenty million people. His second recuperation began on October 28, 1921, when he returned from the hospital with polio. He never fully recovered but learned to overcome his disability. He resumed his political career and became New York governor in 1929 and president in 1932.

142* East 65th Street

Former president Richard Nixon returned to New York City after his self-imposed exile over the Watergate Scandals at San Clemente, California, and lived in this townhouse for about a year and a half until 1981. He had tried to buy several co-op apartments in the neighborhood but was rejected by the buildings' co-op boards on the grounds that his celebrity would be too disruptive to the other tenants.

EAST 66TH STREET

1 East 66th Street

A Romanesque-style mansion, complete with its own moat, that once stood on this corner was the home of Mr. and Mrs. Henry Havemeyer. With money made

in the sugar business and the advice of Mary Cassatt, they collected one of the world's greatest art collections. In 1929 their collection was given to the Metropolitan Museum of Art. It included El Greco's *View of Toledo* and Goya's *Women on a Balcony.*

3 East 66th Street

A brownstone that once stood at this address was the home from 1881 to 1885 of retired president Ulysses S. Grant. It was during this time in New York that Grant invested in a brokerage partnership with his son and Ferdinand Ward. The venture was a financial disaster and bankrupted Grant, his friends, and several banks. He spent the last years of his life writing his best-selling *Memoirs* to recoup his family's fortune.

Movers loading a truck at the East 65th Street home of President-elect Franklin D. Roosevelt on March 2, 1933. The family's possessions were being moved to their new home in the White House. *(FPG)*

4* East 66th Street

This was the home of Bernard Baruch, presidential adviser and financier. He lived here from 1948 until his fatal heart attack on June 20, 1965.

57* East 66th Street

Artist Andy Warhol bought this 1911 Georgian-style townhouse in 1974. Warhol, an eclectic collector, used the house as a combination art warehouse, flea market, and living quarters. After his death in 1987, his estate had Sotheby's auction the contents of the house. The nearly ten thousand items in the ten-day sale raised $25.3 million. The treasures ranged from antique jewelry to his cookie-jar collection.

200 East 66th Street

*Manhattan House**—Big-band musician Benny Goodman lived and died in this apartment house. He had a fatal heart attack here on June 13, 1986. Found by his side was his clarinet and a music stand holding a Brahms composition.

WEST 66TH STREET

7 West 66th Street

American Broadcasting Company—Once a stable called Durland's Riding Academy, this television studio was the site of the fourth and final debate between Vice President Richard Nixon and Massachusetts Senator John F. Kennedy on October 21, 1960. These debates, which would forever change American presidential campaigns and establish television as the definitive media for reaching the voters, helped elect Kennedy two weeks later. The most heated of the debates, this one was devoted to foreign policy, particularly America's dealings with Fidel Castro.

57 West 66th Street

St. Nicholas Skating Rink—America's earliest indoor ice-skating rink was built on this site in 1896. The building later became an arena important in the history of boxing. Jack Johnson, Jess Willard, Floyd Patterson, and Cassius Clay Jr. (later Muhammad Ali) all fought matches in the St. Nicholas Ring. It is now the site of American Broadcasting Company headquarters.

EAST 67TH STREET

136 East 67th Street
Soviet Mission to the United Nations*—It is here that Soviet leaders have stayed while in New York City. Nikita Khrushchev first stayed here in September of 1960, as did Mikhail Gorbachev in December of 1988, during their first visits to New York.

WEST 67TH STREET

1 West 67th Street
Hotel des Artistes*—Harry Crosby, a tortured poet of the 1920s, killed himself and his girlfriend Josephine Bigelow here on December 10, 1929. These luxurious studio-style apartments have been home to Rudolph Valentino, Norman Rockwell, Isadora Duncan, Fannie Hurst, and Berenice Abbott.

15 West 67th Street
Central Park Studios*—This address was home and studio to artist Stuart Davis from 1955 to 1964. It was also home to poet Robert Lowell. The first issue of the New York Review of Books was born on Lowell's dining-room table in 1963.

33 West 67th Street
Atelier Building*—From 1914 to 1920 apartment 2FE was the home of Walter and Louise Arensberg, among the earliest and most important collectors of modern art in America. In addition to filling this soaring two-story space with art by Marcel Duchamp and Henri Matisse, the wealthy couple made their home a gathering place for the avant-garde. They donated their famous collection to the Philadelphia Museum of Art in 1950. The illustrator James Montgomery Flagg, the creator of the "Uncle Sam Wants You" poster, also lived here.

39* West 67th Street
Author Ben Hecht died of a heart attack here at his home on April 18, 1964.

EAST 68TH STREET

45* East 68th Street
This address was once the home of newspaper columnist and TV personality Dorothy Kilgallen. She died mysteriously here on November 8, 1965.

150 East 68th Street

An apartment building, now gone, at this address was the last home of movie star Joan Crawford. She died of a heart attack in her apartment on May 19, 1977. This had been her home since 1973.

525 East 68th Street

New York Hospital-Cornell Medical Center*—On October 23, 1979, the deposed Shah of Iran was admitted to the seventeenth floor of the George Baker Pavilion under the assumed name of "David Newsome." He had just entered the country secretly from Mexico for cancer treatment and a gallbladder operation. Within hours of his arrival the press broke the story. Two weeks later, "student" demonstrators in Tehran reacted to the news by occupying the U.S. embassy and capturing fifty-two Americans. In return for the hostages, the demonstrators demanded that the Shah be returned to Iran. The Shah died the following year in Egypt, and the hostages were not released until January 20, 1981, moments after the inauguration of President Ronald Reagan.

Eight years later another gallbladder operation at this same hospital would also have tragic repercussions. Pop artist and media star Andy Warhol died in his private room on the twelfth floor in the early-morning hours of February 22, 1987, after complications from his gallbladder operation. The hospital settled a wrongful-death suit with the Warhol estate five years later.

Former president Richard Nixon died here on April 22, 1994. The eighty-one-year-old Cold Warrior and Watergate epicenter was brought here four days earlier after suffering a stroke in his suburban Park Ridge, New Jersey, home.

EAST 69TH STREET

157* East 69th Street

The carriage houses along this block of East 69th Street were built in the 1880s for the mansions and townhouses to the west toward Central Park. All restored and converted to modern uses, number 157 was the home and studio of abstract-expressionist painter Mark Rothko. The brilliant colorist killed himself here on the morning of February 25, 1970.

169* East 69th Street

Rube Goldberg, the creator of cartoons of wonderfully absurd contraptions, died here at his home at the age of eighty-seven on December 7, 1970. In 1948 Goldberg had won a Pulitzer Prize for his editorial cartooning.

WEST 71ST STREET

75 West 71st Street

After living at the Fifth Avenue Hotel in a large suite for two years, Civil War Gen. William T. Sherman bought a four-story townhouse at this address in 1888. He died here on St. Valentine's Day, 1891, a week after his seventy-first birthday. A large funeral was held at St. Patrick's Cathedral to mark the passing of one of the last of the Union generals.

EAST 72ND STREET

East 72nd Street and Madison Avenue, Northwest Corner

A fortress-like Romanesque mansion designed by Stanford White in 1882 was home to the Tiffany family. Father Charles Lewis, founder of the jewelry store, had this eight-story home built for himself, although he never lived here, and his two children and their families, including son artist Louis Comfort. It dominated this corner until it was torn down in 1936.

39* East 72nd Street

The French Jesuit priest Pierre Teilhard de Chardin died suddenly while visiting friends at this address on Easter Sunday, April 10, 1955. He was a brilliant scholar in several fields of study: geology, paleontology, philosophy, and the evolution of early humankind. It was his work in evolution that put him at odds with the teachings of the Church. The Vatican censored many of his works.

141* East 72nd Street

This was the last home of Thomas E. Dewey. He was governor of New York from 1942 to 1954 and twice nominated Republican presidential candidate in 1944 and 1948. He lived here between 1955 and 1971.

190 East 72nd Street

John Steinbeck died here at his home on December 20, 1968. The author had only just recently moved to this address from 206 East 72nd Street, where he had lived since 1951.

WEST 72ND STREET

1 West 72nd Street

The Dakota*—This apartment house, built by Singer Sewing Machine magnate Edward Severin Clark and designed by Henry J. Hardenbergh, was fully rented even before it opened on October 24, 1884. The Dakota quickly overcame two serious obstacles to success: first, that it was too far from the center of town and, second, that apartment buildings were not socially acceptable for the upper classes. Always popular with artists, this building was home for two of the greatest musicians of the twentieth century. John Lennon was shot just inside the entrance gate on December 8, 1980, by Mark David Chapman, and Leonard Bernstein died in his apartment on October 14, 1990, of a heart attack.

253* West 72nd Street

Roseann Quinn, a school teacher for the deaf, was stabbed to death here in her apartment on January 2, 1973. Ms. Quinn's murder by a pickup in a single's bar became a symbol of the dangers of the "sexual revolution." This case became the basis for the novel and movie *Looking for Mr. Goodbar.*

EAST 73RD STREET

11* East 73rd Street

The prestigious firm of McKim, Mead and White designed and built this Venetian palazzo-style mansion to the specifications of the ailing publisher Joseph Pulitzer in 1903. Pulitzer, who was nearly blind, was given a wooden model of the façade so he could judge the design by touch. The publisher was also painfully sensitive to sound and dictated that the house was to be as soundproof as possible. After moving in, he was troubled by the noise of a pump needed to control a spring beneath the house. In frustration, the millionaire had another architectural firm build him a bedroom at the rear of the mansion. This bedroom, supported on its

The crowd of mourners outside the Dakota at 1 West 72nd Street, home of John Lennon, after he was shot on December 8, 1980. The former member of the Beatles and his wife, Yoko Ono, had lived at the Dakota since 1975. *(FPG)*

own foundation, had soundproofed walls, heavy double doors, and some windows with three panes of plate glass. The building was converted into apartments in 1934.

127* East 73rd Street

Stanford White designed this Federal-style townhouse for his close friend the illustrator Charles Dana Gibson. Gibson moved into this house in 1903 with his beautiful wife, Irene, his frequent model and the prototype for the famous "Gibson Girl." The artist died here on December 23, 1944, at the age of seventy-seven.

EAST 74TH STREET

23* East 74th Street

Volney Hotel—This former residential hotel was a one-time home of Richard Rodgers in the 1940s. It was also the last home of Dorothy Parker. She died at this hotel on December 7, 1967. She had been living here since 1963. She wrote the play *Ladies of the Corridor* based on her life and observations here.

East 74th Street and Madison Avenue

John Merven Carrere was fatally injured in an accident at this intersection on February 12, 1911. The celebrated architect was riding in a taxicab on West 74th Street when it was hit by a southbound electric streetcar. Carrere was thrown ten feet from the cab onto the street. He never regained consciousness and died on March 1, 1911. Carrere and his partner Thomas Hastings had designed the New York Public Library building on Fifth Avenue.

55* East 74th Street

Seventy-eight-year-old "First Lady of the World" Eleanor Roosevelt died in her apartment on November 7, 1962. She had lived here since 1959.

128* East 74th Street

Songwriter Jerome Kern spend five years of his childhood at this house. He lived here from 1890 to 1895.

East 74th Street at the East River

Captain Kidd's farm "Saw Kill" was on this site in the 1690s. During the Revolutionary War, this bluff was a battery fortified by the rebels before the British occupation.

WEST 74TH STREET

54* West 74th Street

This was the address of Raphael Soyer's studio. Five weeks after the artist died on November 4, 1987, a burglar broke in and stole between four hundred and five hundred prints valued at up to $200,000.

307* West 74th Street

On October 11, 1984, the police raided the apartment of Sheila Denvin, who was, in fact, socialite Sidney Biddle Barrows. She was charged with running a high-class prostitution ring of twenty to thirty call girls. The thirty-two-year-old Barrows, a descendant of a leading pilgrim family, was quickly titled the "Mayflower Madam" by the tabloid press. She went on to become a celebrity and to write self-help books.

EAST 75TH STREET

130* East 75th Street

This was the home from 1936 until 1950 of America's most celebrated husband-and-wife acting team, Alfred Lunt and Lynn Fontanne.

216* East 75th Street

The basement cold-water flat in this brownstone was artist Andy Warhol's first apartment, in 1952. He wasn't alone here too long, though; a few weeks later his mother sold her home in Pittsburgh and moved in with her son.

WEST 75TH STREET

158* West 75th Street

This was the first-floor home of writer Anaïs Nin and her family from 1914 to 1919. She began her celebrated *Diary* while living here.

EAST 76TH STREET

6* East 76th Street

Franklin D. Roosevelt married his fifth cousin once removed, Anna Eleanor Roosevelt, on St. Patrick's Day, March 17, 1905, at this townhouse of the bride's aunt Mrs. E. Livingston Ludlow. President Theodore Roosevelt, Eleanor's uncle, gave away the bride. "Well, Franklin," the president told the groom and his fifth cousin after the ceremony, "there's nothing like keeping the name in the family."

35 East 76th Street

The Carlyle Hotel—President Harry Truman often stayed at this hotel. It was here during the early days of live television that reporters with their bulky cameras would play catch-up during the president's "constitutionals" around the neighborhood. The Carlyle was also a favorite with President Kennedy during his visits.

215 East 76th Street

On the morning of July 16, 1964, off-duty police Lt. Thomas Gilligan shot and killed James Powell, a fifteen-year-old African American youth, at this address.

The incident had escalated after an apartment house superintendent sprayed water on the youngsters. Powell's death provoked race riots in Harlem and Bedford-Stuyvesant in Brooklyn. There were 520 arrests over a five-day period.

WEST 76TH STREET

42* West 76th Street

Wright-Humanson School for the Deaf—Fourteen-year-old Helen Keller came to this address in October of 1894 to attend school for two years. Her devoted teacher and friend, Anne Sullivan, accompanied her. While here she improved her speech and lip-reading skills and studied French and German.

Publicly, Fanny Brice was always supportive of her dishonest and unfaithful husband, Nicky Arnstein. This publicity shot of the couple at home with a hearth was taken early in their marriage. *(Daily News L. P. Photo)*

306* West 76th Street

Comedian and singer Fanny Brice and her husband, Nicky Arnstein, lived at this address during most of the 1920s. Fanny, the long-suffering wife, was often alone while mobster Nicky was in prison. After he was released from Leavenworth, he showed no sign of reform, and Fanny divorced him in 1927.

EAST 77TH STREET

2* East 77th Street

This was the home of actress Joan Crawford and Pepsi-Cola executive Al Steele from 1959 to 1973.

37 East 77th Street

The novelist and historian Paul Leicester Ford was shot and killed by his unstable brother Malcolm Ford, who then committed suicide. The deaths, the tragic result of a long family feud, took place here in the library of the writer's apartment on the morning of May 8, 1902.

57* East 77th Street

Conductor Victor Herbert collapsed and died of a heart attack while climbing the stairs in this building to visit his physician, Dr. Emanuel Barauch, on May 26, 1924.

63 East 77th Street

The funeral for Boss William M. Tweed was held here at the home of his son-in-law, Frederick Douglas, on April 17, 1878.

WEST 77TH STREET

36 West 77th Street

This was the address of Meyer Guggenheim from 1888 to 1905. He was the founder of the family mining fortune.

44* West 77th Street

In 1909 the sculptor Karl Bitter moved into this newly built neo-Gothic apartment house. He lived here until his death in 1915.

EAST 79TH STREET

2* East 79th Street

Oilman Harry Sinclair lived in this French châteaux-style mansion from 1921 to 1929. Mr. Sinclair was involved in the Teapot Dome Scandal of the 1920s. He refused to testify at U.S. Senate hearings on the government oil leases and was held in contempt of Congress. He went to jail on the contempt charges for three months from this house in 1927, but he was acquitted on charges of defrauding the government. Later it was home to Augustus van Horn Stuyvesant and his sister Ann Stuyvesant, the last direct descendants of Governor Peter Stuyvesant.

39* East 79th Street

This address was the home of etiquette expert Emily Post. Mrs. Post had this stylish apartment house built in 1925 and encouraged her friends to be tenants. America's supreme arbiter of good taste lived here until 1960.

108 East 79th Street

On December 12, 1910, Dorothy Arnold, twenty-five-year-old heiress and niece of U.S. Supreme Court Justice Rufus Reckham, left her parents' home to go shopping downtown along Fifth Avenue. She encountered a girlfriend at Brentano's bookstore on 27th Street, and then she vanished. Miss Arnold's disappearance launched one of America's greatest missing person searches. She was never found.

121 East 79th Street

This was the boyhood home of editor and author Walter Lippmann during the 1890s.

WEST 79TH STREET

168 West 79th Street

Notre Dame Convent School*—The future president of the Philippines and populist answer to corrupt Ferdinand Marcos, Corazon Aquino attended this school from 1947 until 1949.

EAST 80TH STREET

2* East 80th Street

Built by her grandfather F. W. Woolworth as a gift for her mother, this mansion was the birthplace of dime-store heiress Barbara Hutton on November 14, 1912. Always popular copy with the gossip columnists, "the poor little rich girl" was married seven times.

EAST 81ST STREET

151 East 81st Street

Guilford*—Nathan Wallenstein Weinstein, better known as Nathanael West, the writer, was born at this address on December 17, 1903.

WEST 82ND STREET

155* West 82nd Street

Future Cuban dictator Fidel Castro and his bride, Mirta, spent their honeymoon in this brownstone in the fall of 1948. They stayed in the apartment of her brother, Rafael Diaz Balart.

EAST 84TH STREET

128 East 84th Street

Shanley's Laundry Shop*—Next door to this address, a cellar entrance stairway was the drop-off point for $20,000 in blackmail money on Saturday, November 7, 1992. Republican Party fund-raiser and socialite Joy Silverman had been instructed to have her doorman deliver the money in an envelope in exchange for nude photographs. FBI agents, who had been working on the case, were watching the scene. Within moments of the appointed time, 10:30 A.M., a woman picked up the envelope. The woman was only a go-between for New York State Chief Judge of the Court of Appeals Sol Wachtler. The judge, the highest ranking jurist in the state and likely Republican candidate for the New York governorship, was arrested the same day for extortion. Wachtler, resentful after his affair with Silverman ended, had been threatening and harassing his ex-lover and her daughter for months. Wachtler served a fifteen-month sentence in a medium-security prison in North Carolina.

428* East 84th Street

Artist Albert Sterner died here at his home on December 16, 1946.

EAST 85TH STREET

450* East 85th Street

Henry Miller, author of the sometimes-banned *Tropic of Cancer,* was born on the top floor here on December 26, 1891.

WEST 86TH STREET

West 86th Street at the Hudson River

In the fall of 1919 Edward Albert, the Prince of Wales and later King Edward VIII, made his official headquarters on the British warship *Renown* at anchor here. The prince was on his first visit to the United States and Canada. As King Edward VIII in 1937, he abdicated the throne to marry the American divorcée Mrs. Wallis Simpson.

WEST 87TH STREET

26* West 87th Street

This was the last home of jazz singer Billie Holiday, from 1957 until 1959. It was here that she collapsed and sank into a coma on May 31, 1959.

EAST 88TH STREET

57 East 88th Street

On the morning of August 28, 1963, two young women, Janice Wylie and Emily Hoffert, were viciously murdered in their third-floor apartment. The following spring George Whitmore Jr. was arrested, beaten, and coerced into confessing to the crime. Eventually, Whitmore was exonerated, and the killer, Richard Robles, was caught and convicted. Tremendous publicity and two books on the case became major factors in helping to abolish the death penalty in New York State in 1965. Whitmore's treatment at the hands of the police also influenced the U.S. Supreme Court's 1966 "Miranda" decision, which requires the police to advise criminal suspects of their rights to remain silent and to have a lawyer present during questioning.

East 88th Street between York and East End Avenues, South Side

This was the site of John Jacob Astor's summer home "Hell Gate." The financier spent the summers of the 1830s and 1840s here on the thirteen-acre estate. The house lasted until 1869.

EAST 89TH STREET

439 East 89th Street

Printmaker Martin Lewis died here at his home on February 20, 1962. He was seventy-nine years old.

East 89th Street at the East River

This jutting promontory was once known as Horn's Hook. The Americans fortified it in 1776 before the British occupation of the city. It was again fortified against the British in 1814 during the War of 1812.

WEST 90TH STREET

7 West 90th Street

Hetty Green died at the age of eighty-two on July 3, 1916, in her son, Edward's, home, a modest red brick townhouse that was replaced by the current apartment building. She was reputed to be the richest woman in the world. Nicknamed "The

Witch of Wall Street," she made her money with stocks and shrewd investments. A lifelong miser, she left an estate of more than $100 million.

303* West 90th Street

A classic gangster-style shoot-out took place at this address on May 7, 1931. Nineteen-year-old Francis "Two Gun" Crowley fled to the top floor of this five-story elegant townhouse two days after killing a policeman. "Two Gun" fought it out with about three hundred policemen who surrounded the place. He finally surrendered after the police had fired more than seven hundred rounds. His sixteen-year-old girlfriend, Helen, and his partner, Rudolph Duringer, also survived the siege—hiding under a bed.

317* West 90th Street

Patty Hearst, the kidnapped heiress turned revolutionary, spent several days in hiding in this brownstone in June of 1974. Jack Scott, a fellow radical and owner of the apartment, helped Hearst, alias "Tania," drive across the country from San Francisco. Hearst was the object of one of the nation's biggest fugitive hunts for a year and a half before being caught by the FBI. Defended by attorney F. Lee Bailey at her trial for her part in a Symbionese Liberation Army (SLA) bank robbery, she was convicted but later pardoned by President Carter on February 1, 1979.

The legendary Hetty Green, photographed outside her son's home at 7 West 90th Street on her birthday, November 21, 1912. The frugal Green, who lived at her son's home, maintained her legal residence in New Jersey to avoid paying New York taxes. *(FPG)*

EAST 91ST STREET

2 East 91st Street

*Cooper-Hewitt Museum**—Steel magnate Andrew Carnegie built his mansion here in 1901. That same year he retired and sold his interest in his companies for a personal profit of $300 million, which he vowed to give away. When he died eighteen years later, he had managed to give away the astounding sum of $350 million, much of it to public libraries.

24 East 91st Street
This was once the home of Carl Schurz, Civil War general, editor, and namesake of the nearby park. He had bought this house from his friend and neighbor Andrew Carnegie in 1902. Schurz died here on May 14, 1906.

WEST 91ST STREET

West 91st Street, West of Columbus Avenue
Apthorpe House—This mansion, built in 1764 and demolished in 1892, was headquarters for the British during the Revolutionary War. It was jointly occupied by Gen. Sir Henry Clinton and Lord Charles Cornwallis in September of 1776.

EAST 93RD STREET

56* East 93rd Street
Completed in 1932, this elegant curving townhouse was one of the last large private homes to be built in Manhattan. It was built by the wealthy stockbroker William Goadby Loew and was later home to Billy Rose, the theatrical producer. It now serves as an alcoholism center for St. Luke's Hospital.

179* East 93rd Street
This was the boyhood home of the Marx Brothers. The large family lived in a small flat here from 1895 until 1910.

EAST 94TH STREET

14* East 94th Street
From 1932 until 1942 this was the home of playwright George S. Kaufman. In 1944 Kaufman sold this white townhouse to pianist Vladimir Horowitz, who lived here until his death on November 5, 1989.

WEST 94TH STREET

250* West 94th Street

Woman-suffrage leader Elizabeth Cady Stanton lived at this address, her son's home, from 1892 until her death here on October 26, 1902. While here she was visited several times by her old friend and ally Susan B. Anthony. This address was also home to the author Norman Mailer. It was here on November 19, 1960, that a drunken Mailer stabbed his wife Adele with a penknife after a party in their apartment. He was jailed and later released on probation. At a hearing in December, Adele refused to sign a complaint, so no charges were filed.

WEST 95TH STREET

115* West 95th Street

This Queen Anne–style townhouse, sadly deteriorated but still standing, was home to eight-year-old Virginia O'Hanlon in 1897. It was here that Virginia wrote a query letter to the editor of *The New York Sun,* whose reply has been immortalized as a part of American Christmas folklore. The reassuring editorial reply contained the famous line "Yes, Virginia, there is a Santa Claus." Miss O'Hanlon grew up, married, and was regularly interviewed by the press, usually at Christmastime. In the 1920s Virginia moved in with her parents, who were living down the block at number 121, where she raised her own daughter.

EAST 96TH STREET

108* East 96th Street

This apartment building is a rare example of a New York City high-rise that became shorter. Originally thirty-one stories tall, the building was shortened to nineteen stories in the spring of 1993 as a penalty for a zoning violation. After a seven-year court battle, the developer had been ordered by the city to demolish the top twelve floors of this apartment house. The builders attributed the error to a mistake on the city zoning map.

12* West 96th Street
The last home of songwriter Fred E. Ahlert was in this apartment building. He wrote "Walkin' My Baby Back Home" and "I'm Gonna Sit Right Down and Write Myself a Letter."

204* West 96th Street
A fire at this address on December 5, 1947, led the Secret Service to the country's longest-sought and most inept counterfeiter. Seventy-two-year-old forger Edward Mieller, whose two-room flat was destroyed by the fire, was forced to move in with his daughter in Queens. Sometime later, two youths scavenging through the old man's belongings tossed outside by the fire fighters found some of his homemade dollar bills. Their discovery led to his capture. Mieller had started printing his primitive bills nine years earlier, first singles and then larger denominations. Years of practice had not improved his technique. For some time his dollars included the misspelling "Wahsington" for our nation's first president.

West 96th Street at the Hudson River
On September 30, 1880, this was the beginning of the last leg of a journey traversing the centuries and more than six thousand miles. It was here that the 3,500-year-old Egyptian obelisk, a 224-ton granite shaft, nicknamed Cleopatra's Needle, was inched to its current site in Central Park behind the Metropolitan Museum of Art. This gift from Ismail, khedive of Egypt, arrived by the ship *Dessoug* and was tugged night and day over wooden tracks, with the aid of cannonballs, first up 96th Street to Broadway and then south to 86th Street. It continued across town to Fifth Avenue, where it again was turned south to 82nd Street before entering the park, a journey of 112 days.

EAST 97TH STREET

60* East 97th Street
Fashion designer Calvin Klein rescued his daughter Marci at this address ten hours after she was abducted on February 3, 1978. Eleven-year-old Marci, who was on her way to the Dalton School, was persuaded to follow her former babysitter Christine Ransay to her sixth-floor apartment here. Ransay and her half-

336   ■ ALL AROUND THE TOWN

brother Dominique called Klein, demanding a $100,000 ransom. After paying the ransom and learning her whereabouts, the designer, accompanied by the FBI, rushed to this address. The kidnappers, apprehended within hours, received prison sentences.

WEST 102ND STREET

313* West 102nd Street
Elliott Roosevelt, brother of Theodore, future president, and father of Eleanor, future first lady, died at this address on August 14, 1894. Elliott, an alcoholic and an embarrassment to the family, lived in this house with his mistress under the assumed name "Mr. Elliott." After falling, he was knocked unconscious and died. He was only thirty-four years old.

WEST 103RD STREET

150 West 103rd Street
Paul Cadmus, satirist painter, was born on December 17, 1904, in his parents' home at this address.

WEST 108TH STREET

321* West 108th Street
The conductor and composer Victor Herbert lived here for twenty years until his death in 1924.

EAST 112TH STREET

116 East 112th Street
Walter Winchell, newspaper and radio gossip columnist, was born at this address on April 7, 1897.

The Obelisk in Central Park is the oldest humanmade outdoor object in the city. Original sections of the Metropolitan Museum of Art seen in this photograph are now concealed by the Robert Lehman wing. (Author's collection)

A bullring with seating for ten thousand spectators once stood at the corner of West 116th and Lenox Avenue. The broadside promised the "spectacle will be very exciting and extremely agreeable for the ladies." *(Museum City of New York)*

EAST 114TH STREET

239 East 114th Street
Comic Groucho Marx (born Julius Henry) was born at this address on October 2, 1890.

WEST 115TH STREET

601 West 115th Street
The Regnor*—On May 16, 1979, while walking on the sidewalk in front of this 1912 apartment house, Grace Gold, a Barnard college freshman, was struck on the head and killed by a piece of terra cotta. The seventh-floor lintel loosened by age fell from the Columbia University–owned building. The tragedy prompted Local Law 10 of 1980, which required owners to inspect their façades and cornices for repairs once every three years. The law has achieved mixed results. Some owners check and preserve their buildings, while others are removing beautiful decorative stonework rather than repairing it.

EAST 116TH STREET

233* East 116th Street
East Harlem Presbyterian Church—Fresh from Union Theological Seminary, Norman Thomas became the minister at this church, passing up a wealthier parish, in 1911. While here, he helped found the National Civil Rights Bureau (later the American Civil Liberties Union) in 1917. Because of his opposition to American involvement in World War I and membership in the Socialist Party, church administrators and parishioners pressured him to resign in 1918. He gave up the ministry and devoted the rest of his life to social causes, the peace movement, and many unsuccessful attempts to win elective office as a Socialist Party candidate.

WEST 116TH STREET

West 116th Street and Lenox Avenue
Central Park Arena—In 1880 Angel Fernandez built Manhattan's only bull-

ring. Over the summer, eight toreadors, led by the renowned Angel Valdemoro, performed three bullfights with untamed steers shipped from Texas. As a concession to the American audiences, the advertisements promised there would be no cruelty to the animals.

WEST 118TH STREET

68 West 118th Street
Milton Berlinger, who later changed his name to Milton Berle and became a comic, was born at this address on July 12, 1908.

208* West 118th Street
Minton's Playhouse—Opened in 1938 by saxophonist Henry Minton, this jazz club was the birthplace of bebop, a provocative style of jazz with an insistent beat and piercing dissonances ideal for small bands. During the club's peak in the early 1940s, lively jam sessions included such jazz greats as Charlie Parker, Dizzy Gillespie, and Miles Davis. Minton's also attracted the beat writers Allen Ginsberg and Jack Kerouac, who would come here to listen to pianist Thelonious Monk.

WEST 125TH STREET

5 West 125th Street
Young Men's Christian Association, Harlem Branch—On October 22, 1912, Dale Carnegie inaugurated his phenomenal career as the master guru of self-confidence by teaching his first public-speaking course. The twenty-four-year-old entrepreneur had persuaded a reluctant "Y" manager to allow him to teach his course—on a commission basis—to businesspeople. His classes were a tremendous success, and he went on to write *How to Win Friends and Influence People.* The book became the biggest bestselling nonfiction work in modern times, second only to the Bible.

West 125th Street between Adam Clayton Powell Boulevard and Lenox Avenue
This block on Harlem's main business artery was chosen as the first spot for the city's first twenty-five parking meters—sixteen years after the first in the nation

were put in use in Oklahoma City. Acting Mayor Joseph T. Sharkey borrowed a dime, much to the amusement of a crowd of dignitaries and onlookers, to activate the first meter at 12:57 P.M. on September 19, 1951. Ten cents enabled the driver to park here for an hour between the hours of 8:00 in the morning and 6:00 at night.

230* West 125th Street

Blumstein's Department Store—A long-time landmark in Harlem, this department store first opened in 1894. In June of 1934 the store became the major target of the "Buy-Where-You-Can-Work" protest. The African American community, including leaders such as the Rev. Adam Clayton Powell Jr., boycotted and picketed the store for a month until managers agreed to hire thirty-five African American clerks and salespeople. The successful protest forced other major businesses not to discriminate against African Americans and served as a model for later boycotts. By 1943 the store was the first to use black models and mannequins and even the first African American Santa Claus.

One unfortunate incident occurred here on September 20, 1958, when Dr. Martin Luther King Jr., who was autographing copies of his new book *Stride Toward Freedom,* was stabbed by Izola Ware Curry, a mentally unstable African American woman. The twenty-nine-year-old Dr. King was rushed to Harlem Hospital, where he underwent three hours of surgery to remove a steel letter opener. New York Governor W. Averell Harriman and Roy Wilkins of the NAACP both went to the hospital to check on his condition. Although pneumonia slowed his recovery, he was released from the hospital two weeks later.

253 West 125th Street

Apollo Theater*—In addition to being the showcase for African American musical talent, the Apollo is also a Harlem institution. The golden age began in 1934 when the new owners, Frank Schiffman and Leo Brechter, began a "colored revue." Over the years entertainers from Bessie Smith to Ray Charles have performed here. On November 21, 1934, Ella Fitzgerald made her debut in the club's famous amateur contest. She won first prize. Other winners in the Wednesday-night competitions have included James Brown, Sarah Vaughn, and the Jackson Five. The theater has also served as a gathering place for New York's African American community.

On the night of May 6, 1995, it was the site of a historic reconciliation between Dr. Betty Shabazz, the widow of Malcolm X, and Louis H. Farrakhan, the Nation of Islam leader. Dr. Shabazz had repeatedly and publicly declared Farrakhan partly responsible for her husband's murder. Called "A New Beginning," the event was part political rally and part fund-raiser for Malcolm X and Dr. Shabazz's daughter Qubilah, who earlier in the week had agreed to "accept responsibility" for her involvement in a plot to kill Mr. Farrakhan. Federal prosecutors had agreed not to take the case to trial if she sought psychiatric, drug, and alcohol treatment.

WEST 126TH STREET

West 126th Street near Frederick Douglass Boulevard

Hotel Braddock—What began as an argument between the hotel management and a female guest escalated into a full-fledged race riot on August 1, 1943. James Collins, a white policeman, was attempting to arrest the woman for disturbing the peace when Robert Bandy, an African American serviceman, came to the woman's aid. Bandy fought with the officer and hit him before fleeing the hotel. Collins chased and shot Bandy in the shoulder and marched him to nearby Sydenham Hospital. A crowd gathered and grew angry with each retelling of the story and each rumor. Before it was over, six black people were killed, five hundred injured, and more than one hundred jailed.

EAST 127TH STREET

20* East 127th Street

This brownstone row house was home to poet Langston Hughes for some twenty years. He lived on the top floor of what was then a rooming house, beginning in 1947.

WEST 134TH STREET

West 134th Street East of Lenox Avenue

The first apartment houses in Harlem that became available to African Americans are located on this block. In 1910 landlords, unable to find white tenants for their new buildings, permitted Philip A. Payton, an African American realtor, to fill two apartment houses with Black tenants. Several neighborhood white property owners panicked and bought the buildings in order to evict the blacks. In retaliation, Payton and his Afro-American Realty Company purchased several other buildings and made them available to African Americans. Later St. Philip's Episcopal Church, a black congregation, purchased ten apartment houses on West 134th Street. The church paid more than a million dollars for the property, the largest real-estate agreement involving African Americans up to that time. The racial economic warfare ended as whites abandoned Harlem. Long denied descent housing, blacks who had been forced to live in the over-crowded ghetto centered on West 53rd Street, called San Juan Hill, flocked to Harlem. Southern blacks, who came to the city during World War I for better wages and a better life, also moved to Harlem. By 1920 the African American population of New York City had grown four times larger in a decade, and most of this growth was in Harlem. Harlem was well on the way to becoming the heart and capital of Black America.

210 West 134th Street

St. Philip's Episcopal Church*—The African American congregation at this church, one of the first to move to central Harlem in 1909, was established in the early nineteenth century in lower Manhattan on Centre Street. It was instrumental in attracting blacks to the neighborhood. Two African American architects, George W. Foster Jr. and Vertner W. Tandy, the first black architect registered in New York State, designed the landmarked Gothic church.

Not far from where African Americans first gained access to better housing in Harlem a few years earlier, this is the corner of West 134th Street and Lenox Avenue. The photograph was taken during World War I. Note the soldier in the lower lefthand corner. (FPG)

WEST 135TH STREET

103 West 135th Street

The 135th Street Branch of the New York Public Library*—This branch served as the meeting place for the writers of the "Harlem Renaissance" of the mid-1920s. These gifted African American authors began to realistically depict black life and culture in their works, often written in black dialect and reflecting a growing Black pride. The group included Langston Hughes, Jean Toomer, and Countee Cullen. The basement was home to the American Negro Theater, where actors Harry Belafonte and Sidney Poitier made their debuts. This branch, still standing, served as the initial repository for Arthur Schomburg's extensive archive and history of black life. The collection, now named in honor of Schomburg, is housed next door on Lenox Avenue.

180 West 135th Street

The Harlem Young Men's Christian Association*—After outgrowing the branch across the street at 181 West 135th Street, this structure was built in 1932. The "Y" served as first home for many African American men moving to the city during the mass migration of Southern blacks to Northern cities during the 1920s and 1930s. These two branches were the first New York homes to Langston Hughes, Ralph Ellison, and Claude McKay.

187* West 135th Street

A national historic landmark, number 187 was the last home of James Weldon Johnson from 1925 until his death in 1938. Johnson was an author and poet during the Harlem Renaissance and a noted African American political leader. While attending Columbia University, he supported Theodore Roosevelt in the presidential election of 1904 and wrote a campaign song, "You're All Right Teddy." He was rewarded for his efforts with two consular posts in South America. His poem "Lift Every Voice and Sing" was later set to music and was known as the Negro National Anthem.

West 135th Street at the Hudson River

On April 7, 1917, one day after Congress declared war on Germany, the collector of the Port of New York, Dudley Malone, and six hundred of his customs agents boarded the German passenger ship *Vaterland,* docked here. The ship was declared interned. This quiet drama, performed with dignity and cooperation by both parties, was the United States's first act of war against Germany and the beginning of U.S. involvement in World War I.

Three years later, in September of 1919, these piers anchored the S.S. *Yarmouth,* owned by the charismatic African American leader Marcus Garvey and his Black Star Shipping Line. This small steamship was intended to be the first link between his black followers and the "African motherland." Garvey planned to use this and other ships for his "Back to Africa" campaign. This campaign proved to be his undoing. Garvey's financial dealing with the Black Star line led to a prison term for mail fraud and his deportation to Jamaica.

WEST 136TH STREET

108 West 136th Street

This address was once the elegant home of Madam C. J. Walker, a very successful African American woman who sold hair-care products. The Georgian-style home was constructed from two existing townhouses by the black architect Vertner Tandy in 1915 shortly after African Americans starting buying Harlem real estate. After her death in 1919, her daughter A'Lelia Walker Robinson lived in the house and created a lively literary salon for the Harlem Renaissance writers of the 1920s. She named it the Dark Tower Tea Club, after a monthly column, "The Dark Tower," written by her friend the poet Countee Cullen. The townhouse was demolished in 1941 for the Countee Cullen Branch of the New York Public Library, an addition to the branch on West 135th Street.

WEST 138TH STREET

120* West 138th Street

Liberty Hall—This was the site of the first International Convention of Negroes Peoples of the World. In August of 1920 more than three thousand delegates ratified a "Declaration of Independence" with sixty-six articles and a universal anthem and colors—red, black, and green. Marcus Garvey was elected "provisional President of the Republic of Africa." Garvey and his powerful newspaper, *The Negro World,* were influential in furthering the cause of African American rights and African Nationalism. The month-long convention culminated in a mass meeting at Madison Square Garden. The building later became the headquarters for the Universal Negro Improvement Association (UNIA).

132 West 138th Street

Abyssinian Baptist Church*—This neo-Gothic-style church was once the power base for the Reverend Adam Clayton Powell Jr., Harlem's controversial and flamboyant congressman from 1945 to 1970. Powell, a leading voice for African Americans in the civil-rights era, built his major Harlem following here through his father's Abyssinian pulpit. The congregation, the largest black congregation in the United States, was founded in 1808 in lower Manhattan.

WEST 145TH STREET

West 145th Street and Convent Avenue

This intersection at 9:00 A.M. on November 27, 1924, was the starting point for the first R. H. Macy's Thanksgiving Day Parade, then called the "Christmas Parade." The guest of honor, then as now, was Santa Claus. But in this first parade, St. Nick

On November 29, 1934, during the Macy's Thanksgiving Parade, a balloon floats down Broadway at West 67th Street. The Cambell's funeral chapel in the Hotel Welden is on the west side of Broadway in the far right of this photograph. *(FPG)*

was really given the royal treatment. After riding his sleigh float along the long and roundabout route, Santa was crowned "King of Kiddies" while seated on a gold throne on the marquee over the entrance to the 34th Street store. The Thanksgiving Day Parade has been a beloved New York City tradition every year since, except for several years during World War II.

WEST 148TH STREET

437 West 148th Street
This was the home of journalist and author of the *Wolfville* books Alfred H. Lewis. He died here on December 23, 1914.

WEST 155TH STREET

West 155th Street between Frederick Douglass Boulevard and Harlem River Driveway
Polo Grounds—After the stands at the old Polo Grounds on Central Park North were torn down in 1890, the Giants baseball team moved their games uptown to this location a year later. In addition to the Giants, who played here for sixty-seven years, this field was home to the Yankees for about a decade beginning in 1912 and also the first home to the Mets in 1962. In the 1890s Harry Magley Stevens, the director of catering, popularized (some say invented) the hot dog. He called them "red hots." The site is now a housing project of four towers of more than thirty stories.

■ SELECT BIBLIOGRAPHY

Anderson, Jervis. *This Was Harlem: A Cultural Portrait, 1900–1950*. New York: Farrar, Straus & Giroux, 1982.

Allenman, Richard. *The Movie Lover's Guide to New York*. New York: Harper & Row, 1988.

Beard, Rick, and Leslie Cohen Berlowitz, eds. *Greenwich Village: Culture and Counterculture*. New York: Museum of the City of New York, 1993.

Browning, Judith H. *New York City, Yesterday and Today: 30 Timeless Walking Adventures*. City, Conn.: Corsair Publications, 1990.

Chauncey, George. *Gay New York: Gender, Urban Culture, and the Making of the Gay Male World, 1890–1940*. New York: Basic Books, 1994.

Cooke, Hope. *Seeing New York: History Walks for Armchair and Footloose Travelers*. Philadelphia: Temple University Press, 1995.

Devorkin, Joseph. *Great Merchants of Early New York, "Ladies Mile."* New York: Society for the Architecture of the City of New York, 1987.

Diamonstein, Barbaralee. *The Landmarks of New York*. New York: Harry Abrams, 1997.

Dolkart, Andrew S., and Gretchen S. Sorin. *Touring Historic Harlem: Four Walks in Northern Manhattan*. New York: New York Landmarks Conservancy, 1997.

Douglas, Ann. *Terrible Honesty: Mongrel Manhattan in the 1920s*. New York: Farrar, Straus & Giroux, 1995.

Dunlap, David W. *On Broadway: A Journey Uptown Over Time*. New York: Rizzoli, 1990.

Dunshee, Kenneth Holcomb. *As You Pass By*. New York: Hasting House, 1952.

Eastman, John. *Who Lived Where: A Biographical Guide to Homes and Museums*. New York: Facts on File, 1983.

Edmiston, Susan, and Linda D. Cirino. *Literary New York: A History and Guide*. Boston: Houghton Mifflin, 1976.

Ellis, Edward Robb. *The Epic of New York City*. New York: Coward-McCann, 1966.

Fifty Years on Fifth. New York: Fifth Avenue Association, 1957.

Gaylord, R. Bruce. *The Picture Book of Greenwich Village*. New York: Citadel Press Books, 1985.

Goldberger, Paul. *The City Observed: New York.* New York: Random House, 1979.

Grafton, John. *New York in the Nineteenth Century: 317 Engravings from Harper's Weekly and Other Contemporary Sources.* 2nd ed. New York: Dover Publications, 1980.

Gray, Christopher, ed. *Fifth Avenue, 1911 From Start to Finish in Historic Block-by-Block Photographs.* New York: Dover Publications, 1994.

The Great East River Bridge. New York: Brooklyn Museum (Abrams, Inc.), 1983.

Heide, Robert, and John Gilman. *Greenwich Village: A Primo Guide to Shopping, Eating and Making Merry in True Bohemia.* New York: St. Martin's Griffin, 1995.

Hurewitz, Daniel. *Stepping Out: Nine Tours through New York City's Gay and Lesbian Past.* New York: Henry Holt, 1997.

Jackson, Kenneth T., ed. *The Encyclopedia of New York City.* New York: Yale University Press, 1995.

Kinkead, Eugene. *Central Park, 1857–1995: The Birth, Decline, and Renewal of a National Treasure.* New York: W. W. Norton, 1990.

Klein, Carole. *Gramercy Park: An American Bloomsbury.* Athens, Ohio: Ohio University Press, 1992.

Limmer, Ruth. *Six Heritage Tours of the Lower East Side.* New York: New York University Press, 1997.

McDarrah, Fred W., and Patrick J. McDarrah. *The Greenwich Village Guide: Sixteen Historic Walks: Includes Soho, Tribeca, and the East Village.* Chicago: Cappella Books, 1992.

Marinac, Paula. *The Queerest Places.* New York: Owl Books, 1997.

Miller, Terry. *Greenwich Village and How It Got That Way.* New York: Crown Publishers, 1990.

Morgan, Bill. *The Beat Generation in New York: A Walking Tour of Jack Kerouac's City.* San Francisco: City Lights Books, 1997.

New York Then and Now: 83 Manhattan Sites Photographed in the Past and Present. New York: Dover, 1976.

New York, N.Y. New York: American Heritage Publishing, 1968.

New York Panorama: A Companion to the WPA Guide to New York City, with a New Introduction by Alfred Kazin. New York: Pantheon Books, 1984.

Postal, Bernard, and Lionel Koppman. *Jewish Landmarks in New York: An Informal History and Guide.* New York: Hill and Wang, 1964.

Plumb, Stephen. *The Streets Where They Lived.* St. Paul: MarLor Press, 1989.

Reed, Henry Hope. *Rockefeller New York.* New York: Greensward Foundation, 1988.

Roth, Andrew. *Infamous Manhattan: A Colorful Walking History of New York's Most Notorious Crime Sites.* New York: Citadel Press Books, 1996.

Salwen, Peter. *Upper West Side Story: A History and Guide.* New York: Abbeville Press, 1989.

Tauranac, John. *Essential New York: A Guide to the History and Architecture of Manhattan's Important Buildings, Parks, and Bridges.* New York: Holt, Rinehart & Winston, 1979.

Willensky, Elliot, and Norval White. *AIA Guide to New York City.* 3rd ed. San Diego: Harcourt Brace Jovanovich, 1988.

Wolf, Marvin J., and Katherine Mader. *Rotten Apples: True Stories of New York Crime and Mystery, 1689 to the Present.* New York: Ballantine Books, 1991.

Wolfe, Gerard R. *New York: A Guide to the Metropolis.* New York: McGraw-Hill, 1988.

Yeadon, David. *Nooks and Crannies: An Unusual Walking Tour Guide to New York City.* New York: Charles Scribner's Sons, 1979.

■ INDEX

Numbers in italics indicate illustrations/captions.